W9-COZ-531

PSYCHOLOGY
AS A
BIOLOGICAL
SCIENCE

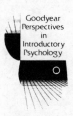

Goodyear
Perspectives
in
Introductory
Psychology

Series Editor   *Richard F. Thompson*
HARVARD UNIVERSITY

PSYCHOLOGY AS A SOCIAL SCIENCE
Fred R. Fosmire
UNIVERSITY OF OREGON

PSYCHOLOGY AS A BIOLOGICAL SCIENCE
Daniel P. Kimble
UNIVERSITY OF OREGON

PSYCHOLOGY AS A BEHAVIORAL SCIENCE
James F. Voss
UNIVERSITY OF PITTSBURGH

PSYCHOLOGY AS A BIOLOGICAL SCIENCE

Daniel P. Kimble

University of Oregon

Library
S.W. Ok. St. U.
Weatherford, Oklahoma

Goodyear Publishing Company, Inc.   PACIFIC PALISADES, CALIF.

Copyright © 1973 by

GOODYEAR PUBLISHING COMPANY, INC.
Pacific Palisades, California   90272

All rights reserved. No part of this book may be
reproduced in any form or by any means without
permission in writing from the publisher.

Current printing (last digit):   10 9 8 7 6 5 4 3 2

Library of Congress Catalog Card Number: 73-78901

Y-6658-2

ISBN: 0-87620-665-8

Printed in the United States of America

PROJECT SUPERVISOR: *Nat LaMar*

EDITOR: *J. W. Maisel*

DESIGNER: *Ben Kann*

COVER PHOTO: *Leonard Lee Rue III
from National Audubon Society
and Ben Kann*

152
K5op5

dedicated to
Reeva, Matthew,
Evan, Sara,
and
Jessica

200204

CONTENTS

CREDITS

Figure 1
Theodor W. Blackstad, Cortical Grey Matter, In H. Hyden, The Neuron, Elsevier, Amsterdam (1967), Figure 24, page 87.

Figure 2, Figure 4, Figure 21, Figure 23, and Figure 24
Ernest Gardner, M. D., "Fundamentals of Neurology," Fifth Ed., 1968. W. B. Saunders Co., Reprinted by permission of publisher.

Figure 3C
William Bloom, M. D., and Don W. Fawcett, M. D. "A Textbook of Histology." Ninth Ed., 1968, W. B. Saunders Co., Reprinted by permission of publisher.

Figure 5
A. Hirano and H. M. Dembitzer. A structural analysis of the myelin sheath in the central nervous system. *J. Cell Biol.* **34:**553–567, 1967. Reprinted by permission of publisher.

Figure 6, Figure 7, and Figure 57.
William Bloom, M. D., and Don W. Fawcett, M. D. *A Textbook of Histology.* Ninth Ed., 1968, W. B. Saunders Co., Reprinted by permission of publisher.

Figure 9, Figure 10, and Figure 15
Charles F. Stevens, "Neurophysiology: A Primer." 1966, John Wiley & Sons, Inc., Reprinted by permission of publisher.

Figure 8 and Figure 11
Theodore C. Ruch, Ph. D., and Harry D. Patton, Ph. D. "Physiology and Biophysics," Nineteenth Ed., 1965. W. B. Saunders Co., Reprinted by permission of publisher.

Figure 12
A. L. Hodgkin and A. F. Huxley. A quantitative description of membrane current and its application to conduction and excitation in nerve. *J. of Physiol.* (London) **117:**500–544, 1952. Reprinted by permission of publisher.

Figure 17
Myron S. Jacobs, P. J. Morgane, and Willard L. McFarland, "The Anatomy of the Brain of the Bottlenose Dolphin (Tursiops truncatus), Rhinic Lobe (Rhinencephalon). I. The Paleocortex." *J. of Comp. Neur.*, V, 141, (2), 1971, p. 223, Reprinted by permission of publisher.

Figure 19, Figure 25, Figure 26, and Figure 27
Copyright 1953, 1962 CIBA-GEIGY Corporation, reproduced, with permission, from THE CIBA COLLECTION OF MEDICAL ILLUSTRATIONS by Frank H. Netter, M.D.

Figure 22
Modified from Wolfgang Zeman and James Robert Maitland Innes. *Craigie's Neuroanatomy of the Rat.* Academic Press (1963).

Figure 29
Beidler, L. M., and Reichardt, W. E. (1970): Sensory Transduction. *Neurosciences Res. Prog. Bull.* 8(5): 459–560. Also in: *Neurosciences Research Symposium Summaries,* Vol. 5. Schmitt, F. O. et al., eds. Cambridge, Mass.: M.I.T. Press, pp. 441–538.

Figure 30
J. E. Dowling and B. B. Boycott, "Organization of the primate retina: electron microscopy," Proceedings of the Royal Society, B., 1966, 80–111, 1966. Reprinted by permission of publisher.

Figure 34
S. W. Kuffler. Discharge patterns and functional organization of mammalian retina. *J. Neurophysiol.* **16:**37, 1953. Reprinted by permission of publisher.

Figure 38
From Poggio, Gian F.: Central neural mechanisms in vision. In Mountcastle, Vernon B., editor: Medical physiology, ed. 13, St. Louis, The C. V. Mosby Co.

Figure 40
C. G. Gross, C. E. Rocha-Miranda, and D. B. Bender. Visual properties of neurons in inferotemporal cortex of the macque. J. Neurophysiology **35:**96–111, 1972. The American Physiological Society. Reprinted by permission of publisher.

Figure 41
R. W. Goy, "Experimental Control of Psychosexuality," Phil. Trans. Roy. Soc. Lond., B. 259, 149–162 (1970). Reprinted by permission of publisher.

Figure 42
Photograph courtesy of H. Wehksein, Oregon Regional Primate Center.

Figure 43 and Figure 46
GENERAL ENDOCRINOLOGY, by C. D. Turner and J. T. Bagnara, 5th edition, W. B. Saunders Co., 1971. Reprinted by permission.

Figure 44
Courtesy of Eugene, Oregon Register-Guard.

Figure 45
G. W. Harris "Neural Control of the Pituitary Gland," 1955, Edward Arnold
Publishers. Reprinted by permission of publisher.

Figure 47
R. W. Sperry. Mechanisms of neural maturation, Chapter 7 in *Handbook of
Experimental Psychology*, S. S. Stevens, Editor. John Wiley and Sons, Inc. Publishers,
1951. Reprinted by permission of publisher.

Figure 48
Geoffrey Raisman "Neuronal Plasticity in the Septal Nuclei of the Adult Rat,"
Brain Research 14 (1969), 25-48. Reprinted by permission of publisher.

Figure 49
G. Adrian Horridge, "Interneurons: Their Origin, Action, Specificity, Growth,
and Plasticity," 1968, W. H. Freeman and Company. Reprinted by permissions
of the publisher.

Figure 50
Leo V. DiCara and Neal E. Miller. Changes in heart rate instrumentality learned
by curarized rats as avoidance responses. *J. Comp. and Physiol. Psychol.* **65**:8–12,
1968. Reprinted by permission of publisher.

Figure 52 and Figure 53
R. W. Sperry, "Hemisphere deconnection and unity in conscious awareness,"
American Psychologist, 23, 723–733, 1968. Reprinted by permission of publisher.

Figure 54
Doreen Kimura. "Right Temporal Lobe Damage," *Arch. of Neurol.* **8**:264–271,
1963. American Medical Association, Publishers. Reprinted by permission of
publisher.

Figure 55
Norman Geschwind. The organization of language and the brain. *Science*
170:940–944, 1970. Reprinted by permission of publisher.

Figure 56
Elizabeth C. Crosby, Tryphena Humphrey and Edward W. Lauer. *Correlative
Anatomy of the Nervous System*. MacMillan Company, New York (1962), Figure
303. Reprinted by permission of publisher.

Figure 57
Madge E. Scheibel and Arnold B. Scheibel, "Elementary Processes in Selected
Thalmic and Cortical Subsystems—the Structural Substrates" in The Neuros-
ciences Second Study Program, Francis O. Schmitt, Editor-in-Chief, 1970, The
Rockefeller University Press. Reprinted by permission of publisher.

Figure 60
W. Penfield and T. Rasmussen. *The Cerebral Cortex of Man*. MacMillan Publishing
Co., 1950. Reprinted by permission of publisher.

Figure 61
Mary A. B. Brazier. *Electrical Activity of the Nervous System.* Pitman Medical and Scientific Publishing Co., Ltd. London and Williams & Wilkins, Baltimore, 1968. Reprinted by permission of publishers.

Figure 62
Michel Jouvet, "The states of sleep" *Scientific American 216* (2): 62–72, 1967. W. H. Freeman and Co., Publishers. Reprinted by permission of publisher.

FOREWORD

Richard F. Thompson, Series Editor

The growth in psychology since 1850 has been so rapid and complex that it is very difficult to teach an introductory psychology course that fairly and competently presents the student with a unified conceptual understanding of the discipline. The Perspectives in Introductory Psychology Series attempts to deal with this problem by focusing on specific psychological fields by presenting the content of psychology through particular viewpoints. In this manner, a consistent and relatively unified framework can be created with which the introductory student can begin to grasp a knowledge of psychology.

Increasingly, psychology departments are offering alternative courses to the traditional survey of general psychology. A sequence of beginning courses, each emphasizing a particular psychological veiwpoint such as biological, behavioral, social, developmental, or applied, enables the student to study the approach most closely allied to his major and facilitates the reality of the instructor's actual training and orientation. For just as the body of knowledge in psychology has nearly exceeded the limits of practical expectations for the teacher, very few of the psychologists teaching introductory psychology today are trained in or are doing research in all areas of psychology covered by the general survey course. Even in departments that do not formally offer sequences of introductory courses, a viewpoint approach is reflected in the selection of texts. After all, every text effectively structures the psychological information the student reads.

Daniel Kimble's *Psychology as a Biological Science* will reveal to the introductory student the fascinating world of physiological and comparative psychology—the importance of understanding the human nervous system in order to understand human behavior. Kimble explores man's acquisition of language, sexual differences, human nature, mental retardation, human development, and other topics within the domain of psychobiology. Beginning with the neuron and the brain, the discussion moves on to treat sensory processes, hormones and behavioral changes, basic behaviors—hunger, thirst, and sex—the biological basis of learning, the special properties of the human brain, and neuromuscular correspondence, and concludes with biological explanations of sleeping, dreaming, and altered states of consciousness.

PREFACE

This book grew out of 10 years of experience teaching physiological psychology with undergraduates at the University of Oregon. As every college instructor knows, undergraduate teaching is (or should be) a two-way interchange, and I have learned much from my students. Hopefully, this book reflects some of those things. It is designed to be useful for students in Introductory Psychology, or in an Introductory Physiological Psychology course. It presupposes no more than a high school background in either biology or other sciences.

Most students who take introductory psychology are not psychology majors. I have kept this fact in mind while writing, and the book is oriented toward a general liberal arts undergraduate, regardless of his or her specialty. Within that framework, the primary focus is on behavior, and the way in which the nervous system and the endocrine system interact in producing behavior. In all cases where it is possible, I have chosen aspects of human behavior as examples of such interaction. In some cases, however, the behavior of other species is discussed, reflecting the nature of the research which forms the foundation of this field.

It will become apparent, upon reading this book, that physiological psychology is an incomplete science, that many important questions have as yet no answer. I have found that while this may be frustrating to some students, to the great majority, it is both exciting and challenging. Ours is not only an incomplete science, it is also an eclectic one, and the findings of anatomists, anthropologists, biochemists, ethologists, linguists, neurologists and psychiatrists, as well as psychologists have contributed to the research reported in this book. I think that in the future development of both Biology and Psychology, we shall see even more "cross-talk" among the existing disciplines. I certainly hope so, for it is my strong belief that through such interaction lies the most rational course for truly understanding ourselves. Such interdisciplinary communication is often difficult to generate and it would be very gratifying if this book could contribute to furthering that communication. Each chapter contains a list of suggested additional readings, and these titles reflect diverse disciplines.

I would like to acknowledge the helpful comments and ideas contributed by several of my colleagues here at Oregon and elsewhere. In particular, I would like to thank Ruth BreMiller, Alan Epstein, John Fentress, Barbara Gordon, Steve Keele, Marvin Lickey, Roger Sperry and Richard Whalen. Much of the time to write this book has been provided due to the understanding of my chairman, Robert Fagot. Monique Prevost typed the manuscript. A special word of thanks should go to Richard F. Thompson for having confidence in my ability to write this book in the first place, as well as for his numerous helpful comments along the way. I would also like to acknowledge my friends at Goodyear, particularly my editor, Clay Stratton.

Also, I wish to thank my parents, Ralph and Ruth Kimble, who taught me to love learning. Finally, the most necessary and most constant help was (and is) provided by my wife, Reeva Jacobson Kimble. She contributed many of the illustrations, long hours of proof-reading, helpful comments, and a truly incredible amount of patience.

PSYCHOLOGY
AS A
BIOLOGICAL
SCIENCE

Chapter 1

INTRODUCTION

Psychology can be defined as the study of behavior, which is an adequate definition as far as it goes. But there are many different kinds of animals that behave and many different ways that behavior can be studied. Psychology is a diverse discipline, with a great variety of techniques and approaches. For example, if one is interested in studying egg-laying behavior, the subjects and experimental methods one chooses will be different than if one wishes to study the acquisition of concepts of formal logic. The biological approach to the study of behavior has been important since the beginnings of academic psychology in the late nineteenth century. Man, like other animals, is a product of evolution; and to understand man's behavior fully, it is helpful to understand his biological heritage. I believe behavior can be more deeply understood by considering psychology as a biological science, which does not deny that man also has cultural heritages which profoundly influence his behavior. This particular book stresses the importance of understanding the human nervous system in order to understand human behavior.

Biological psychology is a hybrid field, taking ideas and experimental techniques from other disciplines: anatomy, physiology, and biochemistry, as well as experimental psychology and ethology (the naturalistic study of animal behavior). Out of this mixture is developing a vigorous science. The past few years have seen a rapid, almost explosive, growth in this exciting field of study, but our knowledge of how the activity of nerves and hormones determine our behavior is still fragmentary. In some areas the information is richer than in others. For example, we now know at least the outlines of how individual nerve cells transmit messages to each other. In other areas, our ignorance is almost perfect. For example, we cannot say why man, of all the mammals, has developed written language.

As we learn more about how neurons transmit messages to each other, we will be in a much better position to understand what goes wrong in the garbled messages which are experienced as hallucinations by the mentally ill. As we learn precisely how the cerebral cortex functions, we will come to understand how language is possible, and we may unlock secrets concerning the causes of mental retardation. As we discover how the presence or absence of certain substances in the embyro (for example, the male hormone testosterone) affect the later sexuality of the individual, we will be able to understand more fully the nature of the psychological differences between male and female. Knowledge is indeed power. As we learn the details of our biological nature, we will learn better how to cure the sick, strengthen the weak, and educate the ignorant.

But the practical applications of knowledge are only one aspect of the potential significance of a better understanding of the biological heritage of man. In order to be truly free, we need to understand ourselves, to determine what it means to be human—what constitutes "human nature." The biological approach to the study of behavior can help us to understand the most complex of all the products of evolution, the human brain and behavior.

The next chapter in this book (Chapter 2) deals with the fundamental building blocks of the nervous system, the nerve cells, or neurons. These are the smallest functional unit of the brain, the basic "elements." Thanks to a large number of investigators all over the world, we can piece together a rather good picture of how the individual units of the nervous system work. The principles are not entirely known, but considerable progress has been made over the past half-century. Chapter 2 may seem somewhat removed from the direct observation of behavior; but the understanding of how individual neurons work may, in fact, provide the necessary insights into understanding behavior. The principles of inhibition and excitation as outlined in Chapter 2 become important, for example, in understanding how our sensory receptors respond to changes in the environment and thus how we experience the world around us. Chapter 3 outlines the basic anatomical plan of the mammalian nervous system. Chapter 4 describes how vision is dependent upon both physiological principles of excitation and inhibition as described in Chapter 2 and on anatomical principles of the convergence and divergence of neuronal connections.

There is a temptation (which we shall resist) to draw analogies between the brain and modern general-purpose computers, and thus between neurons and the on-off switching elements in such computers. There are several reasons why such analogies may be misleading. One major fact is that not only are neurons capable of functioning as "electrical" on-off switches but they are extremely complex biochemical devices. As such, they are exquisitely sensitive to a wide spectrum of biochemical substances, including the *hormones*, products of the endocrine system of the body. Chapter 5 describes some of the effects of hormones on the brain and on behavior. Some statements about hormonal action are still controversial, such as the suggestion that the presence of minute amounts of testosterone in the circulation of embryonic animals can profoundly alter the developing nervous system, "biasing" it toward a more masculine direction. Recent experiments concerning the experimental control of psychosexuality in monkeys are compared with clinical cases of pseudohermaphrodism in Chapter 5 in an attempt to shed light on concepts of "maleness" and "femaleness" in primates. Hormones are important biological triggers. The presence of certain hormones can produce sexual behavior in many species, while the absence of hormones can inhibit the expression of sexual behavior. Maternal behavior and aggressive behavior may also be at least partially controlled by hormone levels in the brain. Chapter 5 also discusses the behavioral changes which can be observed in animals as a function of hormone fluctuations. How much our own sexual, parental, and aggressive behaviors may be related to hormonal levels is still largely undetermined, but it is unlikely that we have completely escaped the influences of our ancestors.

The brain is involved in the regulation of basic behaviors such as eating and drinking, and Chapter 6 discusses how this regulation may be accomplished. As we all know, however, human beings do not always regulate their food intake properly; and experiments have indicated that with certain procedures, experimental animals can be made to eat much more than they need and thus become obese. The possibility of a relation between obese humans and obese rats is discussed in Chapter 6.

As does everything else, the brain changes. As it changes, the behavior it is capable of producing changes as well. In fact, it is often the case that it is only the changes in behavior which are directly observable. Recently, however, new experimental techniques have allowed for a more detailed and precise analysis of nervous system changes. Chapter 7 describes some of these techniques. Our brains change as a result of many factors, including age, injury, and disease. Some changes are more subtle. It is generally assumed that learning produces changes in the brain. So far, however, no one has been able to specify just what these changes may be. Chapter 7 describes a few of the different kinds of experiments which have been designed to try to unravel this most complex biological and psychological problem—the biological basis of learning. Although brain scientists have yet to solve the problem, experimenters in this area have shown considerable imagination and ingenuity in trying to "ask the right question" of nature."

The most complex product of evolution is the mammalian cerebral cortex. This sheet of billions of highly organized nerve cells is the outstanding characteristic of the mammalian brain. The presence of a highly developed cortex distinguishes the brains of mammals from those of birds, reptiles, amphibians, and fishes. Is it the presence of the cerebral cortex which has allowed mammals to show more flexibility, that is, more adaptability, than the birds or fishes? Both birds and fishes can learn, and both show quite complicated behavior, but in comparison with mammalian behavior, both fishes and birds appear more stereotyped and less adaptable—in short, less intelligent than mammals. The human brain displays one of the more complex brains among the mammals (along with the dolphin and chimpanzee brain), but so far no really overwhelming difference between the structure of the human brain and that of other mammals has been demonstrated. Chapter 8 asks the question: Are there special properties of the human brain which allow for the development of language and the complex symbol manipulation ability of humans? The answer is not yet available, but a few extremely interesting reports do exist. One fact which emerges from several different sources is that the human brain is functionally asymmetrical: the major (typically but not always the left) half of the human cortex is more capable of producing language, whereas the other hemisphere has its own special skills. As far as we know now, this asymmetry is not present in the brains of other mammals (although we should not rule out the possibility just yet). In Chapter 8 the relationship between the evolutionary development of the cortical systems and those of another brain region, the thalamus, is also discussed.

Chapter 9 deals with the problem of the production of movement and posture by the brain. Behavior is, or course, composed of movements. Even speech and writing depend on the movement of the appropriate muscles in the correct sequence.

Chapter 10 is devoted to the possible biological explanations of sleeping, dreaming, and other altered states of consciousness. It is only in recent years that these topics have been seriously considered in the laboratory. At the present, considerable progress is being made, and at least three different states of consciousness can be discerned from brain wave records and other measures.

There are many topics in physiological psychology which can be covered only briefly in this introductory book, and some which cannot be covered at all. Hopefully, there will be particular topics which stimulate your curiosity to read additional materials not included. For this purpose, recommended readings are provided at the end of each chapter. Still other references to material discussed in the book are to be found at the back of the book. If the present material is successful, it will prove only a beginning to your exploration of psychology as a biological science.

Chapter 2

NEURONS: BUILDING BLOCKS OF THE BRAIN

The basic mission of any nervous system is communication. In complex animals such as ourselves, there must be a "central command center" in which messages from one part of the body can be received, appropriate decisions reached, and movement commands sent out. Our eyes cannot directly tell our feet that a car is coming; the brain must process the visual information, make a decision, and send messages to our legs to "move, now!" In such a case, speed is essential. We must have a nervous system that allows for accurate and rapid communication among the different parts of the body. For normal behavior, the system must integrate the movement of the various parts into a harmonious whole. In order to accomplish this, some muscles must relax at the same time that others are contracting. The movements of the head and eyes must be coordinated with the movements of the body and the messages coming from other sense organs. The types of cells which are most important in bodily communication are the nerve cells, or *neurons*. They are the building blocks of the brain.

The human brain contains several billion cells. There is general agreement that at least 10 billion of these cells are neurons. In addition to the neurons, there are at least another 50 billion *glial* cells in the brain. The glial cells are more numerous, but less is known about them than neurons. They provide nutrients to neurons and assist in carrying away waste products from neurons. It is not yet known whether glial cells participate more directly in the communication function of neurons. The large number of cells in our heads may cause you to wonder how there is enough room for all of them. One answer is that neurons and glial cells are very small: the cell body of even a large neuron is only about 100 microns in diameter (1 micron is 1/1,000 of a millimeter), just barely visible to the naked eye. On the other hand, neurons can be extremely elongated, in some cases as much as a meter in length. Another explanation for the large number of cells in our brain is that they are packed together very tightly. There is very little extracellular space between cells within the brains of vertebrates. The vertebrate

Figure 1.   An electron micrograph of brain tissue showing packing density of cells. Abbreviations (see text for explanation): a = unmyelinated axons; d = dendrite; g = glial cell; gf = glial filiments; s = spine on dendrite; s′ = spine head; tb = neurotubules in axon; * = end feet of axons, with flattened synaptic vesicles. x39,100. (Blackstad, 1967.)

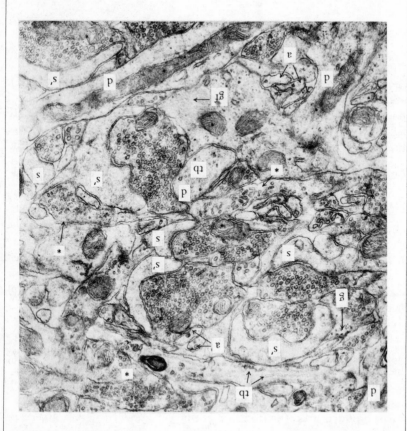

brain thus consists of an organization of billions of cells packed very closely together. Photographs taken with an *electron microscope*, which allows for clear resolution of objects as small as 15 to 20 angstrom units (1 angstrom, or Å, is 1/10,000,000 of a millimeter) provide an idea of the packing density of brain tissue (see Figure 1).

In addition to the neurons and glial cells, blood vessels penetrate the brain and spinal cord, providing the means for transport of nutrients and waste products in and out of the brain (see Figure 2). The brain and spinal cord are known collectively as the *central nervous system*.

Neurons never rest: they work from the time they are formed until they die. Some neurons are active continually, during the time the animal is sleeping as well as waking, and sometimes for 100 years or more until death quiets the cell at last. Unlike most other cells in the body (and unlike brain cells in simpler vertebrates and invertebrates), neurons in the central nervous system of mammals do not divide for more than a short time after birth. As they have become more and more specialized

Figure 2. Schematic representation of *meninges* (coverings of the brain), blood vessels, and nervous tissue. The blood vessels pierce the outer covering layer (*dura mater*) and travel in the *subarachnoid space*. The blood vessel branches that penetrate into the brain are enclosed in a sheath of the inner-covering layer (*pia mater*). (Gardner, 1968.)

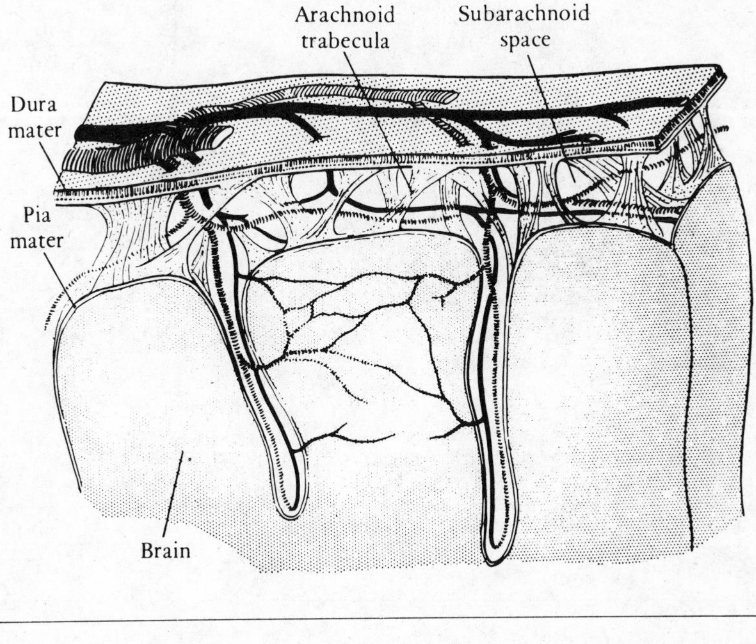

Figure 3. (*A*) Diagram of a peripheral motor neuron. *a* = naked axon; *b* = axon with myelin but without Schwann's sheath (a thin sleeve of flattened cells around the myelin); *c* = normal myelinated axon; *d* = axonal endings, covered only with Schwann's sheath; *e* = naked end feet, *f* = broken lines indicate great length of these axons. (*B*) Purkinje cell from the cerebellum of man. Note complexity and beauty of dendritic tree. There may be as many as 200,000 synapses on such a neuron. *a* = axon; *b* = axon branch; *d* = dendrites (Golgi silver stain, after Ramon y Cajal). (*C*) Pyramidal neuron from cerebral cortex of rabbit. Only a small part of the axon is shown. It may run for a considerable distance in the white substance which underlies the cortex. (Bloom & Fawcett, 1968.)

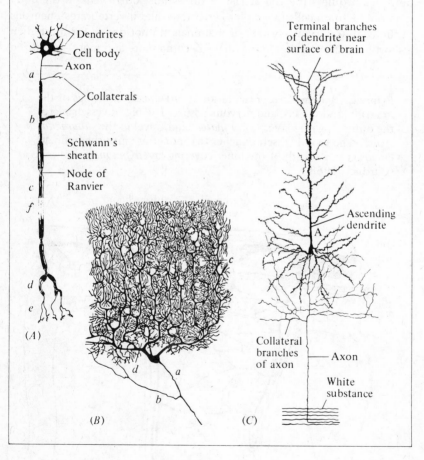

during evolution, mammalian neurons have apparently lost the capacity for continual cell division, or *mitosis*. It may be that they are inhibited from dividing by the dense packing of other cells around them. Whatever the explanation, we are born with virtually all the neurons we will ever have. When neurons die, as they do throughout the life of an animal, they are not replaced. This is an important realization, with implications with respect to aging and recovery of functioning (or lack of it) following brain damage. Neurons do retain some ability to heal themselves if they are injured, however, even though they cannot divide. These comments do not apply to glial cells, which retain the capacity for cell division.

WHAT DOES A "TYPICAL" NEURON LOOK LIKE?

It is as difficult to select a "typical" animal as it is to describe a "typical" neuron. Neurons come in a great variety of sizes and shapes. Figure 3 shows three different types of neurons that can be found in the central nervous system of all mammals.

It is a good idea to keep this diversity of structure in mind, even while we discuss the general features of neurons, because diversity in anatomical detail probably means diversity in function. However, in order to discuss some of the general properties which are true of all neurons, we will imagine a "representative" neuron as pictured in Figure 4.

It is characteristic of vertebrate neurons that the cell body branches out and forms a treelike structure. These branches are called *dendrites*. The Purkinje cell, a type of neuron found in all mammalian brains, has a very elaborate dendritic structure (Figure 3B). One of the branches from the cell body is usually longer than the others. Instead of tapering to a point, it forms small *end feet*, which terminate in close proximity to other cells. This is called the *axon*. The axon may branch several times and form axon collaterals. The axon is the part of the neuron which carries messages from the cell body to the end feet. The end feet, in turn, form functional junctions with other cells. While dendrites do not extend for more than a few millimeters from the cell body, it is not uncommon for the axon of a neuron to extend for a meter or more.

Many neurons have their axons encased in a white material called the *myelin sheath* or, simply, myelin. Myelin is actually the cell body and cell membrane of a type of glial cell. Outside the central nervous system these cells are known as Schwann cells (after their discoverer, Theodore Schwann, a nineteenth century German physician). As illustrated in Figure 5, each Schwann cell forms a complete segment of myelin

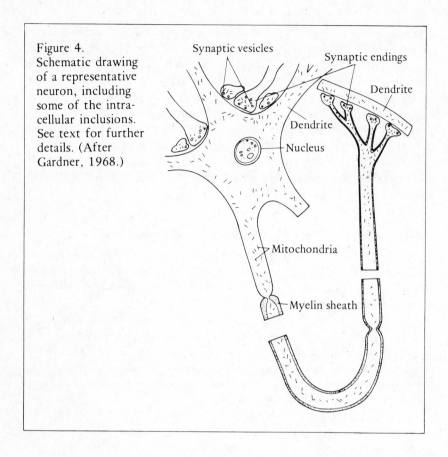

Figure 4.
Schematic drawing
of a representative
neuron, including
some of the intra-
cellular inclusions.
See text for further
details. (After
Gardner, 1968.)

around the axon of the neuron. Between these segments of myelin are gaps where there is little or no myelin over the membrane of the axon. These small gaps, which occur at regular intervals along myelinated axons, play an important part in the conduction of nerve impulses down the axon, as will be discussed later in this chapter. The gaps are called the *nodes of Ranvier,* after their discoverer, Louis Ranvier, a French anatomist. Not all neurons have such an arrangement of individual myelin sheath and nodes of Ranvier. These neurons are usually called "unmyelinated," but the term is not strictly accurate, inasmuch as such axons do usually share the myelin from a single Schwann cell, as pictured in Figure 6.

Myelinization from Schwann cells is more common in neurons outside the central nervous system, in the *peripheral nervous system,* such as on the axons bringing sensory signals from the skin. Myelinization is found throughout the brain and spinal cord. Here the wrapping cells are not strictly termed Schwann cells, they are another type of glial cell, but

Figure 5. Diagram to illustrate the hypothetical unwrapping of a myelin sheath from an axon. It is important to realize that this is a purely hypothetical unrolling to show the mature anatomy of the sheath; it does not represent the developmental process. (Hirano & Dembitzer, 1967.)

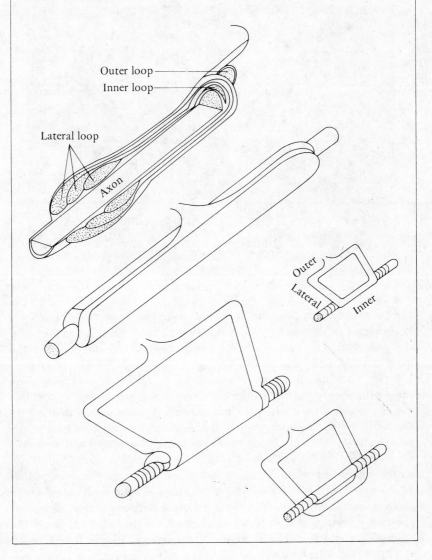

Figure 6. Electron micrograph of unmyelinated nerve from a rat. A single Schwann cell (nucleus of cell shown in upper left) wraps itself around many different axons. x25,000 (Bloom & Fawcett, 1968.)

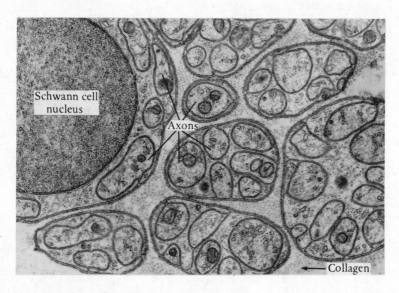

the process is very similar. In every myelinated neuron, the myelin is restricted to the axon. It does not extend onto the cell body or onto the end feet. The part of the cell body that tapers out to form the axon is known as the *axon hillock.*

Inside each neuron is an endlessly busy biochemical factory. The most prominent structure in the cell body is the *nucleus,* which contains the *chromosomes,* the carriers of the hereditary information that guides the cell's function. Surrounding the nucleus in the cell body is the *intracellular fluid,* a rich broth of all the many molecules and elements necessary for the life of the cell. [A consideration of the detailed biology of the cell is important for more advanced work; an interested reader is referred to J. D. Watson, *Molecular biology of the gene* (1970).] There is an intracellular transport system in most neurons which allows for the transportation of materials manufactured in the cell body down the axon to the end feet. The axon also contains intracellular fluid.

The "skin" of the neuron is called the cell membrane. It is approximately 75 to 100 angstroms thick in most neurons so far examined. Its detailed structure is not precisely known. In addition to forming the outer skin of the neuron, the cell membrane performs a particularly important function: It is quite porous to some particles and less porous to other particles. This type of membrane is called a *semipermeable* membrane. The capacity of the neuron to generate and transmit the nerve impulses which produce behavior depends on this ability of the membrane to discriminate among various particles.

Neurons are the best-studied type of cell in the brain, but they are not the most numerous. The great majority of cells in the brain and spinal cord are glial cells. Several varieties of glial cells are pictured in Figure 7. Each neuron in the central nervous system of vertebrates has some glial cells associated with it, typically clustered around the cell body. Because of this type of glial "packing," the cell bodies of neurons only rarely touch one another.

Figure 7. Drawings of various types of glial cells in the nervous system based on light microscopy. (A) Protoplasmic astrocyte; (B) fibrous astrocyte; (C) microglia; (D) oligodendroglia. (Bloom & Fawcett, 1968.)

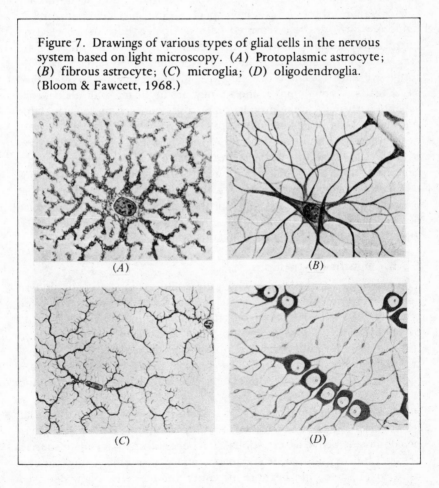

(A)

(B)

(C)

(D)

Are there special "mind-producing" features of neurons?

It has sometimes been assumed that neurons must differ from all other cells in nature in some critical fashion because their combined, organized activity in our own heads (and, we infer, in the heads of other human beings) produces a certain insistent belief that we are conscious. Is there some single physiologic characteristic which sets neurons apart from all the other types of cells which have evolved? The answer seems to be "no" or, at least, "not one that can be specified so far." Neurons, as we shall see, produce electric signals in response to stimulation, but so do muscle cells. Neurons manufacture and secrete some very potent chemical substances, but so do cells in the adrenal gland, the anterior pituitary, and elsewhere. Neurons possess a metabolic "pumping" system which allows them to pump some particles from a region of lesser concentration into a region of greater concentration, but so do kidney cells. Perhaps there is no one, special, mind-producing feature of neurons which can be discovered with microelectrodes or the electron microscope. Yet unless we are deluded in our conviction that we are conscious—and such an argument is often difficult to squash satisfactorily—we must conclude that neurons, in the aggregate, have evolved some features not found in the kidney or the heart. Not all neurons seem to participate in the production of consciousness, by the way: large portions of our brains seem to operate quite effectively without any need to intrude on our awareness. Perhaps it is the unique combination of biological capabilities which neurons have evolved that give us the capacity to think about our own thoughts. To understand the operations of the brain better, there are two features of neurons in particular that we need to consider in some detail; the ability of neurons to produce electric signals; and their ability to secrete "messenger" molecules which allow for the transmission of signals to other cells.

Electric signaling by neurons

You may have seen articles in which the brain is compared with modern general purpose computers. In such comparisons, the neuron is often regarded as analogous to an on-off switch, having only the capacity to be either active (on) or resting (off). There is not much merit in this analogy. Neurons are not simple on-off devices. Neurons are extraordinarily complex products of evolution, products that our modern technology cannot yet begin to match. We will, from time to time, find it useful to describe neurons as being on or off, as resting or active, but these are simplifying terms, or sometimes useful fictions. Neurons never rest. They are not turned off until they die. To be alive is to be continually active and continually dependent upon adequate sources of food and oxygen. Neurons, for example, have only a few minutes of oxygen reserve; they begin to die within minutes after being deprived of an oxygen supply. Even in deep sleep or coma, the brain does not "shut down." Other explanations, as described in Chapter 10, must be sought for such quiet states.

As mentioned above, one of the important characteristics of the membrane of the neuron is that it is semipermeable. Among the small particles to which the membrane is differentially permeable are *ions*. An ion is an electrically charged particle, formed in several ways. In water, substances such as salt (sodium chloride, abbreviated NaCl) break apart, or *dissociate*, to form two or more ions. There are two formed as NaCl dissociates: the sodium ion, Na^+, and the chloride ion, Cl^-. (The abbreviation Na for sodium comes from the Latin word *natrium*, for sodium.) You will notice that the symbols for ions include either a positive ($+$) or a negative (–) part. The sign indicates whether the ion carries a positive or a negative electric charge. An ion is positively charged (as, for example, Na^+) if it has lost one or more electrons in the process of dissociation. An ion is negatively charged (as, for example, Cl^-) if it has added one or more electrons during the process of dissociation. Electrons are one of the fundamental constituents of matter. They have a negative electric charge.

Positively charged ions are called *cations* because they are attracted to the *cathode*, or negatively charged pole, of a battery. Negative ions are known as *anions* because they are attracted to the *anode*, or positive pole, of a battery. (All this terminology may not be of overwhelming interest to you at the moment, but it will be useful from time to time. It may also be useful to consult an introductory chemistry text for further details regarding ions and related matters.)

Since the brain is basically a liquid medium, substances such as NaCl and potassium chloride (abbreviated KCl, the Latin word for potassium being *kalium*) do not exist. Instead, the ions Na^+, K^+, Cl^- are found. With respect to the electric signaling of neurons, three kinds of ions are particularly important: Na^+, K^+, and a group known collectively as the *organic anions* (A^-). The *organic* anions (so-called because they contain carbon) are relatively large as ions go; they are found mainly within the neurons. The amount of charge carried by a particular ion is indicated by the number of charge signs it has. Organic ions have varying amounts of negative charge. The fact that ions possess electric charge is of fundamental importance in understanding the nerve impulse. One more fact to consider is that positive ions, or cations, repel each other but are attracted to anions. Likewise, negative ions, or anions, repel each other but are attracted to cations.

THE RESTING VOLTAGE ACROSS THE MEMBRANE OF THE NEURON

Because it is not equally porous to the different kinds of ions in its environment, the cell membrane of the neuron produces an unequal distribution between the different types of ions inside the neuron and those outside the neuron. Some ions can cross the membrane more easily than others. For example, Na^+ ions penetrate the resting membrane with much greater difficulty than do K^+ ions. The larger organic anions inside the cell cannot penetrate to the exterior of the membrane at all under normal conditions. In addition, there are biologic devices located within the cell membrane which actively transport some types of ions from the inside of the cell to the outside as well as transport other types of ions from the outside of the cell membrane to the interior. The consequence of the combined forces on the ions is an unequal distribution of ion types on the inside as compared with that existing on the outside. Figure 8 shows a hypothetical diagram which summarizes the situation as it seems to be in most neurons studied so far. Several facts are worth emphasizing here. The intracellular fluid inside the neuron contains a higher concentration of K^+ ions than does the extracellular fluid immediately surrounding the neuron. The intracellular fluid, on the other hand, contains a lower concentration of Na^+ ions than does the extracellular fluid immediately surrounding the neuron. The intracellular fluid contains a number of large organic ions (A^-), whereas there are virtually none of these molecular fragments outside the neuron. There are "pores," or channels, in the membrane to allow for the passage of Na^+, K^+, and Cl^- ions.

Overall there is a slight excess of negatively charged ions on the interior of the membrane as compared with the number of positive ions on the interior. There is a slight excess of positively charged ions on the exterior surface of the membrane as compared with the number of negatively charged ions on the exterior surface of the membrane. It should be pointed out that the size of these excesses is very small when compared with the number of positive and negative charges available in the intracellular and extracellular fluid. Nevertheless, these excesses are sufficient to produce a *voltage difference* (or *potential*) across the membrane of the cell of approximately 70 millivolts (1 millivolt is equal to 1/1,000 volt). Stated in a slightly different way, the extent to which the electric charges carried by the ions are separated by the membrane can be measured as an electric voltage across the membrane. In the case of the neuron's membrane, the inside of the membrane is negatively charged with respect to the outside, and the amount of the voltage is 70 millivolts. A resting voltage across the membrane has been found in every neuron that has been examined, from those in the abdomen of a sea slug to those in the frontal cortex of a monkey. In some neurons, this resting potential is as great as –90 millivolts and in others, as low as –50 millivolts. The minus sign is with respect to the inside of the neuron. It indicates that the inside of the membrane is always negative with respect to the outside during the resting state.

Figure 8. Hypothetical diagram to illustrate separation of ions by the semipermeable membrane of the neuron. Sizes of symbols in left- and righthand colums indicate relative concentrations of the ions. K^+ = potassium ion; Na^+ = sodium ion; A^- = large organic anions; Cl^- = chloride ion. The hypothetical membrane illustrated here contains "pores" or ion channels, such that K^+ and Cl^- can move through them relatively easily, Na^+ with difficulty, and A^- not at all. (After Ruch & Patton, 1965.)

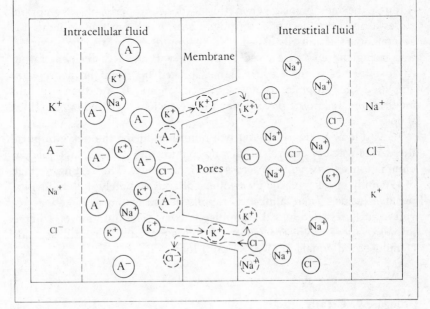

NEURONS IN ACTION: THE NERVE IMPULSE

Neurons do not usually remain at rest for very long. In response to stimulation or "spontaneously," neurons become active. They produce *nerve impulses,* which are also called *action potentials.* This is indicated when the resting voltage across the membrane is replaced by a voltage which momentarily reverses the negative charge inside the axon and replaces it with a positive charge. This voltage reversal of the action potential lasts only a fraction of a second. The neuron then recovers the resting voltage and is ready to respond to further stimulation. Meanwhile, the original action potential is transmitted down the axon to the end feet. This fundamental biological event can occur in an individual neuron thousands of times each hour and countless millions of times in the lifetime of the cell. Multiplied by roughly 10 billion, these voltage changes are what constitute our sensations, feelings, thoughts, emotions, dreams, fears, movements. They are the stuff of our mind. The action potential is, as far as we know, the only way in which excitation reaching the cell body and dendrites of a neuron can be transmitted down the axon of a cell and prepare it to communicate with another.

The tiny electric nerve impulses of neurons can be readily recorded with various electronic devices developed over the past forty or so years. Figure 9 is a simplified diagram which shows only the major elements in a typical recording setup. The electrical activity of a neuron can be measured by inserting a tapering microelectrode directly into the neuron through the membrane. When this is done properly, the membrane closes around the electrode, forming a seal which can remain intact for several hours if not disturbed. Nerve impulses can also be recorded by placing the electrode close to the cell without actually penetrating it. In either case, the electric signals picked up from the neuron are amplified (the amplifier is not shown in Figure 9) and then fed into an electronic recording or a display device such as a cathode ray oscilloscope.

As you look at Figure 10 you will note that during the nerve impulse there is an actual *reversal* of the normal resting voltage, not just an elimination of any voltage across the membrane. The resting voltage of –70 millivolts is replaced by a voltage of approximately +30 millivolts, positive inside. Then, almost as rapidly as the resting voltage was reversed, it is restored and the impulse is over. The duration of a nerve impulse varies in different neurons, but it is typically 1 to 2 milliseconds (1 millisecond equals 1/1,000 second) long.

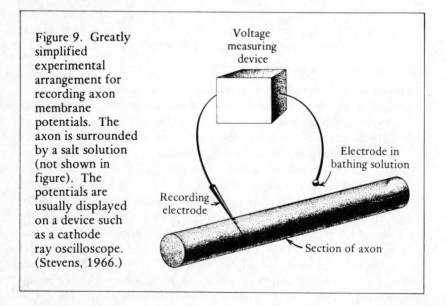

Figure 9. Greatly simplified experimental arrangement for recording axon membrane potentials. The axon is surrounded by a salt solution (not shown in figure). The potentials are usually displayed on a device such as a cathode ray oscilloscope. (Stevens, 1966.)

Voltage measuring device

Electrode in bathing solution

Recording electrode

Section of axon

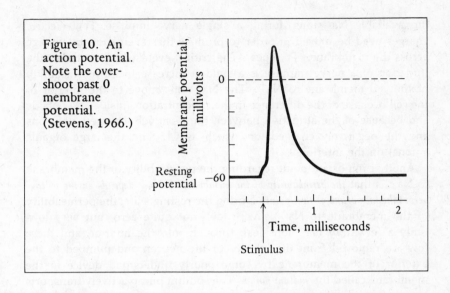

Figure 10. An action potential. Note the overshoot past 0 membrane potential. (Stevens, 1966.)

The Hodgkin cycle: the role of Na^+ in the initiation of the nerve impulse

In his superb book *The conduction of the nervous impulse* (1964), Professor A. L. Hodgkin of Cambridge University, England has written an account of the experiments and theory which propose to explain the nerve impulse and some related phenomena. Hodgkin presents the diagram from which Figure 11 was adapted. This diagram represents what is commonly called the Hodgkin cycle. As Figure 11 indicates, *the critical event underlying the initiation of the nerve impulse is an increase in the permeability of the membrane to Na^+ ions.* The molecular change which allows for this increased permeability to Na ions is not known. It presumably involves some reversible structural change in the cell membrane. Whatever the underlying molecular cause, the response of the membrane to appropriate stimulation is to suddenly become much more permeable to Na^+ ions. Immediately, Na^+ ions begin to penetrate to the interior of the neuron. They enter the neuron for two reasons: First, because the concentration of Na^+ is greater outside, and ions always move from regions of high concentration to lower concentration if not opposed by other forces; second, because the positively charged Na^+ ions (in common with other cations) are attracted to the negatively charged anions on the interior, such as Cl^- and the organic anions. For a brief period of time, perhaps less than 0.5 millisecond, the membrane becomes very permeable to Na^+. It is important to point out, however, that the number of Na^+ ions that actually penetrate the membrane to the interior is very small. This number has been calculated to be less than 1/50,000 of the available Na⁺ ions during a single nerve impulse. Few electric charges need be moved in order to produce the reversal of the voltage across the membrane. To repeat: The critical event which underlies the initiation of a nerve impulse is a sudden increase in the permeability of the cell membrane to Na⁺. The Na⁺ ions move to the interior of the cell because of the difference in the concentrations inside and outside and because of the attraction between the positively charged Na⁺ ions and the negatively charged ions (such as Cl⁻ and the large organic anions) on the interior.

Another important point regarding the permeability of the membrane to Na⁺ is that *the permeability of the membrane to Na⁺ depends on the voltage across the membrane at that point.* During the resting state, the permeability of the membrane to Na⁺ is very low—not quite zero, but very low. Only a few stray Na⁺ ions leak through into the interior; and these few are removed from the interior of the neuron and pumped to the exterior of the membrane by some poorly understood device in the membrane called the *sodium pump.* The sodium pump actively transports Na⁺ ions "uphill" from a region of lower Na⁺ concentration inside the neuron to a region of higher concentration of Na⁺ outside the neuron. However, when a nerve impulse occurs and the permeability of the

Figure 11. The Hodgkin cycle. A positive-feedback situation develops when the membrane is sufficiently depolarized. At this point the membrane becomes increasingly permeable to sodium, which enters the neuron and further depolarizes the membrane. This process is stopped by another process known as sodium inactivation. (Modified slightly from Hodgkin, 1964.)

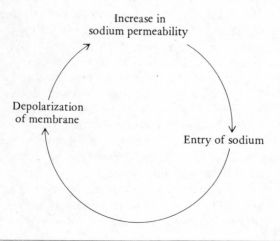

membrane to Na^+ increases, more Na^+ ions begin to enter the cell. As the Na^+ ions enter the neuron, the positive charge that they carry alters the voltage across the membrane at that point, making the interior more positive. This rapidly reduces the resting potential from -70 millivolts inside to -60 millivolts, then on to -40, -10 to 0, and past 0 (without stopping) to about +30 millivolts inside—a *reversal* of the resting potential. This process whereby the voltage across the membrane is reduced toward zero is called *depolarization*. The membrane is said to be depolarized as the voltage across it approaches zero. In other words, as Na^+ ions begin to enter the axon, the membrane becomes slightly depolarized at that point. This slight depolarization in turn further increases the permeability of the membrane to Na^+ at that point, so that still more Na^+ ions rush in. There is, for a short time, a *positive feedback* situation such that the more Na^+ ions that enter the neuron, the more depolarized the membrane becomes at that point; and the more depolarized the membrane becomes, the more permeable it becomes to Na^+ ions. Nothing succeeds like success! Obviously, this positive feedback could go on only until the membrane is completely open to the passage of Na^+ ions. Suddenly, as the internal voltage reaches about +30 millivolts, the permeability of the membrane to Na^+ suddenly returns to a low level. It is not known what breaks the positive feedback of the Hodgkin cycle. Almost as rapidly as the permeability of the membrane to Na^+ has increased, it is shut off. This phase of the nerve impulse is called *sodium inactivation*. It refers to the sudden *inactivation* of the permeability of the membrane to Na^+ ions. Na^+ ions on either side of the cell membrane are now nearly totally blocked again from moving across the membrane to the other side. In another half millisecond or so, the voltage across the membrane has been restored to the original resting voltage of -70 inside. The nerve impulse is over.

RECOVERY: THE ROLE OF K^+ IN THE RESTORATION OF THE RESTING POTENTIAL

The recovery of the resting voltage across the cell membrane is due in large part to a change in the permeability of the membrane to another ion, K^+. Figure 12 illustrates how the changes in the permeability of the Na^+ and K^+ ions is related to the production of the action potential.

At this point, it is necessary to introduce a new term, that of *conductance*. The conductance of ions and the permeability of the membrane to ions are very closely related concepts. In fact, they are often used as though they mean the same thing, even though this is not exactly the case. But for our immediate purpose of considering the rapid changes underlying the action potential, we can treat the two terms as approximately the same. Strictly speaking, conductance is a measure of the ability of a substance to conduct electric current. In the case of the

Figure 12. Relationships among the action potential in an axon and the membrane conductance changes for Na$^+$ (gNa$^+$) and K$^+$ (gK$^+$). Note that the rising phase of the action potential is primarily due to the conductance change to Na$^+$, while the falling phase is primarily due to the conductance change to K$^+$. We owe these insights to A. L. Hodgkin and A. F. Huxley (1952).

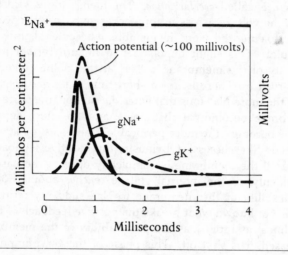

cell membrane, the conductance refers to the ability of the membrane to conduct ionic current carried by various ions, such as Na$^+$ and K$^+$. Figure 12 is adapted from the classic work of A. L. Hodgkin and A. F. Huxley, who along with B. Katz and J. C. Eccles have received Nobel prizes for their scientific contributions to our understanding of the action of neurons. The Hodgkin-Huxley theory of nerve action employs the use of ionic conductance rather than ionic permeability; we will follow their usage. Figure 12 shows the relationship among the action potential and the membrane conductance changes. Note that the conductance of a substance is measured in *mhos* [in this case, millimhos (1 millimho is equal to 1/1,000 mho)].

The increased conductance of the membrane to K$^+$ follows a different time course than is the case with Na$^+$. The peak of the conductance for K$^+$ does not occur until after the sodium inactivation phase has begun and Na$^+$ ions can no longer readily get across the membrane. Let us focus for the moment on the conductance curve for K$^+$. As the conductance (permeability) for K$^+$ increases, K$^+$ ions move *out of the neuron,* because the concentration of K$^+$ ions inside the neuron is much greater than the concentration of K$^+$ ions outside the neuron. Although the negative charge on the organic anions and C1$^-$ ions still exerts an attractive force on the K⁺, there is so much K⁺ inside that the outward movement of K⁺ ions is greater than the force exerted on them by the anions on the interior. There is thus a net outflow of positive charge carried by the K⁺ ions. *This outflow of positive charge carried by the K⁺ ions counteracts the inward flow of positive charge carried by the Na⁺ ions and restores the voltage across the membrane to its original −70 millivolts inside.* Both the initial reversal of the membrane's resting voltage and the subsequent restoration of the original resting voltage are due to sudden and brief increases in the membrane's permeability to the flow of Na⁺ and K⁺ ions. *Na⁺ is the critical ion for the initial rising phase of the action potential. K⁺ is the critical ion for the falling phase of the action potential.*

You may wonder what happens to the Na⁺ ions trapped inside the neuron when the sodium inactivation phase occurs and what happens to the K⁺ ions which have migrated to the outside of the neuron during the action potential. The first thing to point out is that there are actually very few Na⁺ ions responsible for the rising phase and a very small number of K⁺ ions responsible for the restoration of the resting voltage. Even if the Na⁺ ions and K⁺ ions were not returned to where they came from, it would not make any real difference in the amplitude of the nerve impulse until thousands of impulses had occurred. The relatively few extra Na⁺ ions inside the neuron are presumably pumped back to the exterior of the cell by the sodium pump. But it is important to realize that the recovery of the resting voltage is not dependent upon returning the few Na⁺ ions to the outside. The recovery of the resting voltage is accomplished by the outflow of K⁺ ions. Likewise, some of the K⁺ ions lost by the neuron during the action potential are transported back into the cell by an active pumping process. It is also possible that additional K⁺ ions may be taken in by surrounding glial cells. Under normal circumstances, the supply of both Na⁺ and K⁺ is more than ample to allow neurons to fire thousands of times per hour for a lifetime.

REFRACTORY PERIODS

What happens if a second stimulus is applied to the neuron before the resting voltage has been fully restored? Can the neuron respond to this fresh stimulus? The answer is no if the second stimulus is applied during the early part of the sodium inactivation phase. This period of time following the initiation of one nerve impulse during which no stimulus, no matter how strong, can produce another nerve impulse is called the *absolute refractory period.* If we consider the fact that during the sodium inactivation phase no Na⁺ ions can cross the membrane, it is understandable that no nerve impulse could be initiated. If, however, the second stimulus is applied a short time later, *and the stimulus is strong enough,* then the neuron can produce a second nerve impulse. This later period of time during which the stimulus must be stronger than normal is called the *relative refractory period.* The absolute refractory period places a ceiling on the frequency of action potentials with which a neuron can respond to stimulation. For example, if the absolute refractory period for a particular neuron is 0.5 millisecond, the maximum frequency that is theoretically possible for that neuron is 2,000 impulses per second.

One of the implications of the existence of a relative refractory period is that a stronger stimulus which lasts for a period of time will be able to produce a more rapid *rate* of action potentials than will a weaker stimulus of the same duration. This fact provides the nervous system the physiologic basis for a "code" whereby it can code the intensity of a stimulus into the frequency of nerve impulses. There is no question that this code is operative. However, in many of the cases in which this matter has been examined, the frequency code seems to operate in a range of frequencies below those which would involve the relative refractory period. It may be that our nervous system has evolved in such in way as to be able to code most intensities satisfactorily without "pushing the limits" of the system.

THE "ALL-OR-NONE" NATURE OF THE NERVE IMPULSE

If a stimulus is strong enough to evoke a nerve impulse in a neuron, the *strength* of that nerve impulse is always the same. Stronger stimuli do not produce stronger nerve impulses, although they can produce more of them. The strength of a nerve impulse, measured in the amount of the voltage change, is constant for a given neuron and not dependent on the strength of the event that initiates the nerve impulse. This characteristic of neurons is referred to as the *all-or-none law.* Either the neuron "fires" with all its available energy during a nerve impulse or it does not fire at all. While this law is true across wide varieties of neurons, there are some necessary qualifications, as we shall see.

PROPAGATION OF THE NERVE IMPULSE DOWN THE AXON

The Hodgkin-Huxley theory of nerve action also provides an explanation of how the nerve impulse is propagated down the axon to the end feet, where it then stops. This process is diagrammed in Figure 13. A nerve impulse usually starts at or near the axon hillock, where the cell body begins to taper out into the axon. It has been demonstrated in some neurons that the membrane has a lower *threshold* at this point than elsewhere. The threshold of a neuron is the minimum depolarization necessary to trigger a nerve impulse. Another way of thinking about the threshold is as the degree of voltage change required to bring the membrane into the Hodgkin cycle.

Let us consider the situation in which a nerve impulse has been initiated near the axon hillock. As you know, the rising phase of the nerve impulse is produced by the inflow of Na^+ ions at the point of initiation. This flow of ions produces an electric current or, more precisely, an

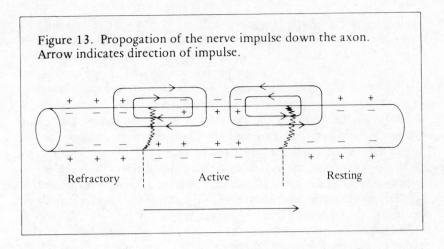

Figure 13. Propogation of the nerve impulse down the axon. Arrow indicates direction of impulse.

ionic current that by bringing more positive charge into the axon (carried by the Na⁺ ions) serves to depolarize the membrane at that point, causing an even greater inflow of more Na⁺ ions. *This ionic current produced also depolarizes the next adjacent area of the membrane.* It is this depolarization which alters the membrane just ahead of the nerve impulse so that the membrane enters the Hodgkin cycle. This depolarization must be of sufficient size, usually about 10 to 15 millivolts.

As the next region of membrane is sufficiently depolarized, Na⁺ ions begin to enter at that point in the membrane. As this occurs, the ionic current produced at the new point alters the membrane's permeability to Na⁺ still further down the axon to the point where it is now depolarized too. Thus, in this fashion, the nerve impulse "travels" down the axon, the ionic currents produced by the entry of Na⁺ ions at one point in the axon acting as the stimulus for the next adjacent area of axon.

SPEED OF THE NERVE IMPULSE DOWN THE AXON

In warm-blooded animals, the speed with which the nerve impulse travels down the axon varies in different neurons from less than 1 meter per second (about the rate of a leisurely walk) to top speeds of about 120 meters per second. The speed with which a particular neuron conducts nerve impulses is a characteristic of that neuron and depends primarily on two factors: the diameter of the axon and the nature of the neuron—that is whether or not it has nodes of Ranvier. The larger the diameter of the axon, the faster the neuron can conduct nerve impulses. The demands for faster and faster communication among body parts resulted in the evolution of larger and larger diameter axons. For example, the giant neurons of the squid, *Loligo*, which are primarily responsible for supplying the muscles involved in the high-speed escape movements of this animal, are over a foot in length and about one

millimeter in diameter! The speed with which these huge neurons can
carry nerve impulse has, of course, been critical in the survival of this
species, by allowing them to escape rapidly from predators. But there
are other demands in the design of neurons as well. For example, we
need fast-conducting neurons from our eyes to our brains in order to
respond to fast-moving objects. If we relied for speed solely on the
diameter of the axons in the optic nerve from the eye to the brain,
we would need optic nerves several feet in diameter in order to contain
the million or so axons that we have in each optic nerve. The answer
to this problem was the evolution of myelinated fibers with nodes. In
heavily myelinated axons, in which nodes of Ranvier are present at
regular intervals, the nerve impulse skips or jumps from one node to
the next, as shown in Figure 14. This type of impulse conduction is
called *saltatory* conduction (from the Latin word *saltare,* "to dance"). This
type of conduction increases the speed of the nerve impulse twentyfold.
The fastest conducting axons in warm-blooded animals are all myelinated. The nodes are typically about 1 millimeter apart. It is at these
nodes that the ionic current works to produce the depolarization necessary for the production of a nerve impulse. Since the current produced
at one node can travel through the core of the axon much faster than
would be the case if it traveled down the membrane itself, the time
necessary for the nerve impulse to reach the end feet is shortened.
The myelin wrapping between the nodes serves to prevent the current
from leaking out there, and the impulse is thus initiated at the next
point where the spike threshold is lowest, the next node. This is a
much faster process than the propagation of the nerve impulse in unmyelinated axons.

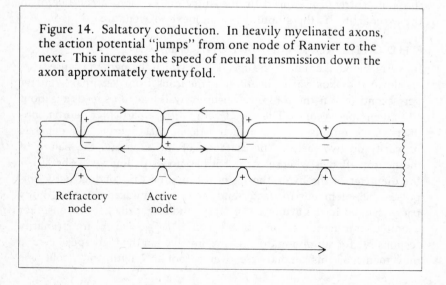

Figure 14. Saltatory conduction. In heavily myelinated axons,
the action potential "jumps" from one node of Ranvier to the
next. This increases the speed of neural transmission down the
axon approximately twentyfold.

Refractory   Active
node   node

TRANSMISSION AT THE SYNAPSE

In mammals, neurons influence other cells by means of chemical substances that they secrete from their end feet. If the cell adjacent to the end feet is a muscle cell, the point of interaction is called a *neuromuscular junction*. If the adjacent cell is another neuron, the point of interaction is called a *synapse*. (The term synapse was coined by the great English physiologist Sir Charles Sherrington long before there was any anatomical evidence available.) The major outlines of the structure of synapse can now be observed by means of the electron microscope. Figure 15 is a schematic drawing of a synapse.

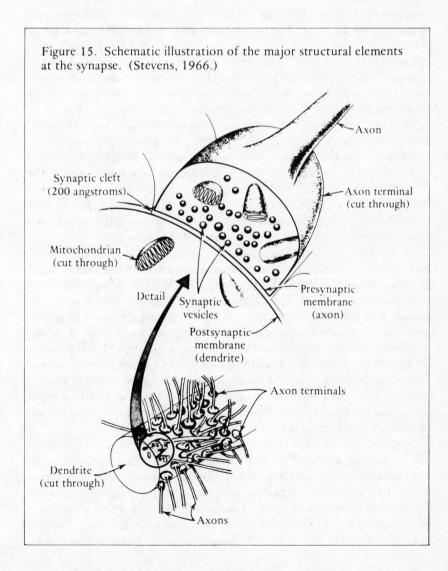

Figure 15. Schematic illustration of the major structural elements at the synapse. (Stevens, 1966.)

Axon

Synaptic cleft
(200 angstroms)

Axon terminal
(cut through)

Mitochondrian
(cut through)

Presynaptic
membrane
(axon)

Detail   Synaptic
vesicles

Postsynaptic
membrane
(dendrite)

Axon terminals

Dendrite
(cut through)

Axons

The end foot of the *presynaptic* neuron is separated from the patch of dendrite, or cell body, of the postsynaptic neuron by a space of 200 to 300 angstroms. This space between the two neurons is called the *synaptic cleft*. The three elements—the presynaptic end foot, the synaptic cleft, and the postsynaptic receptive site—are collectively known as a *synapse*. There are billions of synapses in the human brain. They are certainly the main (and possibly the only) points of communication between one neuron and another, as well as between neurons and muscle cells.

The critical event at mammalian synapses is the release of a particular chemical substance, termed the *transmitter*, from the end foot of the presynaptic neuron. This release is caused by the arrival of the nerve impulse at the end foot. The transmitters are either manufactured directly in the presynaptic end feet or in the cell body and transported down the axon to the end feet. They are stored in small packages called *synaptic vesicles*. These vesicles are large enough to be readily identified in pictures taken with an electron microscope, and an accumulation of them in an end foot serves to mark the presence of a synapse.

Even at "rest," there is a leakage of a small amount of the transmitter into the synaptic cleft (Katz, 1966). When the presynaptic end foot is invaded by a nerve impulse, however, the rate at which the transmitter is released into the synaptic cleft is increased many times. Once it is released, the transmitter diffuses across the synaptic cleft where it comes into contact with receptor molecules in the postsynaptic membrane. The exact nature of these receptor molecules is not presently known, but rapid progress is being made in research along these lines.

At some synapses, called excitatory synapses, the result of the interaction between the transmitter and the receptor molecules is a small depolarizing current which can be recorded from the postsynaptic cell with a microelectrode. This depolarizing current is called an *excitatory postsynaptic potential*, abbreviated *epsp*. At other synapses, other transmitters produce a hyperpolarizing current. A hyperpolarizing current is one which makes the interior of the cell even more negative than the resting voltage of –70 millivolts. It is directly opposite to a depolarizing current. The hyperpolarizing current is called an *inhibitory postsynaptic potential*, or *ipsp*. The terms excitatory and inhibitory reflect the fact that epsps encourage the postsynaptic neuron to produce nerve impulses and ipsps discourage nerve impulses.

In some cases, there is another chemical in addition to the transmitter which must be available for normal synaptic function. This additional substance serves to inactivate the released transmitter after it has produced its postsynaptic potential, allowing the postsynaptic receptor to become ready again to accept a fresh surge of transmitter. One transmitter which has been identified in the mammalian nervous system is acetylcholine. The substance which inactivates the acetylcholine is acetylcholine esterase. Obviously, any drug which interferes with either acetylcholine or acetylcholine esterase will change the function of the nervous system. One class of drugs which inactivates the acetylcholine esterase is the highly toxic organophosphates, which include many pesticides as well as the group of potential chemical warfare agents known as "nerve gas." Such substances (for example, parathion) are extremely lethal, acting not only on the central nervous system but at other points as well (see Goodman and Gilman, 1970, for more detailed information).

There are several different transmitters. The best-documented ones are acetylcholine, norepinephrine, and gamma amino butyric acid (GABA). GABA has been identified as the transmitter at inhibitory synapses, while both acetylcholine and norepinephrine are generally associated with excitatory synapses. Acetylcholine, however, is known to be an inhibitory transmitter at neuromuscular junctions in the heart because of a difference in the properties of the postsynaptic heart muscle cell membrane. Although there are a few exceptions, it is a *general* rule that a particular synapse is either excitatory or inhibitory.

Postsynaptic potentials, whether excitatory or inhibitory, decay with time. Subsequent release of more transmitter from the presynaptic end feet can augment these decaying potentials. The process is called *summation.* The combined effect of both epsps and ipsps on the postsynaptic cell determines how that cell will respond. The effect of an epsp is excitatory because it moves the voltage across the membrane toward the threshold for a nerve impulse (see Figure 16).

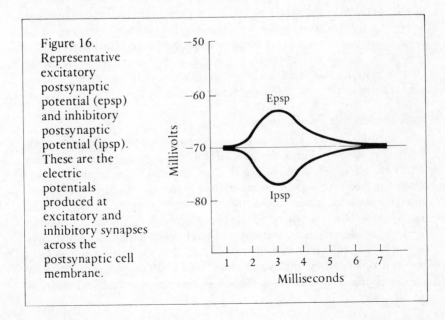

Figure 16. Representative excitatory postsynaptic potential (epsp) and inhibitory postsynaptic potential (ipsp). These are the electric potentials produced at excitatory and inhibitory synapses across the postsynaptic cell membrane.

Although the epsp alters the membrane in a depolarizing direction, as does the nerve impulse, the shape and time course are different. It is important to note that these two kinds of excitation, epsps and nerve impulses, are produced at different sites on the postsynaptic cell, and by different ionic mechanisms. Although the ionic movements underlying both the nerve impulse and the epsp are somewhat similar, they are not identical. For example, the epsp does not obey the all-or-none law. The size and duration of an epsp is dependent on the amount of transmitter released as well as related factors. Also, the epsp although depolarizing, is not regenerative. That is, it does not cause the membrane at that point to enter the Hodgkin cycle and thereby propagate the impulse into the cell body as is true for the propagation of the nerve impulse down the axon.

Synapses at which the transmitter produces a hyperpolarizing current (see Figure 16) are inhibitory. Since the hyperpolarizing current moves the voltage across the membrane further away from the firing threshold, an ipsp reduces the likelihood that the postsynaptic cell will produce a nerve impulse.

Ionic movements during an epsp

The action of an excitatory transmitter on the postsynaptic membrane apparently increases the permeability of the membrane to one or more ions. When this was first studied at the neuromuscular junction, it was found that the permeability of the membrane increased for both Na^+ ions and K^+ ions, with the inflowing Na^+ ions dominating the voltage change. However, it now appears that the particular ions to which the transmitter causes increased permeability vary from one type of synapse to another, although it is the Na^+ ion which is usually involved in an epsp. The epsp is not a nerve impulse itself, however. The epsp contributes to excitation by contributing to the overall depolarization of the neuron. The level of depolarization from a particular epsp may or may not be sufficient to reach the threshold of that cell.

Ionic movements during an ipsp

Inhibitory transmitters also alter the permeability of the postsynaptic membrane to ions. But in the case of inhibitory synapses, the two ions which are selectively affected are K^+ and Cl^-. At some inhibitory synapses, the permeability of the membrane is increased only for K^+ ions. Since they are in greater concentration inside the neuron than outside, the K^+ ions flow out, carrying positive charge with them and making the interior slightly more negative. This hyperpolarization constitutes the ipsp. At still other synapses, it seems that the critical ion is Cl^-. In this case, opening the membrane to Cl^- allows Cl^- ions to flow *into* the neuron, since Cl^- is in higher concentration outside the neurons than inside (see Figure 8). The inflow of a negative ion such as Cl^- also produces a more negative interior, a hyperpolarization. The inhibitory current of an ipsp is therefore due to the movement of K^+ or Cl^- ions or both, which tend to hyperpolarize the membrane. This hyperpolarization moves the voltage across the membrane even farther away from the nerve impulse threshold. Thus, depolarization is exciting, whereas hyperpolarization is inhibiting.

NEURONS AS COMPUTERS OF SYNAPTIC POTENTIALS

Neurons in the central nervous systems of mammals are typically encrusted with hundreds or thousands of presynaptic end feet. It would not be unusual to find 10,000 or more end feet on a single neuron. These end feet are arriving from a variety of other neurons, more than one ending from each presynaptic neuron in many cases. Some of these synapses are excitatory, some are inhibitory. The two opposing influences often act simultaneously on the postsynaptic neuron, and thus the postsynaptic cell must "compute" the net effect of these combined influences. There are three possible answers: excitation that can increase the cell's spontaneous rate of nerve impulses; inhibition that can decrease the cell's spontaneous rate of nerve impulses; or excitation and inhibition that can balance each other out for no net change. Which answer is given in a particular situation depends on the moment-to-moment balance that is struck between inhibition and excitation. If enough excitatory synapses are active to cause the overall depolarization of the neuron to exceed the cell's threshold, then there will be one or more nerve impulses produced. If the ionic currents at the inhibitory synapses are sufficient to counter the effect of the excitatory synapses, there will be no change in the firing rate of the neuron. If the hyperpolarizing currents produced at the inhibitory synapses alter the neuron sufficiently, the neuron will fall silent, dropping in its firing rate below the resting or spontaneous rate. In each case, the postsynaptic cell is a decision maker in the nervous system, one among billions of decision makers in our brains.

SUGGESTIONS FOR FURTHER READING

Katz, B. *Nerve, muscle and synapse.* New York: McGraw-Hill, 1966.

Watson, J. D. *Molecular biology of the gene.* (2nd ed.) New York: W. A. Benjamin, Inc. 1970.

Chapter 3

STRUCTURAL ORGANIZATION OF THE MAMMALIAN BRAIN

The behavior of an advanced mammal such as a chimpanzee, dolphin, or human being is more complex than that of lower vertebrates. The brain of advanced mammals is also more complex than that of lower vertebrates. We assume that these two facts are related, but at the present there is insufficient evidence to demonstrate *how* the structure of the brain of more advanced mammals is related to their behavior. There is a basic structural similarity among all vertebrate brains, including that of man. Very few parts of the brain are present in man but missing in other primates. The outstanding characteristic of the mammalian brain as contrasted with other vertebrate brains is the development of the massive *cerebral cortex*, as seen in Figure 17. The development of the cerebral cortex is of particular significance in the evolution of mammalian behavior, a topic that is discussed more fully in Chapter 8.

We need to know the structure of the nervous system of any animal if we wish to fully understand its behavior. It does not follow, however, that if we are to gain detailed knowledge of the brain of a particular species, we should then expect that the anatomy will, by itself, explain the behavior of that species. Neuroanatomy is necessary, but not sufficient, for understanding behavior. In this chapter, we will consider some relevant anatomical facts which are useful in any general discussion of vertebrate behavior.

Figure 17. Brain of the bottlenose dolphin. The lateral part of the brain has been dissected away to show underlying structures. (Jacobs, Morgane, & McFarland, 1971.)

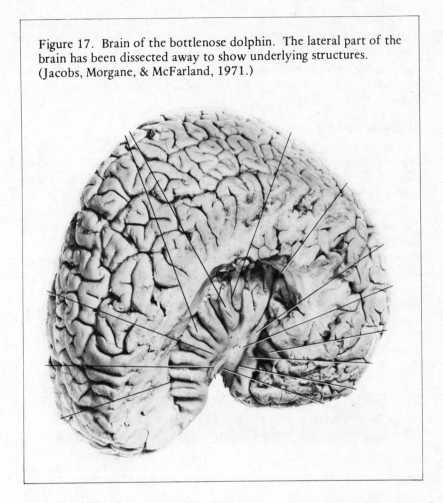

DISTINCTION BETWEEN PERIPHERAL AND CENTRAL NERVOUS SYSTEMS

Neuroanatomists divide the vertebrate nervous system into two basic components: the *central nervous system* (abbreviated CNS), which includes the brain and the spinal cord; and the *peripheral nervous system*, which includes the rest of the nervous tissue of the body. These two components are not totally separate; the axons of motor neurons (supplying the muscles) whose cell bodies are in the spinal cord form part of the peripheral nervous system, and the end feet of sensory neurons whose cell bodies are in the peripheral nervous system make synaptic contacts within the spinal cord. The distinction between central and peripheral is made by man, not nature. The CNS is the main focus of attention in this book, but the peripheral nervous system is also important because it executes the movement commands issued by the CNS. The peripheral system also receives and carries sensory information to the CNS. The peripheral nervous system is simpler and composed of many fewer neurons than the CNS.

Organization of the peripheral nervous system

The major parts of the peripheral nervous system are twelve pairs of cranial nerves and thirty-one pairs of spinal nerves. Nerves are collections of the axons of neurons bundled together like wires in a telephone cable. Large nerves, such as the optic nerve in man, contain about one million axons. Small nerves may contain only a few hundred axons. The nerves in which the axons are conducting sensory impulses toward the CNS are called sensory, or *afferent*, nerves. Nerves that conduct impulses away from the CNS to the muscles and glands of the body are called motor, or *efferent*, nerves. See Figure 18.

Most nerves contain both sensory and motor axons and are thus mixed nerves. Mixed nerves typically contain mostly sensory *or* motor axons, however. The cranial nerves are good examples.

ON OLD OLYMPUS' TOWERING TOPS

There are twelve pairs of cranial nerves that serve the head and neck regions. Some of these can be seen in Figure 19. These nerves are as follows: (1) The *olfactory* nerves. These are principally sensory nerves whose axons come from receptor cells in the mucous membrane of the nose, and are concerned with conducting afferent impulses associated

Figure 18. Greatly simplified diagram of the cross section of the human spinal cord. The swelling in the dorsal root contains the cell bodies of the sensory neurons.

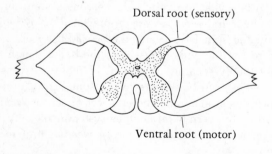

Dorsal root (sensory)

Ventral root (motor)

Figure 19. Schematic illustration of autonomic nervous system. The parasympathetic division is represented by the four cranial nerves, III, VII, IX, and X, and S1-5 and Cx (sacral and coccyx nerves). The sympathetic division is composed of the remainder of the nerves shown. The first eight cranial nerves not included in the parasympathetic division are not pictured. (Netter, 1962.)

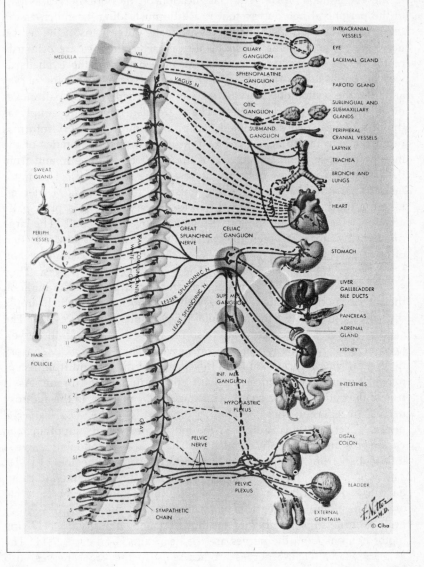

with the sense of smell. (2) The *optic* nerves. In man, monkey, and other animals with well-developed eyes, the optic nerves are very large, containing more axons than any other nerve. These nerves are mostly afferent [but in most mammals probably contain a small percentage (2 to 3 percent) of efferent axons] that carry impulses from higher centers in the brain to the eye. The exact function of these outgoing fibers to the eye is not known. The classification of the optic nerves as part of the peripheral nervous system is a little misleading inasmuch as the retina of the eye and the optic nerves are really outgrowths of the central nervous system. (3) The *oculomotor* nerves. These nerves are primarily motor nerves whose axons control the movements of the eyeballs as well as pupil size. (4) The *trochlear* nerves. These are motor nerves and, like the oculomotor nerves, are also concerned with eyeball movement. (5) The *trigeminal* nerves. These are also referred to simply as the fifth nerves. They are mixed nerves, transmitting sensory information from skin in the head region, from the mucous membranes of the mouth and nose, from the cornea of the eye, from the teeth, and from the *dura mater* (the tough outer membrane of the brain itself). The motor neurons go principally to chewing muscles. (6) The *abducens* nerves. Like the third and fourth cranial nerves, the sixth nerve is principally a motor nerve supplying the muscles which move the eyeball. The large number of neurons devoted to control of eye movements is a reflection of how man evolved from creatures which depended heavily on vision for survival. (7) The *facial* nerves. These are also mixed nerves. They contain sensory neurons conveying information from the taste buds on the anterior portion of the tongue as well as motor neurons which supply the salivary glands and the lachrymal (tear) glands of the eyes. (8) The *auditory* nerves. These nerves are also referred to as the eighth nerves. Precisely, they are the *vestibulocochlear* nerves. They are mainly sensory nerves, carrying information from the cochlea of the ear and from receptors in the inner ear concerned with equilibrium to the brain. As is true of the optic nerves, a small percentage of the neurons in the auditory nerves are efferent; their function is unclear. (9) The *glossopharyngeal* nerves. These are mixed nerves, the motor components supplying the vocal cords and some salivary glands. The sensory component conveys information from taste buds in the posterior part of the tongue. (10) The *vagus* nerves. These are mixed nerves and, as their name indicates, have a wide distribution to the tongue, throat, and various internal organs, including the heart. Their sensory components bring sensory input from a large number of locations. Among the organs receiving motor neurons from the nerves are the heart and vocal cords. (11) The *accessory* nerves. These nerves are accessory to the vagus nerves, also supplying motor axons to the vocal cords as well as to some other muscles. The accessory nerves are mainly motor nerves. (12) The *hypo-*

glossal nerves. These are motor nerves supplying the muscles of the tongue.

It is traditional among medical students, anatomy students, and others faced with the task of memorizing the names of the cranial nerves to use the following mnemonic: *On Old Olympus' Towering Tops, A French And German Viewed And Hopped.* It's a difficult line to forget, I agree, but it is sometimes hard to remember if "Towering" means "trochlear" or "trigeminal." (It's trochlear!)

THE SPINAL NERVES

The cranial nerves provide input and output paths for the head, neck, and many internal organs. The rest of the peripheral nervous system consists of thirty-one pairs of spinal nerves. Figure 18 shows a cross section of the human spinal cord cut at the point where a pair of spinal nerves are attached. The butterfly-shaped darker region constitutes the *gray matter* of the cord, composed mostly of neuronal cell bodies and dendrites together with their surrounding glial cells. The rest of the cord is *white matter*, composed primarily of neuronal axons wrapped in their whitish myelin sheath.

It appears from Figure 18 that there are actually two pairs or four separate nerves attached to the spinal cord. However, the two branches from each side actually join together a short distance from the cord and are thus considered as one nerve with two branches, or *roots*. There are two roots for each nerve, a dorsal root (closer to the back) and a ventral root (closer to the stomach). Charles Bell discovered in 1811 that these two roots have quite different functions, and Francois Magendie confirmed this fact a few years later. It was an important discovery that helped later investigators understand such phenomena as reflex activity. The dorsal root is sensory in function, carrying afferent impulses from sense receptors in the body to the spinal cord. The ventral root is motor, carrying impulses from the CNS to the muscles of the body. There is one apparent exception to this rule of "dorsal-sensory, ventral-motor." There is a set of small motor neurons in the ventral root that go *to a sense organ*, the muscle spindle organ, which is a stretch receptor organ located in the belly of muscles. This might seem to break the rule, but since these so-called "gamma efferents" actually do activate small muscle fibers in the sense organ, they too follow the *law of roots.*

The dorsal root looks different from the ventral root because of the swelling in the dorsal root near the point where it joins the spinal cord. This swelling is the *dorsal root ganglion*, which contains the cell bodies of the sensory neurons. The sensory neurons in general have two long processes, one specialized into a particular sort of sensory receptor and the other an axon. These neurons convey sensory information from sense receptors in the skin, muscles, joints, tendons, and various internal organs and tissues into the spinal cord where they synapse with neurons of the central nervous system. Some of these processes must be quite long indeed to stretch, for example, from the toe of a human being to the level of the spinal column where it enters the cord. The dorsal root neurons serving the hoof of a giraffe or the tail fin of a whale must be impressive neurons indeed!

The ventral root has no swelling, for the cell bodies of the neurons whose axons make up the ventral roots are in the spinal cord in the ventral "horn" of gray matter. The axons of these "ventral horn cells" typically go to the muscles that they activate before synapsing. A particular ventral horn cell may branch into many axon collaterals, which go to as many as several hundred different muscle fibers and thereby cause the simultaneous activation of the muscle fibers. The group of muscle fibers activated by a single ventral horn cell is called a *motor unit*.

THE AUTONOMIC NERVOUS SYSTEM

Some of the cranial and spinal nerves are also classified as belonging to the *autonomic nervous system*. Autonomic implies that the system is somehow independent, or autonomous, in function, but such is not the case. It was generally believed until recently that the responses of this system, such as modulation of blood pressure and heart rate, were beyond conscious control and thus involuntary. Over the past few years, however, Neal Miller and some of his students at Rockefeller University have demonstrated that man and other animals may be able to learn to bring some of these involuntary responses under control. We shall discuss some of these experiments in Chapter 7.

Figure 19 shows the major connections made by the autonomic nervous system. Most of the internal organs of the body receive input from the autonomic nervous system, including the heart, stomach, pancreas, bladder, intestines, adrenal medulla (the inner portion of the adrenal gland), and parts of the genital organs. The entire autonomic nervous system is composed of branches of four of the twelve cranial nerves—the oculomotor (3), facial (7), glossopharyngeal (9), and the vagus (10)—and branches of most of the spinal nerves. There are two subdivisions of the autonomic nervous system recognized: the *sympathetic* and the *parasympathetic*.

The branches of the four cranial nerves, together with a few thousand axons which emerge from the sacral portion of the spinal cord, compose the parasympathetic division. Because of the origin of the neurons of which this system is composed, it is also referred to as the *craniosacral* division. All the other neurons of the autonomic nervous system belong to the sympathetic division. The axons of these neurons emerge from branches of the spinal nerves in the middle regions of the spinal column, which are named the thoracic and lumbar regions. The sympathetic division is thus also called the *thoracolumbar* system. (It would be considerably easier if everything had just one name, but in neuroanatomy there are often two or more names for the same thing.)

The axons of the neurons which compose the parasympathetic division go directly to their destinations before synapsing. Axons of the sympathetic division, on the other hand, enter one of two chains of *ganglia* (called the *chain ganglia*), which lie along either side of the spinal column. The sympathetic axons either synapse onto neurons in the ganglion they enter or onto neurons in nearby ganglion; or in some cases, they pass through the ganglion to synapse outside the chain ganglia, closer to the organ they supply.

Functional interaction of the sympathetic and parasympathetic divisions

Most internal organs receive a nerve supply which includes contributions from both the sympathetic and parasympathetic divisions of the autonomic nervous system. As a general rule, the action of these two sets of neurons oppose one another. For example, the effect of activity of the sympathetic system on the heart is to increase the pumping of the heart—it beats faster and more forcefully. The effect of the parasympathetic division, via the vagus nerve, is to slow down the heart beat and inhibit the force of each individual contraction. The heart does not depend upon the nervous system in order to beat; it contains its own "pacemaker" cells which cause it to beat. The activity of the autonomic nervous system is to *modulate* the heart's own intrinsic beat, either by sympathetic acceleration, parasympathetic braking, or as is more typically the case, their combined action.

Another example of the functional interaction of the two opposing effects can be seen in the processes of erection and ejaculation in most male mammals. In male human sexual behavior, for example, the erection of the penis is dependent upon the rush of blood into the spongelike tissue of the penis. This response is partly one of vasodilation of the blood vessels, under the control of parasympathetic division neurons. If, for some reason, the activity of the sympathetic system dominates, erection is diminished or impossible. *Ejaculation,* however, is dependent upon a series of events which is primarily under sympathetic control; and a dominance of parasympathetic activity at this point interferes with ejaculation. The processes of erection and ejaculation, both critical to normal sexual behavior, are controlled via autonomic nervous system neurons, but the timing and dominating activity is different for the two processes. In the human female, the effect of parasympathetic activity in the vagina is that of vasodilation, whereas sympathetic activity constricts the small blood vessels in the vaginal wall. In the male, *orgasm* is a separate phenomenon from ejaculation, although both typically occur close together in time. The biological basis for orgasm is obscure, except that one assumes that it must involve activity in the brain.

FUNCTIONS OF THE SYMPATHETIC DIVISION

There are some organs which do not receive dual nerve supply from both the sympathetic and parasympathetic divisions. The sweat glands of the skin, for example, receive only sympathetic neurons. It is the activity of these sweat glands in emotional excitement which is monitored as the GSR (galvanic skin response). This change in the electrical resistance of the skin is one of the most widely used indicators for such inferred psychological phenomena as emotional excitement and attention to stimulation. The GSR is one of the components of the so-called "lie detector," which measures a variety of bodily responses such as heart rate, blood pressure, respiration pattern, and the GSR in response to various questions. Presumably, in our culture, if a person is consciously lying, this will be an "emotional" situation for him and will show up on one or more of the bodily response measures assumed to be beyond conscious control. The assumptions underlying the use of such devices can be seriously questioned.

Another organ supplied exclusively by the sympathetic division of the autonomic nervous system is the *adrenal medulla.* This is the inner portion of the adrenal glands, one of which is located on top of each kidney. When stimulated, the cells of the adrenal medulla secrete two substances of considerable importance for understanding the functions of the sympathetic division. These substances are epinephrine and norepinephrine. The compounds, together with others, are liberated from the adrenal medulla directly into the circulation and can thus rapidly reach a wide range of target tissues. Both substances are quite similar in chemical structure and in many (but not all) cases have quite similar effects on various tissues of the body. The total "package" of substances released by the adrenal medulla is usually called simply *adrenalin.* The released substances produce a very vivid, conscious sensation—a surge of adrenalin which accompanies a loud, unexpected noise, for example. Normally, both the release and the metabolic destruction of these substances is rapid, although the aftereffects of an emotional situation may be directly related to these circulating substances for many minutes. The impact of these substances on various tissues of the body, together with the other more direct neural effects of the sympathetic nervous system, is widespread. There are changes in heart rate and contraction force and effects on the smooth muscles of various internal organs and on constriction and dilation of blood vessels. One of the most noticeable consequences of adrenalin is the stimulating effect it has on the heart, increasing both the force and frequency of the beat. Adrenalin also dilates some of the blood vessels through which the heart is pumping blood, particularly those supplying the larger muscles of the body. The overall effect is to raise the blood pressure as well as speed up the pulse. In addition, one of the adrenalin components, epinephrine (and to a much lesser degree, norepinephrine), increases the amount of sugar released into the blood stream from various storage depots, where it becomes more readily available for use by the muscles.

THE "FIGHT-OR-FLIGHT" CONCEPTS OF SYMPATHETIC ACTIVATION

The most durable generalization describing the overall effects of activation of the sympathetic division is that of W. B. Cannon's. Cannon, an American physiologist whose work on the function of the autonomic nervous system remains one of the classic research projects of physiology, summarized the role of sympathetic activation as *preparing the animal for immediate emergency action: for "fight or flight"* (Cannon, 1929). Such bodily changes as the increased pumping action of the heart and the mobilization of blood sugar reserves for quick distribution to the large skeletal muscles do seem very adaptive to the ancient and continuing drama of prey and predator. The sympathetic division and the adrenal medulla are activated in man as in many other animals by a wide variety of events, including pain, threat of injury, emotional excitement (both pleasant and unpleasant), vigorous exercise, exposure to cold, etc. Attacks of nonspecific fear or anxiety in man are typically characterized by sympathetic activation and adrenal medullary secretion. Such effects certainly must contribute to the often acute bodily distress associated with anxiety. A question of considerable relevance is: To what extent is this "emergency" response of the body, which evolved in earlier forms of life, still useful in our modern society? There is no question but that the ability to mount sudden, lethal attacks on animals and against other men was one of the factors which contributed to the survival of our ancestors, both remote and recent. Yet it can be argued that our civilization hovers on the brink of incredible holocaust largely because of our enormous destructive capacity. It may also be that the activation of sympathetic nervous system responses in situations of personal threat may be incompatible with the evolution of a more peaceful society that must increasingly find nonviolent ways to solve conflict or otherwise destroy itself. It is a sobering thought that the time which seems necessary to evolve such complicated biological mechanisms as the autonomic nervous system is much longer than what appears to be needed to solve the problems in our civilization. We cannot rely on natural evolution. In any event, however, we should try to understand the biological potential which we have inherited from our ancestors.

THE "CONSERVATION OF ENERGY" CONCEPT OF PARASYMPATHETIC ACTIVATION

In contrast to the quite widespread distribution of axons belonging to the sympathetic division, the neurons of the parasympathetic division form a much more restricted, discrete pattern of distribution to the organs they supply. Also, there is no activation of the adrenal medulla or other secretory organs and thus no release of activating substances into the general circulation as a result of parasympathetic activation. The "mass effect" on the body during emergency conditions has no parallel when parasympathetic neurons are activated. Cannon's generalization regarding the parasympathetic division is that it acts in a complementary way to the sympathetic division, operating to protect and conserve the energy resources of the body. This generalization is a little hazy, but it covers such diverse effects as the slowing of the heart rate, the stimulation of digestive processes (which will increase the usable energy available to the body), the secretion of saliva, and the movements of the esophagus important in swallowing.

"SEEK SIMPLICITY, AND DISTRUST IT"

It is important not to let the anatomical and proposed functional distinctions among the various components of the nervous system mislead us about the nature of the whole integrated system. As we mentioned earlier, the autonomic nervous system is not autonomic. It is not separated from the central nervous system; it serves simply as one of the major output paths available to the central nervous system. Either the neural activity in *any* peripheral nervous system neuron is part of a reflex which must include neurons within the spinal cord or (more typically) peripheral activity is part of complex behavior "programs" organized at various levels of the brain and spinal cord. In order to begin to understand the ways in which the nervous system works, we must sometimes ignore, temporarily, the "wholeness" of its function as a concession to the limited attention with which our nervous system provides us. Philosopher A. N. Whitehead's advice is useful here: "Seek simplicity, and distrust it."

It will be helpful to later discussions if we can gain at least a superficial appreciation of some relevant neuroanatomy. Neuroanatomists often devote their entire working careers to the detailed knowledge of small parts of particular brains, and it may be wise to keep the truly staggering complexity of "brains in general" in perspective as you read through the following very simplified outline. (Since the neuroanatomical picture presented here must be quite limited, you might consider having a more sophisticated text handy as an additional source. Two such sources are listed at the end of this chapter.)

The basic plan for the mammalian central nervous system

It is possible to discern a basic organizational plan for the mammalian central nervous system from comparative studies of various mammalian species. Evolution has wrought great differences in the brains of rats and men, but there are even greater similarities. The differences seem to be primarily due to the fact that in higher land-dwelling mammals, such as the chimpanzee and man, there is a great increase in the development of those parts of the brain devoted to processing input from the *distance sense organs*, the eye and ear. Coupled with this growth is an even more profound increase in the area of the brain that we believe to be most concerned with more complex information processing and logic functions—the cerebral cortex.

Figure 20 illustrates some anatomical terms. In an animal that walks on four legs, the back side is referred to as the *dorsal* surface, the belly side as the *ventral* surface, and the sides as the *lateral* surfaces. The

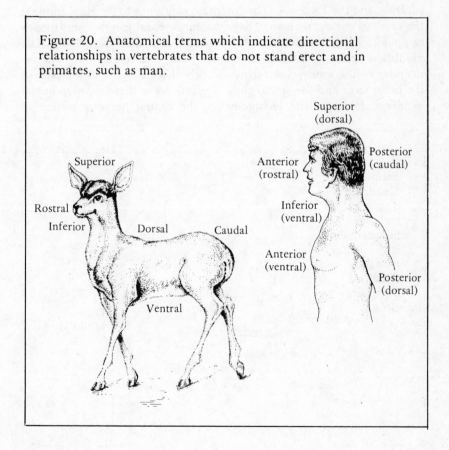

Figure 20. Anatomical terms which indicate directional relationships in vertebrates that do not stand erect and in primates, such as man.

head end of the animal is referred to as in the *rostral* direction, and the tail end as in the *caudal* direction. In an animal that walks upright, such as man, the ventral surface is called the *anterior* surface, and the dorsal surface is called the *posterior* surface.

In cutting sections through the brain, three orientations, or *planes*, are most common. A slice which divides the brain into left and right sections is in the *sagittal* plane. A plane at a right angle to the sagittal, which divides the brain into anterior and posterior portions, is in the *frontal* plane. A slice which divides the brain into upper and lower portions is the *horizontal* plane.

PORTRAIT OF THE BRAIN AS A YOUNG TUBE

The human brain develops from a tube of cells which eventually becomes sealed at both ends. See Figure 21. As the neural tube of the growing embryo develops, it pushes out into three main swellings that go on to develop into the three basic divisions of the brain—the *forebrain,* the *midbrain,* and the *hindbrain.* The forebrain continues to develop, forming the cerebral cortex, thalamus, hypothalamus, basal ganglia, and hippocampus. The midbrain forms the superior and inferior colliculi. The hindbrain forms the medulla oblongata, pons, and cerebellum. The remainder of the embryological neural tube becomes the lower part of the brain stem and the spinal cord. Despite all of these developmental bendings, foldings, and enlargements, the central nervous system of

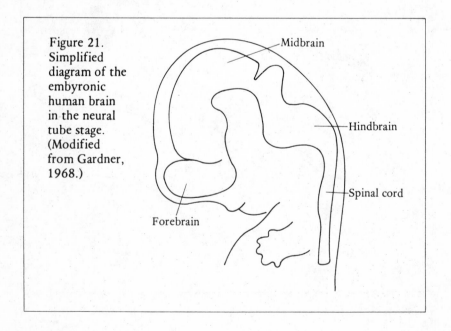

Figure 21. Simplified diagram of the embyronic human brain in the neural tube stage. (Modified from Gardner, 1968.)

Midbrain

Hindbrain

Spinal cord

Forebrain

vertebrates retains its basic characteristic as a tube. As Figure 22 illustrates, the original simple tube shape is best seen at the spinal cord level. More anterior, the canal widens out and forms the fourth ventricle, then narrows again (the narrowing is called the aqueduct of Sylvius) and widens out again to form the third ventricle and finally the lateral ventricles. The ventricular system is filled with a clear, almost colorless, liquid called the *cerebrospinal fluid.*

The brain and spinal cord are covered with three tightly connected membranes, or *meninges.* (See Figure 2 in Chapter 2.) The outermost of these three membranes is the *dura mater* ("hard mother"). The dura mater is remarkably tough in most species. The inner membrane, which directly envelops the brain tissue, is the pia mater ("tender mother"). Between these two is the arachnoid ("weblike") layer. The blood vessels which supply the brain with the necessary stream of nutrients and dispose of the waste products are critical for the brain to function normally. Neurons die within minutes of being deprived of oxygen. The condition of asphyxia (too little oxygen, too much carbon dioxide) is very often the major factor in the brain damage encountered during difficult births, certain diseases, and episodes of carbon monoxide poisoning.

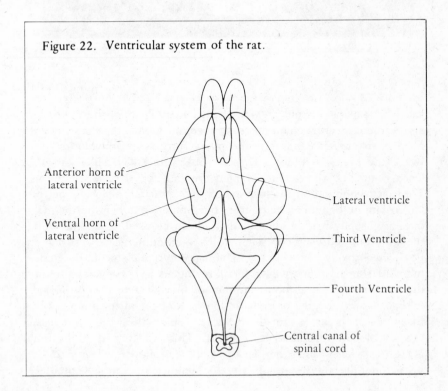

Figure 22. Ventricular system of the rat.

Anterior horn of
lateral ventricle

Ventral horn of
lateral ventricle

Lateral ventricle

Third Ventricle

Fourth Ventricle

Central canal of
spinal cord

Figure 23. Photograph of lateral surface of left hemisphere of human brain. The dura mater, arachnoid, and pia mater coverings have been stripped off. (Gardner, 1968)

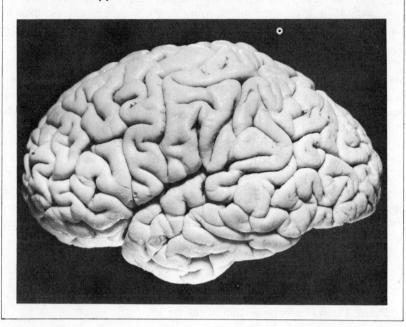

Figure 23 shows a human brain which has been removed from the skull and separated from the spinal cord at the level of the brain stem and with the covering membranes stripped off. One of the characteristics of most mammalian brains is the many furrows or convolutions into which the brain is folded. These furrows are called sulci (singular, sulcus), and the ridges thus created are called gyri (singular, gyrus). The exact configuration and location of these gyri and sulci is not perfectly constant in the human being from one brain to another, but the major ones are usually readily identifiable and can be used as landmarks (although every neurosurgeon seems to have encountered at least one patient where this is not really so). The major gyri and sulci in the human brain are shown in Figure 24. Not all mammals have convoluted brains; the rat and rabbit are good examples of *smooth-brained*, or *lissencephalic*, mammals. The degree of convolution is so great in the human brain that some of the surface of the brain is visible only if the overhanging temporal lobe is displaced to reveal it. This hidden part of the brain is the *insula* (also called the *island of Reil*); it is shown in Figure 25.

Anatomically, the brain is bilaterally symmetrical, and a sagittal sec-

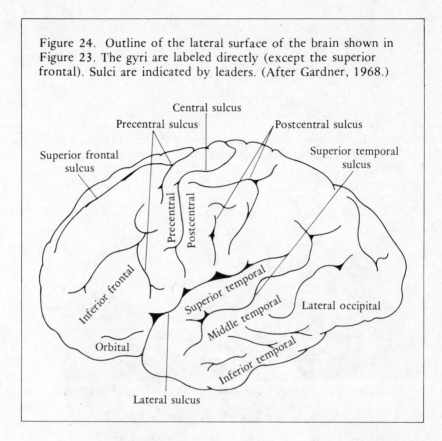

Figure 24. Outline of the lateral surface of the brain shown in Figure 23. The gyri are labeled directly (except the superior frontal). Sulci are indicated by leaders. (After Gardner, 1968.)

tion cut on the midline divides the brain into two halves which look very much alike. However, clinical experience and experiments with brain-damaged humans have revealed that the two halves of the human brain are not precisely alike in structure, and are quite different in function! We will discuss these findings in more detail in Chapter 8.

Just anterior to and dorsal to the medulla oblongata is the "little brain," or cerebellum. In man, the cerebellum is tucked up under the occipital lobes of the cerebral hemispheres. It is about the size of a baseball. The cerebellum is involved in the modification and guidance of movements of the body and postural adjustments. It receives sensory input from the senses of vision, audition, and touch and sends many neurons out to synapse with other neurons throughout the central nervous system. Its function in behavior is not entirely clear, but an elegant treatment of the anatomy and physiology of the cerebellum can be found in Eccles et al. (1967).

Located forward of the cerebellum are the superior colliculus, the inferior colliculus, and the pineal gland. The superior colliculus seems to control visual orienting and following responses. It receives input from the auditory system as well as visual input; and there are bimodally responsive cells in the superior colliculus of cats which respond to both auditory and visual stimuli (Wickelgren, 1971).

Figure 25. Drawing of the lateral aspect of the human brain, showing the island of Reil hidden beneath the temporal lobe. (Netter, 1962.)

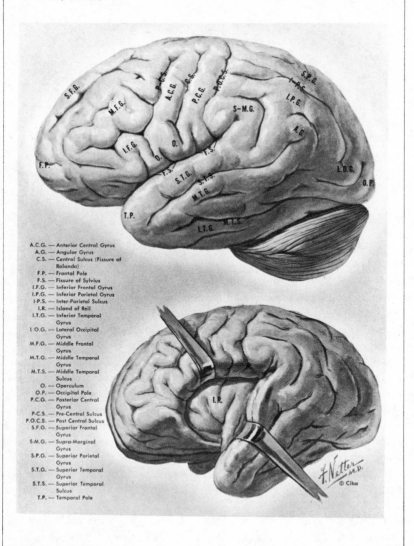

A.C.G. — Anterior Central Gyrus
A.G. — Angular Gyrus
C.S. — Central Sulcus (Fissure of Rolando)
F.P. — Frontal Pole
F.S. — Fissure of Sylvius
I.F.G. — Inferior Frontal Gyrus
I.P.G. — Inferior Parietal Gyrus
I-P.S. — Inter-Parietal Sulcus
I.R. — Island of Reil
I.T.G. — Inferior Temporal Gyrus
L.O.G. — Lateral Occipital Gyrus
M.F.G. — Middle Frontal Gyrus
M.T.G. — Middle Temporal Gyrus
M.T.S. — Middle Temporal Sulcus
O. — Operculum
O.P. — Occipital Pole
P.C.G. — Posterior Central Gyrus
P.C.S. — Pre-Central Sulcus
P.O.C.S. — Post Central Sulcus
S.F.G. — Superior Frontal Gyrus
S-M.G. — Supra-Marginal Gyrus
S.P.G. — Superior Parietal Gyrus
S.T.G. — Superior Temporal Gyrus
S.T.S. — Superior Temporal Sulcus
T.P. — Temporal Pole

The inferior colliculus is a processing station in the auditory pathway. Axons from the inferior colliculus project to the medial geniculate nucleus of the thalamus. There are also projections from the inferior colliculus to the superior colliculus.

The pineal gland is generally regarded as a sort of transducer that mediates the effects of light on hormonal secretions, which in turn influence the gonads (ovaries and testes). Light striking the eye produces a variety of effects in the brain, one of which is to alter the rate of manufacture and release by the pineal gland of a substance called *melatonin*. Melatonin is then carried by the bloodstream to other parts of the body. It has different effects on the gonads in different species. It is not yet known whether these effects are produced directly by the effects of melatonin on the gonads or indirectly by altering the rate of hormone release from the pituitary gland which in turn regulate the activity of the gonads.

In the middle of the mammalian brain is the thalamus. The thalamus is more highly developed in more advanced mammals such as the primates. The development of the thalamus is related to the development of the cerebral cortex, the massive covering of the brain so characteristic of mammalian brains. The anatomical and functional relationships between the thalamus and the cortex are discussed in greater detail in Chapter 8.

Anterior to and partly surrounding the thalamus is a group of brain structures known collectively as the *basal ganglia*. Figure 26 shows these structures in a highly simplified form, as if they had been dissected out from the human brain. The basal ganglia are concerned with the movements and postural adjustments of the body, but their role is not yet entirely clear. Damage or disease in the basal ganglia lead to distur-

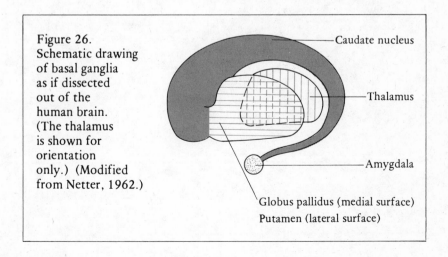

Figure 26. Schematic drawing of basal ganglia as if dissected out of the human brain. (The thalamus is shown for orientation only.) (Modified from Netter, 1962.)

Caudate nucleus

Thalamus

Amygdala

Globus pallidus (medial surface)
Putamen (lateral surface)

Figure 27. Drawing of the human brain dissected partly away and viewed in a horizontal plane to reveal hippocampus and related structures. (Netter, 1962.)

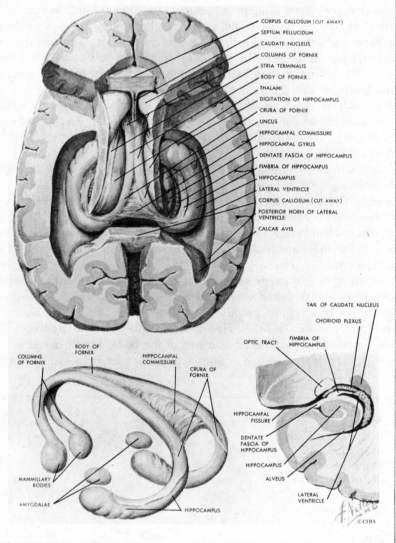

bances in various aspects of movement (to be discussed further in Chapter 9).

Lying beneath the thalamus is an area of the brain known as the hypothalamus. It is a major crossroads in the vertebrate brain, receiving input from widely distributed parts of the central nervous system. It contains neurons whose function is to regulate such activities as eating, drinking, and temperature control. In addition, neurons from the hypothalamus secrete materials necessary for the release of hormones from the anterior pituitary, a small button of tissue connected to the base of the brain. The significance of some of these hormones for behavior is discussed in Chapter 5.

There is also a set of forebrain structures known as the *limbic system*, so-named because it forms a border (the Latin word for border is *limbus*) surrounding the thalamus. The largest structure in the limbic system is the *hippocampus*, a curiously shaped brain structure which was named by an imaginative anatomist for its supposed resemblance to a sea horse. The hippocampus is connected to the hypothalamus (as well as to other parts of the lower brain) by a massive bundle of fibers called the *fornix*. There are well over two million axons in the human fornix, slightly more than the number of axons in the two optic nerves. The *septal area*, which forms a wall or *septum* in the middle of the brain just anterior to the thalamus, is also considered part of the limbic system, and is closely related to the hippocampus, both anatomically and functionally. The two structures are connected by the fornix and another system of axons, the *fimbria*. These systems will be discussed in greater detail in Chapter 7. One other part of the limbic system deserves mention. This is the *amygdala* (from the Latin word for "almond"), a group of tightly clustered cell bodies in the tip of the temporal lobe of the brain. As is true for all of the structures in the limbic system, the function of the amygdala is under intensive investigation. It may be involved with the regulation of hypothalamic neurons concerned with fighting, eating, and other activities. Certainly its anatomical connections with the hypothalamus would indicate that such a role is possible. Figure 27 illustrates these limbic system structures.

SUGGESTIONS FOR FURTHER READING

Gardner, E. *Fundamentals of neurology.* (5th ed.) Philadelphia: Saunders, 1968.
Zeman, W., & Innes, J. R. M. *Cragie's neuroanatomy of the rat.* New York: Academic, 1963.

Chapter 4

OF SENSE ORGANS AND BRAINS

Our knowledge of the world around us is based on the nerve impulses which flow into our brains from a variety of sensory receptors. These receptors are strategically located throughout our body. Some are embedded in the skin, muscles, and joints; others are organized into complex *sense organs,* such as the eyes and ears. Although receptors have evolved into a rich variety of sizes, shapes, and types in various animal species, all retain certain basic receptor characteristics. One defining characteristic of all receptor cells is: *they are capable of responding to a change in some form of energy with a change in their resting membrane potential.*

SENSORY RECEPTORS AS BIOLOGICAL TRANSDUCERS

Receptors vary in the type of energy change to which they are particularly sensitive. In mammals, it is possible to identify four basic types of receptors: pressure receptors, chemical receptors, light (electromagnetic) receptors, and temperature receptors.

A word about pain is in order here. Although some scientists would add to our list a fifth class of receptors, pain receptors, it is still not entirely clear just what form of stimulation produces pain. In some cases, pain may be produced by tissue injury (or the release of some chemicals by tissue in response to injury). In other cases, pain may be due to the excitation of a subclass of pressure receptors. There appear to be some receptors which can respond to both pressure and temperature, and these may be important to an understanding of pain. Thus, it seems premature to group pain receptors in a separate and distinct class of sensory receptor.

It may not be obvious into which category sound receptors fit. The receptor cells in our ears which are responsible for hearing are a type of pressure receptor. These cells have become quite specialized, but they evolved, it is believed, from pressure receptors in the skin, and they retain many features in common with skin touch receptors (Békésy, 1969).

Whatever the specialization of receptor cells, however, the outstanding characteristic of all is that they respond to one form of energy and transmit another form. Such cells can be accurately described as *biological transducers*. A transducer is a device which changes one form of energy to another. The common form of energy into which various receptor types convert one or another form of energy is the electrochemical energy represented by the flow of ions across the cell membrane, as outlined in Chapter 2. In the current chapter, we will consider two examples of sensory receptors: a touch receptor and a "light" receptor.

Biological transduction in the Pacinian corpuscle

Figure 28 illustrates a type of pressure receptor found in widespread areas of the skin and internal tissue of many mammals, including man. This is the Pacinian corpuscle, which changes pressure into nerve impulses and thereby provides a good example of biological transduction. Pacinian corpuscles are responsible for sensations of pressure from such areas as the fingers, inner lining of the body wall, intestines, and other locations. The Pacinian corpuscle is a specialized receptor, with the area

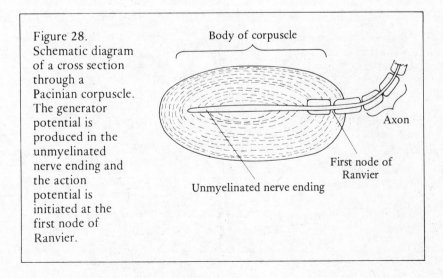

Figure 28. Schematic diagram of a cross section through a Pacinian corpuscle. The generator potential is produced in the unmyelinated nerve ending and the action potential is initiated at the first node of Ranvier.

Body of corpuscle

Axon

First node of Ranvier

Unmyelinated nerve ending

of pressure-sensitive membrane located at the tip of a long extension of the cell body. This area of the Pacinian corpuscle, the unmyelinated nerve ending, responds to pressure on the many-layered body of the corpuscle by producing a slow depolarization at that point. This slow depolarization, very similar in appearance to an epsp, is termed the *generator potential.* In some sensory systems, there is one or more potential change prior to the production of the generator potential. The earlier changes are usually called *receptor potentials.* The term generator potential should be reserved for the potential that is eventually directly responsible for initiating a nerve impulse. Figure 29 illustrates the more complex situation that involves both receptor potentials and the generator potential (epsp) in a receptor cell from the lateral line organ. This is an organ of equilibrium sense (balance) found in many species of fish. In the lateral line organ, the stimulus produces first a receptor potential and then the slow depolarization of the generator potential, which occurs

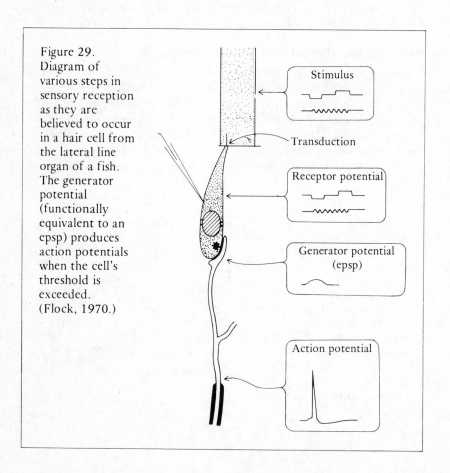

Figure 29.
Diagram of various steps in sensory reception as they are believed to occur in a hair cell from the lateral line organ of a fish. The generator potential (functionally equivalent to an epsp) produces action potentials when the cell's threshold is exceeded. (Flock, 1970.)

in the dendrite of the immediately postsynaptic neuron. The nerve impulse or action potential is then initiated in the axon of that postsynaptic cell. In the Pacinian corpuscle, however, the entire process takes place within the single receptor cell.

The generator potential is a slow, graded depolarization lasting from 1 to 100 milliseconds. It is "graded" in size depending upon the strength of the stimulus. It is in many cases functionally equivalent to an epsp, although the ionic currents which underlie the generator potential may or may not be identical to those which underlie the epsp. (For that matter, as you will recall, all epsps may not be due to identical ionic currents.) If the depolarization produced by the generator potential is large enough to exceed the threshold of the cell for the production of a nerve impulse, then there will be one or more nerve impulses initiated at the first node of Ranvier. The nerve impulse is then transmitted into the spinal cord.

The sequence of events can be outlined as follows: pressure on the body of the corpuscle → generator potential → nerve impulse initiated in the first node. From this point on, synaptic transmission carries the impulses into the spinal cord and to various destinations in the cord and brain. The impulses may or may not evoke a sensation of pressure, depending on other factors, such as the amount of distracting stimulation and whether or not the animal is "conscious." These other "central" factors of consciousness and attention are much more poorly understood than are the beginning steps of sensory reception (see Chapter 10). We would be wise not to develop a false sense of security from the sequence of events outlined above: the nervous basis of sensation is not completely understood; we can say some things about the process, but (not surprisingly) the further we probe into the brain itself, the less we can say with assurance.

In the Pacinian corpuscle, we know that both the generator potential and the nerve impulse are produced within 0.5 millimeter of each other. But we do not know how the generator potential is produced. We do not understand the transduction process—how the mechanical energy change resulting from pressure on the body of the corpuscle is turned into an alteration of the voltage across the membrane of the cell. Once produced, the generator potential, if of sufficient size, initiates nerve impulses at the first node. The way in which this occurs is analogous to the way in which epsps produce nerve impulses in neurons, by depolarizing the membrane sufficiently to bring about increased Na^+ permeability. We can assume that from this point on, normal neural transmission carries the information into and through the brain. Although not completely understood, the transduction process in the Pacinian corpuscle is fairly straightforward. Let us now consider a much more elaborate sense organ, the vertebrate eye.

Transduction in the vertebrate eye

The portion of the vertebrate eye which contains all of the receptor cells is called the *retina,* and the retina of a vertebrate is an extremely complex organ. In the primate retina, as in most other vertebrate retinas,

Figure 30. A summary diagram of the major types of cells present in the primate retina. R = rod; C = cone; MB = midget bipolar; RB = rod bipolar; FB = flat bipolar; H = horizontal cell; A = amacrine cell; MG = midget ganglion cell; DG = diffuse ganglion cell. (Dowling & Boycott, 1966.)

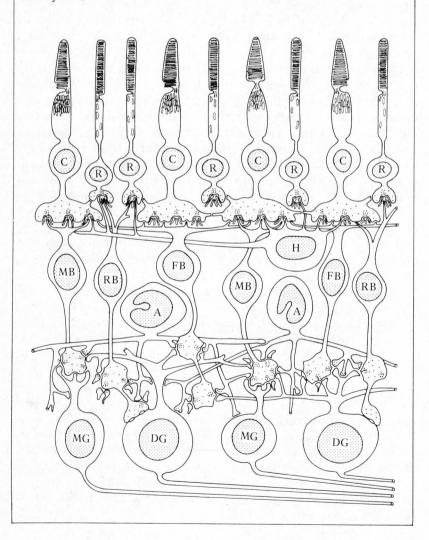

there are five major types of cells: rods, cones, amacrine, bipolar and ganglion cells. Subtypes are identified in Figure 30. The final details of this process have not been worked out, but a considerable body of facts has been compiled. One of the immediate effects of light on the rods and cones is to alter the molecular structure of the *visual pigments* contained in these cells. The term pigment is used because the substances absorb light. Both rods and cones contain a visual pigment, but not the same one. Rods are the more numerous type of receptor in the primate eye, and in many other vertebrate eyes. It is estimated that there are about 120 million rods in each of your eyes (assuming that you are a human being reading this). There are many fewer cones than rods, about 5 million; but for normal daylight vision, it is the cones which are most important. The visual pigment in primate rods is called *rhodopsin.* Rhodopsin is a compound made up of two main parts, a *retinene* part and an *opsin* part. The retinene part is structurally similar to vitamin A, from which, in fact, it is derived. The opsin part is a complex protein. The retinene part of the rhodopsin molecule can exist in several different shapes, called *isomers.* Two of these isomers are of particular interest in the transduction of light to nervous energy. The first step in the transduction of light in rods occurs when the light penetrates the various materials of the eye and is absorbed by the rhodopsin. The light has the immediate effect of changing the retinene part of rhodopsin from one isomer, named *11-cis retinene,* to another isomer, *all-trans retinene* (Wald, Brown, & Gibbons, 1963). Figure 31 shows these two isomers. There are additional chemical reactions that occur spontaneously in the dark once this change from 11-*cis* retinene to all-*trans* retinene has occurred; and in ways not yet understood, these changes lead to the changes in membrane potential of the receptor cells.

Unlike the Pacinian corpuscle, neither the rods nor cones are capable of producing nerve impulses themselves, although they do produce a slow, graduated receptor potential that is hyperpolarizing in the cases studied so far. Both rods and cones form synapses with other cells in the retina, including *bipolar* cells, *horizontal* cells, and *amacrine* cells. Very little is known about how these synapses work, but true nerve impulses are apparently not produced until the amacrine cell level. The axons of the ganglion cells, of which there are two recognizable subtypes, midget ganglion and diffuse ganglion cells, emerge from the retina a million strong and form the optic nerve.

Thus, both the Pacinian corpuscle and the rods and cones of the retina are transducers. Both respond to particular forms of energy changes in the environment by producing slow, graded electric potentials. In the case of the Pacinian corpuscle, this potential is depolarizing and generates nerve impulses directly in the same cell. In the retina, the receptor potential in the rods and cones is hyperpolarizing (we don't

Figure 31. Structural formula for two of the isomers of the retinene part of rhodopsin. The 11-*cis* isomer is pictured above and the all-*trans* isomer is pictured below. Light has the effect of changing the 11-*cis* isomer to the all-*trans* isomer. This is the only action of light in vision. (Wald, Brown, & Gibbons, 1963.)

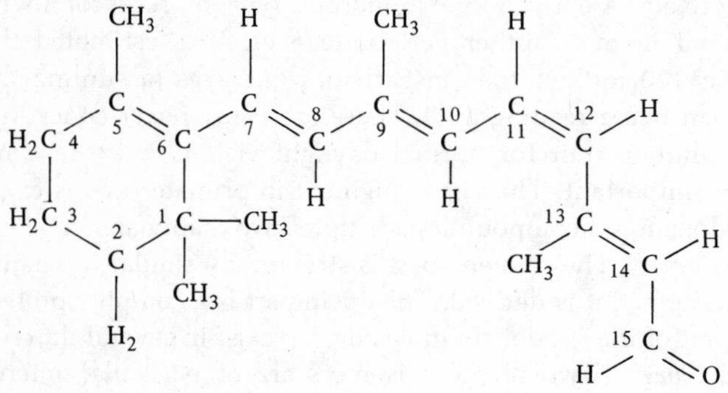

11-*cis* retinene

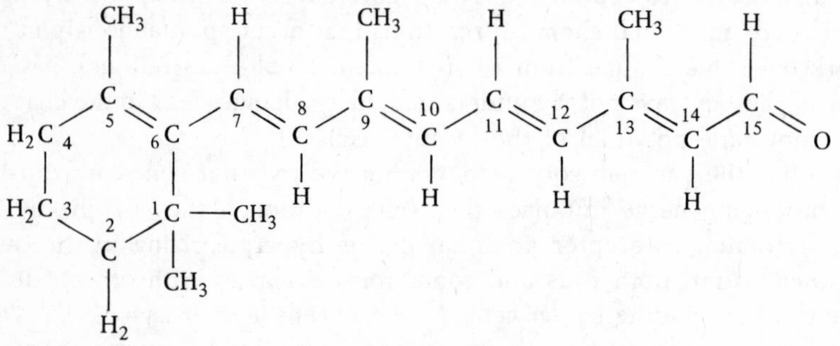

all-*trans* retinene

know why) and does not generate a nerve impulse in that cell. There are many variations on the basic theme of biological transduction.

How eyes talk to brains: the eye

Figure 32 is a simplified diagram of the human eye. Figure 33 shows how the light which is reflected from an object in the visual field is focused so that the light from a small portion of the visual field is

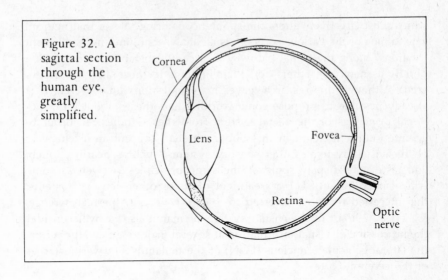

Figure 32. A sagittal section through the human eye, greatly simplified.

Cornea

Lens

Fovea

Retina

Optic nerve

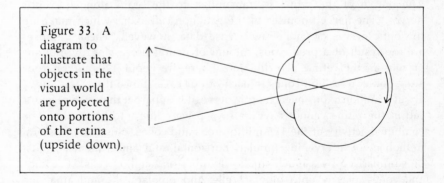

Figure 33. A diagram to illustrate that objects in the visual world are projected onto portions of the retina (upside down).

projected onto a small part of the retina, affecting a small number of rods and cones. Most of the actual bending of the light rays entering the eye is accomplished by the cornea, but the lens is critical in helping to focus the light rays by changing their shape. This is called *accommodation*. Because of the large number of rods and cones, each point in the visual world excites a slightly different population of rods and cones in the retina. The number of receptors which will be excited by a visual stimulus depends on several factors, including the size of the object and the location on the retina that it is focused.

One of the most significant developments in the analysis of the visual system has been the identification and description of the response of single cells in that system. By recording with microelectrodes placed close to or within individual neurons in the visual pathway between the eye and the brain, it has been possible to describe the stimulation which most effectively alters the spontaneous firing rate of that neuron. The catalog of the various sorts of visual analyzers found in the different "stations" along the visual pathway is already substantial, and growing rapidly as new researchers add their findings to those already discovered. Although this research leaves many questions unanswered, it is already possible to propose some working hypotheses about the functional principles of the visual system from these studies. In order to go into sufficient detail in this book, we shall concentrate exclusively on the visual system. Other sensory systems, such as hearing, touch, and taste may display some of the same principles, as well as some which are different. For a treatment of these other sensory systems, the interested reader is referred to *Sensory processes* (Alpern, Lawrence, & Wolsk, 1967). In the visual system of mammals, we will consider the processing of visual information at several major stations: the retina, the lateral geniculate nucleus (LGN) of the thalamus, and various areas of the cerebral cortex.

PROCESSING OF VISUAL INPUT IN THE RETINA

The output of the retina is transmitted to the brain along the optic nerves. The nerve impulses in the ganglion cell axons which make up the optic nerves are not "raw" sense data, however. These impulses are the result of a prodigious amount of neural processing by millions of cells in the retina. To illustrate, there are about 120 million rods and another 5 million cones in each of our eyes. Since there are "only" about 1 million axons in each optic nerve, it is apparent that each receptor cell in the retina cannot have its own private line into the brain. The combined activity of the 125 million rods and cones, plus that of several million more intervening bipolar, horizontal, and amacrine cells, must be summarized by a much smaller number of ganglion cells. The rods and cones *converge* onto bipolar cells, and bipolar cells and amacrine cells in turn converge onto ganglion cells. The nerve impulses carried to the brain by a single ganglion cell may represent the combined activity of a wide "net," or receptive field, represented by many rods and cones. The receptive field of a cell is *that area of the retina within which light alters the firing rate of the cell.* A single ganglion cell thus serves as the "representative" of some patch of receptor cells in the retina.

In order to gain understanding of the functional result of the convergence of receptor cells onto ganglion cells, investigators such as Kuffler (1953) and others have recorded the nerve impulses occurring in ganglion cells. This can be done by inserting an electrode through the eye of an anesthetized experimental animal (Kuffler used cats in this case) and recording from single ganglion cells in the retina. Figure 34 shows the pattern of response of a single ganglion cell in the eye of a cat. This receptive field pattern is the result of three different responses which

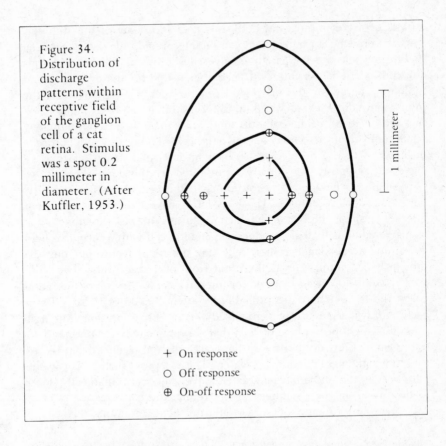

Figure 34. Distribution of discharge patterns within receptive field of the ganglion cell of a cat retina. Stimulus was a spot 0.2 millimeter in diameter. (After Kuffler, 1953.)

1 millimeter

+ On response

○ Off response

⊕ On-off response

the ganglion cell displayed: on responses, off responses, and on-off responses. The term on response was applied when the ganglion cell produced a burst of nerve impulses at the time that the stimulus was first applied. The term off response was used when the cell gave a burst of impulses at the termination of the stimulus. An on-off response described the situation when both the presentation and removal of the stimulus caused a burst of nerve impulses in the ganglion cell. The stimuli used in this type of experiment were small spots of light (0.2 millimeter in diameter) which were directed to small areas of the retina. The overall shape of the receptive field of the ganglion cell was oval. There were three distinct zones within the receptive field. The receptive field had an on center, indicating that within the center of its receptive field, it responded to the stimulating light probe with a burst on the appearance of the first light. In the outer regions of the receptive field the opposite result occurred. Here off responses were the rule, the cell firing a burst of impulses at the termination of the stimulus. In between these two regions was an area in which light caused the cell to produce a burst of nerve impulses at both the onset and offset of the stimulus. This receptive field arrangement can be interpreted only by recognizing that the response of the ganglion cells reflects their input from the rods and cones. Excitatory input must be responsible for the on region and inhibitory input for the off region. In between these two areas, the input from both excitatory and inhibitory input act on the ganglion cell. In addition to on-center, off-surround cells, there is an approximately equal number of off-center, on-surround cells among the ganglion cells in the cat retina. These cells also have an intermediate on-off zone.

Not all receptors are equally represented by the ganglion cells. A very small percentage of the receptors in the primate retina are VIRs (very important receptors). These receptors have their own direct "hot line" to a single bipolar cell which in turn synapses directly with a single ganglion cell. This produces a ganglion cell with a receptive field containing a very small center, reflecting the input from one cone, although its surround reflects the input from other receptors. The VIRs are probably all cones, clustered together in a central region of the retina called the *fovea*. There are probably less than 50,000 of these VIRs in each eye, less than 0.1 percent of all the receptors present, but it is upon this small percentage of cells that we rely heavily for normal daylight vision. Outside the fovea, the degree of convergence from receptors to ganglion cells is much greater. The receptors further out in the periphery of the retina have a greater convergence ratio than cells closer to the fovea. In the periphery of the retina, the convergence ratio of 250:1 receptors to ganglion cells would not be uncommon.

Implications of retinal anatomy for vision   There are some aspects of perceptual experience which may be related to the convergence in the retina. Let us begin by distinguishing between *sensitivity* and *acuity* in vision. Sensitivity refers to the ability to detect the presence or absence of light. Acuity refers to the ability to distinguish the fine features of a stimulus, for example, whether there are one or two fine lines present. The detection of the presence or absence of a dim light depends upon cells in the brain being activated. We do not know *which* cells precisely, but we can be sure that it is the ganglion cells that must bring the information to them. Let us assume that some small subset of the receptors which converge onto a single ganglion cell must be excited by the light in order to change the firing rate of that ganglion cell significantly from its base-line rate. Let us assume further that the number of simultaneously active receptors necessary to affect the ganglion cell firing is nearly constant for all ganglion cells. If such is true, then the more receptors there are which converge onto a particular ganglion cell (ignoring the intervening bipolar cells in this discussion), the more likely it is that a small spot of light will be detected if it excites receptors in a part of the retina in which there is a greater convergence ratio of receptors to ganglion cells. Thus, sensitivity to the presence or absence of light should be greatest in the periphery of the retina, where the convergence ratio is greatest. And it is.

Human observers are much better at detecting the presence of a dim light if that light is focused on the periphery of the retina than nearer the fovea. For example, it is easier to see a dim star by looking not directly at where you think it is but slightly to one side or the other, so that the light from the star will fall on the periphery of your retina. There is also another fact about the retina that contributes to the increased sensitivity of the periphery. Rods are more sensitive to light than cones. Since there is an increasing number of rods in the periphery as compared with the fovea, this too plays a role in the greater sensitivity of the periphery.

In primates, acuity is much better in the fovea than anywhere else in the retina. Let us consider the task of detecting whether there are one or two lines present in a visual stimulus. Our decision must depend on whether or not one or more ganglion cells are simultaneously stimulated. With respect to vision, the brain knows only what the optic nerve tells it. Thus, if the receptive fields provided in the fovea can produce differential stimulation for different ganglion cells, such that two closely adjacent lines will stimulate different ganglion cells, then the brain has the necessary basis to decide "two lines." If these closely adjacent lines both fall in the center of the receptive field of a single ganglion cell, the information from the receptors will be pooled and delivered to a single ganglion cell. This is just the same result (as far as the ganglion cells are concerned) as if there was only one line present; and the information sent to the brain can allow only for the decision "just one line," even when there are, in fact, two lines. An analogous perceptual situation in another sense can be easily demonstrated by touching someone on the skin with two points simultaneously (out of the person's sight). If the points are applied to the skin on the back, there are several areas where the person cannot tell reliably the difference between one point and two unless the points are an inch or more apart. This reflects the receptive field arrangement of touch receptors in the skin on the back. On the lips and fingertips, however, this two-point acuity is much better, and the two points must be very close together before the situation becomes ambiguous. In the eye, the convergence ratio of as little as 1:1 for the center of the receptive fields representing the fovea to several hundred to one in the periphery provides an anatomical basis for the greater sensitivity of the periphery of the retina and the greater acuity of the fovea.

THE LATERAL GENICULATE NUCLEUS OF THE THALAMUS

The axons of the ganglion cells are bundled together as the optic nerve. There is a rather unusual anatomical arrangement in the primate brain with respect to the optic nerve. As is illustrated in Figure 35, part of the optic nerve from each eye (that containing the axons of the ganglion cells from the inner, or nasal, half of the retina) crosses over just after emerging from the eyes and goes to the lateral geniculate nucleus on the opposite side of the brain. The axons from the lateral half of the retina do not cross over; they project to the lateral geniculate nucleus on the same side of the brain. The place where the ganglion axons from the nasal half cross over is known as the *optic chiasm*. This splitting and crossing over of the optic nerve is generally true of most mammals, but the situation is different in other vertebrates.

The lateral geniculate nucleus is the first major processing station in the brain for visual input. There are about one million neurons in the primate LGN, about the same number as there are ganglion cells in the optic nerve. One of the most productive methods in the analysis of sensory systems has been to record the activity of single neurons with microelectrodes. Once the electrode tip has been snuggled down against a cell in the LGN, the experimenter can record the nerve impulse activity from that cell while presenting various stimuli. The animal is

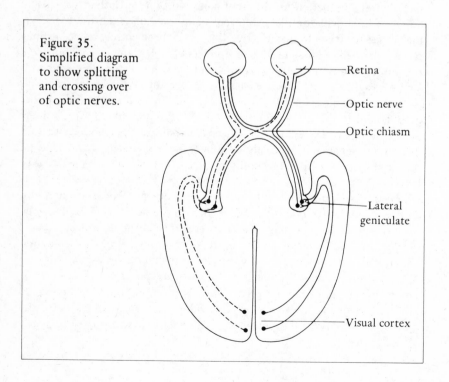

Figure 35.
Simplified diagram to show splitting and crossing over of optic nerves.

Retina

Optic nerve

Optic chiasm

Lateral geniculate

Visual cortex

kept from moving either by an anesthetic or a paralyzing agent such as curare combined with local anesthetics to reduce the discomfort of the restraining device. These devices are called *stereotaxic* instruments. Figure 36 shows a cat in such an experiment. The stereotaxic instrument allows for the accurate placement of electrodes in the brain. This biological "wiretapping" has uncovered a great deal of valuable information about the response of single neurons in various parts of the brain. If one looks at the response characteristics of several hundred neurons, sampled from the total LGN population of a million, it is possible to make reasonable guesses about the rest of the population. The situation is analogous to opinion polling and subject to some of the same problems. In the brain, moreover, it can happen that the size of the electrode, the level or type of anesthesia, or other factors may bias the sample. For example, it is much easier to record from a cell if it is large rather than small. Therefore, in recording the activity of a population of neurons that are of mixed size, one may record only large neurons, which would bias the sample and perhaps distort the accuracy of conclusions regarding the entire population of cells. Despite these possible drawbacks, this recording technique is very valuable, widely used, and

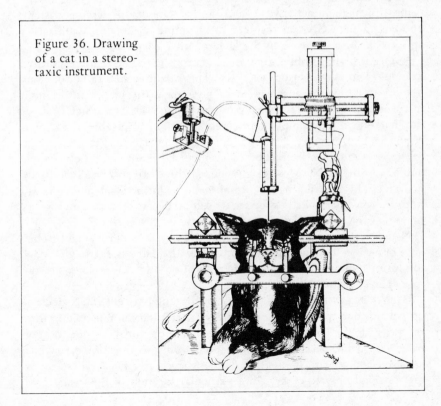

Figure 36. Drawing of a cat in a stereotaxic instrument.

the source of much of our current notions about the response characteristics of neurons in the sensory systems.

Response characteristics of LGN neurons

SPONTANEITY   One of the main characteristics of LGN neurons is that
they are spontaneously active, producing a base level of nerve impulses
even in the dark. This might seem somewhat surprising, but spontaneity
is characteristic of brain cells in general. Neurons are alive; and one
manifestation of this is that most of them appear to have some base
rate of "spontaneous" or "background" activity which we cannot readily
account for in terms of energy changes we observe in the environment.
We use the term spontaneous, but of course, there may be stimulating
events in the local environment of the neuron of which we are unaware.
In any case, there is a constant activity in the brain. One implication of
this fact is that information in the nerve impulses coming in along the
optic nerves does not enter a quiet, passive receiver in the brain. Incoming sensory impulses must impose their "signal" onto the existing background activity of the brain. Although this background activity is probably not strictly "noise" but information coming into the LGN from other
parts of the brain, the incoming messages must be processed in the
context of ongoing activity. As is true throughout the nervous system,
neurons in the LGN can respond to incoming stimulation with either
an increase or a decrease in the level of their base rate.

SPECIFICITY   It is unlikely that most neurons in the LGN are responsive
to input from other sensory systems. This might seem a rather obvious
point, but as it turns out, it is not. There are many places in the brain
(for example in the brain stem, superior colliculus, and other areas of
the thalamus, hippocampus and cerebral cortex) where impulses originating in two or more different sensory systems converge onto single
polysensory neurons. There do not seem to be many such polysensory
neurons in the LGN. Most of the neurons here are specifically "visual"
neurons. This may not be true for all neurons in the LGN, and certainly
not true for other cells in the visual system, because many polysensory
neurons can be found in the "visual" areas of the cortex.

Neurons in the LGN do not respond very well to diffuse light. They
are connected to ganglion cells in a way that allows them to "code"
for various stimulus features such as location and color. They are not
just light detectors.

LOCATION CODING   As is the case with ganglion cells, LGN neurons
do not respond to visual stimuli unless the stimulation falls within their
receptive field. Thus, a particular LGN neuron can code for location
of an object in space because it responds only to those objects which
are projected onto receptors that define its receptive field. These receptors respond only to objects in a particular location of the visual field.

Different LGN neurons have different receptive fields, and the nature of these receptive fields is very similar to those for ganglion cells, except that these receptive fields do not usually have the intermediate on-off zone.

COLOR CODING   Let us return for just a moment to a consideration of the receptor cells in the retina. In the primate retina, it has now been determined by various means that for both man and some monkey species, there are three basic types of color-sensitive receptor cells, all of which are cones. Figure 37 shows that the three types of cones are maximally responsive to light of particular wavelengths. This is because the three types of cones have three different visual pigments in them that absorb light as shown. Of course, rods also contain a visual pigment, rhodopsin, but considerable evidence indicates that rods do not contribute to color vision.

Wavelength of light is measured in units of length. The visible spectrum (to the normal primate eye) runs from about 400 nanometers (nm) at the blue end to about 700 nanometers at the red end. In primates, the three different cones are maximally sensitive to light at approximately 440, 535, and 570 nanometers. It is convenient to apply color names to these cones. Thus, we can think of the 440-nanometer cone as the blue cone, the 535-nanometer cone as the green cone, and the 570-nanometer cone as the red cone. Actually, light at 570 nanometers appears yellow to normal human observers, but since this type of cone is also primarily responsible for our sensitivity to light of wavelengths 570 to 700 nanometers, which appear progressively more red, we can use the term red cone. All these cones respond somewhat to other wavelengths, as Figure 37 indicates; it is the *maximum* wavelength sensitivity which identifies a particular cone type. The three cone types are found primarily in the fovea and in the immediately surrounding region of the retina. It is the combined action of them that provides the brain

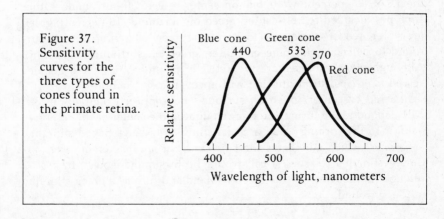

Figure 37. Sensitivity curves for the three types of cones found in the primate retina.

Relative sensitivity

Blue cone   Green cone
440   535   570
Red cone

400   500   600   700
Wavelength of light, nanometers

with the information that we perceive as color. The effect of light of different wavelengths has been studied by recording the activity of single neurons in the LGN in experiments by Russell De Valois (1966) and by Torsten Wiesel and David Hubel (1966).

De Valois discovered that there are cells in the LGN of monkeys that respond with an increase in their base firing rate if the visual field is flooded with red light, but are quieted below their base firing rate if the visual field is illuminated with green light. He called this type of cell an *opponent-process* cell. It would be a red-on, green-off cell. Other opponent-process LGN neurons have also been discovered: green-on, red-off, red-on, blue-off, and blue-on, red-off cells. Neurons in the LGN are connected with the three cone types in the retina in different ways. The overall effect is to produce a population of LGN neurons which are differentially sensitive to different wavelengths, although any given neuron apparently receives input from just two of the three types of cones.

Simultaneous coding of location and color   It is possible, of course, that neurons in the LGN are concerned not only with the color of the stimulus but also with the location of that stimulus in the visual field. Three possible cell types are immediately apparent: strictly opponent-process cells ("color coders"), strictly center-surround cells ("place coders"), and combination neurons, opponent-process–center-surround cells (color *and* place coders). All three types have been discovered in the lateral geniculate of monkeys (Wiesel and Hubel, 1966). Because of the truly striking overall similarity between monkey and human visual capacities, we can expect a very similar situation to exist in our own LGNs. The three basic neuron types are illustrated in Figure 38. The most common type is the combination cell shown at the top of Figure 38. Out of 213 cells recorded by Wiesel and Hubel, 164 (77 percent) were of the combination type I. Various subtypes were discovered. Of the 164 type I cells in the LGN, 35 percent were red on-center, green off-surround. Other subtypes included red off-center, green on-surround (18 percent), green on-center, red off-surround (16 percent), green off-center, red on-surround (6 percent), and blue on-center, green off-surround (1 percent). Although other subtypes are theoretically possible, they were not observed. Perhaps further testing will uncover such examples.

In a red on-center, green off-surround neuron, for example, the cell will respond to the turning on of a red light in the center of the receptive field or to the turning off of a green stimulus (a ring-shaped stimulus, or *annulus*) which stimulates the surround but *not* the center. The optimum stimulus for such a cell would be to simultaneously turn *on* a red light in the center of the receptive field and turn *off* a green stimulus in the surround.

The next most common type of cell to type I was the center-surround only cell, type III, pictured at the bottom of Figure 38. There were 34 (16 percent) of these: 14 on-center, off-surround; and 20 off-center, on-surround cells. The least frequently seen cell type was the opponent-process only type, of which only 15 examples (7 percent) were

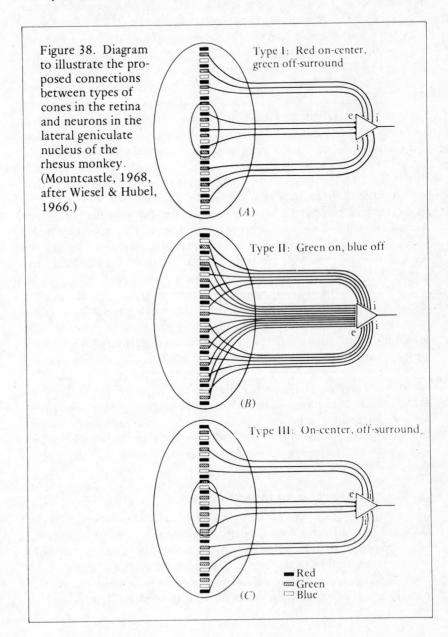

Figure 38. Diagram to illustrate the proposed connections between types of cones in the retina and neurons in the lateral geniculate nucleus of the rhesus monkey. (Mountcastle, 1968, after Wiesel & Hubel, 1966.)

Type I: Red on-center, green off-surround

(A)

Type II: Green on, blue off

(B)

Type III: On-center, off-surround

■ Red
▨ Green
▭ Blue

(C)

noted. Wiesel and Hubel were able to determine both the color- and place-response characteristics of these neurons by using small spots of light at various wavelengths rather than whole-field illumination as was De Valois' technique. Figure 38 also illustrates how Wiesel and Hubel conceived the functional connections between the three cone types and the neurons of the LGN which would produce the observed response characteristics. They ignored the intervening bipolar cells for simplicity.

A cell which responds differently depending upon whether the stimulus is light at a wavelength of 440 nanometers or 535 nanometers and whether the stimulus is located in the center of its receptive field or a fraction of a millimeter away has to be regarded as a rather fancy biological invention. Yet the principles from which this cell derives its response characteristics are straightforward: the physiological processes of excitation and inhibition; and the anatomical principle of convergence. (The *divergence* of the branches of single ganglion cells onto several LGN neurons is a well-documented fact also, but we will have more to say about divergence later.) We can imagine the synaptic arrangements that would produce the cellular response specificity observed, as Wiesel and Hubel have done; but so far, it is not known for sure that this is in fact the way it is done. It is encouraging, however, to be able to make at least intelligent guesses about such synaptic arrangements and to explain the response of these LGN cells in terms of physiological processes and anatomical structure.

Even were we to understand the operations of the LGN cells in great detail, however, it is not likely that we would be in a position to satisfactorily explain *vision* itself. Despite the truly remarkable elegance with which individual neurons in the LGN are tuned to various characteristics of the visual world, the primate retina and the lateral geniculate nucleus *by themselves* cannot produce *vision*. A primate with its eyes and LGN intact but deprived of the rest of the visual system of the brain is, as far as can be determined, blind. This seems to be almost certainly true for human beings, although a documented case of just this sort has not been available for study. To understand vision, we must consider the operations of other portions of the brain, most particularly the cerebral cortex.

OF GRANDMOTHERS AND MONKEY PAWS

In the primate brain, the axons of the LGN neurons emerge from the LGN and form a large bundle known as the *optic radiations,* which eventually synapse with cells in the posterior part of the brain, particularly in the occipital lobes of the brain, in an area called the primary visual projection area, or simply *visual cortex.* A system for numbering various cortical areas, based on differences in cellular appearance, was devised by Brodmann (1914) for the primate brain. In Brodmann's numbering system, the primary visual cortex is given the number 17. In *area 17* the axons of the LGN cells branch, diverge, and synapse with many millions of neurons in the visual cortex. Both divergence and convergence take place so that a given neuron in the visual cortex receives synaptic input from many LGN neurons (as well as neurons from other regions of the brain) and a given LGN neuron contributes synaptic input to many different visual cortex cells. There are at least 100 million neurons in area 17. Only a minute fraction of these have been thoroughly studied to discover their response characteristics. What we do know of these cells is based largely on the research of David Hubel and Torsten Wiesel at the Harvard Medical School (e.g., Hubel & Wiesel, 1968). The basic plan of their research is similar to that used in investigating the response characteristics of neurons in the LGN—to place microelectrodes close to a particular neuron and record its responses to various stimuli. When the cell has been sufficiently examined, or if it is damaged, the electrode can be cranked down a few microns until it encounters another neuron that can be studied. The result of hundreds of such penetrations has revealed that the response characteristics of the cortical neurons can be readily distinguished from those in the LGN from which they receive their input.

Simple cells in area 17   Most of the experiments performed by Hubel and Wiesel were done on the cortical neurons of cats immobilized with barbiturates. It is meaningful to ask if the drugs used to immobilize the cat would not also alter the response characteristics of the very neurons they wished to investigate. It is certainly true that the level of barbiturate used in these experiments renders the animal incapable of responding *behaviorally* to visual stimulation; and from comparable levels in humans, we know that nothing resembling normal perception or memory can occur in individuals so drugged. Fortunately, more recent work (Wurtz, 1969) has shown that the most striking properties of neurons in the visual cortex of the anesthetized cat can also be observed in the visual cortex of behaving unanesthetized monkeys. In describing some of Hubel and Wiesel's findings, we can reasonably expect that the cells in the visual cortex of other mammals, including our own, would show similar response characteristics. It is important to stress, however, that this is merely an expectation based on our belief in the continuity in brain function among species. There have as yet been only preliminary reports of recordings of single neurons in the human brain.

Simple cells in the visual cortex of cats respond most vigorously to *line stimuli.* A particularly effective stimulus for triggering a response from simple cells is a slit or bar presented in a particular part of the visual field of the cat. A dark bar on a light background is effective, as is a light bar on a dark background. The critical features of such line stimuli in exciting the cortical neurons are the *orientation* of the line and the *location* of the line in the cat's visual field. If the "best" (greatest change from base-line firing frequency) response of a simple cell is triggered by a stimulus oriented 10 degrees from perpendicular, moving that stimulus to a different orientation, say, 90 degrees from perpendicular, may result in a loss of all response to that stimulus by that cell. Parenthetically, the most flexible computer so far used to determine a particular neuron's best response is the human brain. In these experiments, the train of nerve impulses recorded from the neuron under study was recorded and fed into an audio-amplifying system so that Hubel and Wiesel could hear the cell firing over a loudspeaker. The sound is a series of "pops," each pop being caused by a nerve impulse. Auditory comparisons of the frequency of cell firing can then be made as the position and orientation of the line are shifted in an attempt to find the maximum response for that cell, thus defining the response characteristic. The human brain is superb at integrating such auditory signals and determining best response. While it is true that nonhuman computers are becoming more essential to many aspects of biological and psychological research, they have not yet replaced the human experimenter.

Orientation and location in the visual field are the features of the environment to which the simple cells are most directly keyed, according to the findings of Hubel and Wiesel. Like retinal neurons, simple cells in the visual cortex also have receptive fields. In the cat, these fields are usually about half a millimeter in length. A large number of different neurons must be available in order to have the necessary coverage for the entire visual field. And a large number of neurons is just exactly what is available in the cortex.

Complex cells   Another type of visually responsive neuron has also been discovered in the visual area of the cat and in the closely associated cortical areas. (The cortical numbering system, devised for the primate brain by Brodmann, can be applied, with limitations, to the cat.) The associated visual areas in the monkey brain are numbered 18 and 19. We will use these numbers for the cortical areas of the cat that are close to the primary visual area, 17. Like simple cells, complex cells are also most responsive to visual stimuli in the shape of lines or bars. Also, like simple cells, each complex cell responds maximally to such stimuli when the stimuli are in a particular orientation. However, complex cells respond to a properly oriented stimulus over much wider areas of the visual field than do simple cells. In other words, *the complex cell generalizes over wider areas of the visual field.* For example, a simple cell will respond maximally to a dark bar only if that bar completely covers the off areas of the receptive field in the proper orientation. A complex cell responding to that same bar will respond over much wider areas.

Complex cells were found in area 17 and even more predominantly in the related areas, 18 and 19; simple cells were not found outside area 17. These two cell types—complex and simple—do not exhaust the types of cells so far discovered. There are cells, for example, which Hubel and Wiesel have termed "lower-order hypercomplex" cells and "higher-order hypercomplex" cells. The response specificity of these cells differs from those of simple and complex cells in some interesting ways; further details can be found in the original articles (e.g., Hubel & Wiesel, 1965.)

CONVERGENCE AND DIVERGENCE IN THE CORTEX   What are the possible anatomical connections that may underlie the response specificity of simple and complex cells? Although much of the detailed neuroanatomy is not known, the way in which a neuron in the cortex responds to visual stimuli depends upon the synaptic input it receives from other neurons. Figure 39 shows how the response characteristics of a simple

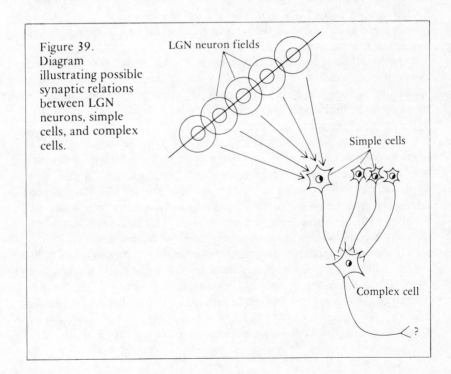

Figure 39. Diagram illustrating possible synaptic relations between LGN neurons, simple cells, and complex cells.

cell could be determined by the pattern of synaptic input it receives from the LGN. The response specificity of a simple cell could be determined by the input from neurons in the LGN because the on centers of an array of LGN center-surround cells corresponded to a line in the visual field. Thus, when the stimulus in the visual field of the animal *was* a line or bar, oriented in the proper direction, this stimulus would stimulate the retina in such a way that all these LGN cells would fire more or less simultaneously. Shortly thereafter, the simple cell in the visual cortex would be excited by the summed activity of the LGN neurons, and a maximum burst of potentials would be recorded by the investigator's electrode. If the line is moved, or oriented differently, the LGN cells stimulated would be different, and the response of *that* particular simple cell in the cortex would diminish (although some *other* simple cell in area 17 would be maximally stimulated by this maneuver). We can speculate that for every conceivable orientation and position, there are some simple cells for which the stimulus would be the "best" stimulus. But even though this sort of anatomical arrangement is very plausible, at the present time we cannot yet *know* if it is true. The technique of tracing individual axons to their terminations in a complex brain such as that of a mammal has so far proved exceedingly difficult. The hypothesis that the response specificity of simple cells is determined by their input from LGN neurons is a good guess, however, because it appears to account for all the known facts so far and does not violate any other known facts.

What about complex cells? The situation is somewhat less clear here, but on the basis of Hubel and Wiesel's work, it appears that the response specificity of complex cells is determined primarily by integrating the input from a number of simple cells.

It appears, therefore, that the neurons in each successive processing stage in the visual system is specified by the just-previous stage. The response characteristics of the ganglion cells are determined by the nature of the convergence of receptors and bipolar cells. At the next level, the response characteristics of neurons in the LGN are determined by the anatomical pattern of the synaptic connections from the ganglion cells. In turn, then, the axons of the LGN neurons determine the response characteristics of the simple cells at the cortical level. And, as we have just noted, the response characteristics of the complex cells are in their turn primarily determined by the input they receive, not from LGN neurons but from the simple cells of area 17. And so on. And so on? Here the trail begins to grow fainter, but there is no reason to expect the complex cells or the lower-order hypercomplex or higher-order hypercomplex cells to represent a final end point in vision. On the contrary, there are good reasons, both theoretical and experimental, to assume that the stages of visual processing so far revealed in the cortex are important but only intermediate, not the final steps in vision. It is more likely that by means of the "cascading" of increasingly speci-fied arrays of neurons, we might expect to find neurons in the brain for which the best stimulus is the letter Z, the number 6, or the image of your grandmother's face! Such a "grandmother cell" would then, perhaps, be the critical cell to be activated to complete the process in the perception and identification of grandmother. A grandmother cell has not (so far) been discovered, but there does seem to be a "monkey's paw" cell!

The inferotemporal cortex and the Klüver-Bucy syndrome There is now over-whelming evidence that in the monkey brain, a region of cortex that is not "classically" identified with the visual system is nonetheless in-volved in vision. It is the inferotemporal cortex, located on the inferior gyrus of the temporal lobe. This portion of the brain receives synaptic input from several other parts of the brain, including areas 18 and 19. The importance of the temporal lobe in vision was dramatically revealed in the late 1930s by the psychologist Heinrich Klüver and the neuro-surgeon Paul Bucy, who had collaborated on experiments examining the behavior of monkeys who had undergone experimental surgery which removed most of both temporal lobes (Klüver & Bucy, 1937). One of the unexpected findings of these experiments was described by Klüver and Bucy as *psychic blindness.* Although these animals could reach for and accurately pick up small objects, and were clearly not blind, they did appear to have lost the ability to identify objects by sight. The flavor of these early discoveries can be best appreciated by a quote from a paper by Klüver and Bucy (1939):

> In the "concentration" test, in which a piece of food or a metal object passes the experimental cage every thirty seconds, the monkey picks up both the food and the metal object until it ceases reacting to both. The food is eaten, whereas the nail or the steel nut is discarded after an examination by mouth. In some experimental periods, both the food and the inedible object are picked up in 100 per cent of the trials. Even after as many as 260 successive trials the monkey may remove the nail each time it passes, so that finally more than a hundred nails may lie on the floor of its cage. As a rule, however, the monkey is not content with removing and examining the metal object in all or practically all trials; it will frequently pick up a nail or steel nut from the floor of the cage in the intervals between removing an object

every thirty seconds. It should be pointed out that the normal monkey in this test situation will let the nail pass by in all trials or pick it up only the first few times.

Since these early reports by Klüver and Bucy, scores of studies have been done in an effort to determine just what portion of the temporal lobe was most critical for this psychic blindness. The answer appears to be that the critical zone is a portion of the lateral surface on the inferior gyrus, identified as *inferotemporal* cortex. Monkeys with this portion of both temporal lobes damaged or removed are virtually unable to learn to discriminate simple shapes by sight, although they are normal in learning discrimination tasks involving touch, taste, hearing, and smell. From such studies, we can conclude that this portion of the brain is part of the brain's visual system too, critical for the identification of objects by sight. Evidence from human brain-damaged patients suggests that a similar area exists in man's temporal lobes.

A monkey's paw in the monkey's brain What are the response characteristics of single neurons in the inferotemporal cortex? There are as yet no data on the human brain, but this region of the monkey brain has been examined using the microelectrode technique and there is some evidence that neurons exist in this part of the brain with rather startling response specificities. Although the research area is only beginning, neurons sensitive to size, shape, color, and orientation and direction of movement have already been discovered. There is even a report that a particular neuron had as its best stimulus the outline of a monkey's paw.

> . . . one day when, having failed to drive a unit with any light stimulus, we waved a hand at the stimulus screen and elicited a very vigorous

Figure 40. Stimuli used to excite a neuron in the inferotemporal lobe of a monkey. The stimuli are arranged from left to right in order of increasing ability to fire the neuron from none (1) or little (2 and 3) to maximum (6, the monkey's paw). (Gross, Rocha-Miranda, & Bender, 1972.)

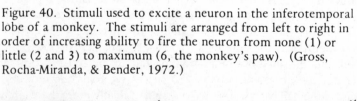

response from the previously unresponsive neuron. We then spent the next 12 hours testing various paper cutouts in an attempt to find the trigger feature for this unit. When the entire set of stimuli used were ranked according to the strength of the response that they produced, we could not find a simple physical dimension that correlated with this rank order. However, the rank order of adequate stimuli did correlate with similarity (for us) to the shadow of a monkey hand. The relative adequacy of a few of these stimuli is shown [Figure 40]. Curiously, fingers pointing downward elicited very little response as compared to fingers pointing upward or laterally, the usual orientation in which the animal would see its own hand. (Gross et al., 1972, pp. 103-104.)

We can anticipate the discovery of single neurons with extremely interesting response specificities as this type of research continues.

SUGGESTIONS FOR FURTHER READING

Alpern, M., Lawrence, M., & Wolsk, D. *Sensory processes.* Belmont, Calif., Brooks/Cole, 1967.

De Valois, R. L. Neural processing of visual information. In R. W. Russell (Ed.), *Frontiers in physiological psychology.* New York: Academic, 1966.

Gregory, R. L. *Eye and brain: The psychology of seeing.* New York: McGraw-Hill, 1966.

Hubel, D. H. Effects of distortion of sensory input on the visual system of kittens. *The Physiologist,* 1967, **10**, 17-45.

Chapter 5

HORMONES, SEXUALITY, AND BEHAVIOR

HOW TO MAKE A MALE

We are generally accustomed to thinking of animals as coming in two basic flavors: male and female. This is, of course, *generally* true. But as with most general propositions, there is considerably more to the story. In this section, we shall consider the development of some behavioral differences which distinguish males from females and the hormones which contribute to the development of these differences.

Just what are the criteria by which we judge the maleness or femaleness of an animal? Ordinarily, we may not be overly concerned with the evaluation of species other than our own, although in many cultures, the question of what characteristics are manly and what womanly is of great significance. And even in our own culture, we are currently experiencing considerable changes in our conceptions of appropriate occupations for men and women, for example, whereas psychologists have for many years been interested in psychological differences between men and women (Maccoby, 1966; Bardwick, 1971). In fact, even making the simple judgment of whether an individual is male or female is not always simple. We think we can tell the differences, despite the illusions that fads and fashions may create. If we cannot always be sure in the case of other species, *they* can tell the difference, we argue, and that is what is important for the survival of their species. With normal individuals under normal circumstances, then, animal species in which there are just two sexes have little difficulty in making this distinction. But individuals are *not* always normal, nor are circumstances. It is not always a simple question to determine "the" sex of an individual, which brings us back to our previous question: What are the criteria by which we judge the sex of an individual?

First, we will give a few definitions that will help the discussion. The *endocrine system* refers to glands in the body that secrete their products, the *hormones,* directly into the bloodstream. Included in the endocrine system are the pituitary gland, the thyroid gland, the parathyroid glands, the adrenal cortex, the ovary and testes, and the pancreas. The brain is also so intimately involved in endocrine function that it too must be included in any discussion of the endocrine system. A useful definition of a hormone is: an organic compound which is manufactured in a particular tissue and after being transported in the general circulation can affect the function of other cells in the body either locally or distant.

Patients with various endocrinological disorders occasionally present ambiguous cases of sex typing; and John Hampson, who has worked with such patients for many years at Johns Hopkins University Medical School, has given considerable thought to this question of the criteria relevant to sex or gender determination (Hampson, 1965). The list that he has compiled of "seven variables of sex" will give a perspective on the problem that is more suitable to our considerations.

1   *External genital morphology.* This is, of course, the most obvious indicator for ordinary distinctions, one which first influences the obstetrician delivering the child to pronounce the words, "You have a fine baby boy (or girl)." In the normal course of events, the obstetrician simply examines the external genitals briefly and makes an immediate sex identification. In some percentage of cases, however, the appearance of the external genitals may be ambiguous, or even misleading, in which case, other indicators must then be considered.

2   *Sex chromatin pattern.* In cases in which the appearance of the external genitals is ambiguous, a few cells from the individual (from the skin, for example) can be analyzed under the microscope to determine whether the chromosome pattern is male, female, or some intermediate case. In humans, as in many other mammalian species, the genetic contribution to the sex of the individual is due to a single pair of chromosomes. Normal men have an XY pair of sex chromosomes, and normal women have an XX pair. This particular fact is not easy to determine directly, but cells from an individual with an XX chromosome pattern also invariably contain a small, dark object located in the nucleus of each cell of their body. This telltale object is called a *Barr body,* after M. L. Barr, who first noted its presence and its significance in sex deter-

mination (Barr, 1966). The presence of a Barr body in a cell is normally taken as definite proof that a cell is from an individual with an XX pair of chromosomes.

3   *Gonadal sex as determined by morphology.* A third variable of sex is the presence of gonads (internal sexual organs) and whether they are morphologically more like ovaries or testes. In some cases, this could be determined only by surgery, and is therefore not very practical in humans.

4   *Hormonal sex, correlated with associated secondary sex characteristics.* Normal men secrete both androgens (the so-called male hormones) as well as estrogen and progesterone (so-called female hormones) from their testes. Normal women also secrete androgens as well as estrogen and progesterone from their ovaries. In addition, both sexes secrete smaller amounts of all these hormones from their adrenal glands. Thus, both sexes normally produce both male and female hormones. The difference between normal men and women is the *balance*, or ratio, in the hormones secreted. In normal men, androgen production dominates over that of estrogen, while in normal women, estrogen and progesterone are produced in greater amounts than are androgens. These hormonal ratios help to determine the secondary sex characteristics that we tend to take for granted, which are so crucially important for our perception of our own and other individuals' masculinity or femininity. Secondary sex characteristics include such things as facial hair, broader shoulders, heavier muscular development in males; breasts, different pelvic structure, and lack of facial hair in females. There is no question that these characteristics represent very potent factors indeed in our self-image of our own sexual identity as well as that of others.

5   *Internal accessory reproductive structures.* In the normal female mammal, the internal structures which are associated with the formation of an ovary, such as the fallopian tube, are derived from what is termed in the developing embryo the *Müllerian duct system.* In males, the development of the Müllerian duct system is inhibited by the presence of androgens, and the male system, called the *Wolffian duct system,* is stimulated to develop. Thus, the morphological appearance of the internal accessory reproductive structures is a relevant consideration in sex determination.

6   *The "society" factor: sex of assignment and rearing.* In most human societies, an infant is identified as either a boy or a girl at birth. The manner in which the parents, the rest of the family, and the society in general treats an infant is strongly influenced by this sex assignment. In some cultures it has literally been a matter of life and death. As the child becomes old enough to understand

(or more probably, before full understanding is possible), the child is made fully aware of the sex category to which she or he belongs. In some societies the distinction is fairly casual, and no great importance is placed on it until the age of puberty is approached. But in most societies, including our own, the label of boy or girl can have a profound effect on what activities are encouraged or allowed, what family role is assumed, what future plans and occupational aspirations are encouraged or discouraged, how punishment and rewards are distributed, and so on. Our society distinguishes between male and female—sometimes with a vengeance. It is also significant that at the present time, society as a whole seems to accept just two adult sex categories as "normal," heterosexual male and heterosexual female. This is not the case in all societies.

7   *Psychologic sex or "gender role."* The last variable of sex to be considered here is the sex identification which the individual makes about himself or herself. The term gender role is often used. Gender role or a person's sexual self-image is not always easy to determine. Clues can be obtained, however, from how a person dresses, what sorts of erotic dreams he or she may report, what conscious fantasies a person has, what individuals a person is sexually attracted to, what activities an individual enjoys; and why an individual enjoys particular activities. All these scraps of information can be useful in inferring how the individual regards his or her own gender role.

Congruity and incongruity of the various variables of sex

It is obvious that in the majority of cases there is great congruity among the seven variables of sex determination. A normal male, for example, has an XY chromatin pattern, normally masculinized genitalia, and male internal sexual organs. His testes secrete predominantly androgens, he is assigned as a boy at birth, he is raised as such, and he regards himself as male throughout life. Likewise, the majority of females have an XX chromatin pattern, Barr bodies in their cells, normal female genitals, and female internal sex organs. Their ovaries secrete the normal female ratio of more estrogen and progesterone than androgen, they develop breasts but little facial hair, they are assigned as girls at birth, and they think of themselves as female.

But it is not always so straightforward. For example, genetic mistakes, as well as events in the uterus, can alter the normal course of the development of the fetus. Errors which affect the sex chromosomes would obviously be likely to have profound effects on later sexuality. Also, because both mother and fetus share a more-or-less common bloodstream, abnormal conditions in the mother's body can often be transmitted to the fetus and affect its development. A variety of clinical cases in which errors in development have occurred have stimulated some experimental work pertinent to an understanding of psychosexuality.

The androgen-insensitivity syndrome

A most dramatic example of abnormal development of psychosexuality occurs in some XY (i.e., genetically male) individuals. Despite the unmistakable male chromosome pattern, such individuals are born with external genitals which are virtually indistinguishable from the normal female. Since the appearance of the external genitals is the factor which typically determines the sex assignment at birth, these individuals are usually identified as female at birth. The gonads are morphologically testeslike but they are either completely undescended, or appear as small lumps near the labia, and are often misdiagnosed as bilateral inguinal hernias. Although these testes are incapable of producing viable sperm, they do secrete normal or near-normal amounts of the primary male androgen—testosterone (as well as normal—for testes—amounts of estrogen and progesterone). But in these individuals, the cells of the body are incapable of responding to androgens; that is, they are androgen-insensitive. The reason for this deficiency is not known. The key to understanding the development of these individuals *is that the cells of their body are insensitive to the effects of testosterone, and they thus cannot develop as normal males. The basic impulse of nature is to make a female; it is necessary to add something—androgens—to make a male.* In the absence of the appropriate androgens, the development of the fetus will follow a more female-like course. As a basic generalization, in man and many other mammals, it is necessary to add androgen at critical times during development in order to make a male.

But it can be pointed out that these feminized individuals with androgen insensitivity syndrome *do* secrete normal levels of testosterone. Whereas this is true, we must assume that the insensitivity of the other cells in the body is functionally equivalent to a reduction or absence of testosterone. The "absence" of testosterone in these cases does not result in a sex "reversal." These individuals are *not* normal females who happen to have an XY chromosome pattern. Nevertheless, the presence of a vagina (often quite short), the development of breasts at puberty, and the general feminization of pelvic structure, body build, etc., clearly illustrate the fundamental differences between these individuals and normal males. A word might be said regarding the development of breasts in these individuals. Since they possess testes, the onset of adolescence for them, as for normal males, is marked by a great surge in the production and secretion of testosterone. To a lesser extent there is also an increase in the amount of estrogen secreted as well, as it is also true for normal males at puberty. But in these individuals with an insensitivity to androgens, the hormone which dominates the developmental changes at puberty is estrogen. Estrogen can have a very dramatic feminizing effect in these people, which typically includes breast development. Some of these individuals have been feminized in bodily characteristics to a degree compatible with a successful career as fashion models (Money, 1970). But feminization, it must be emphasized, is not complete. The uterus is not fully formed, menstruation is impossible, and since there are no ovaries or sperm-producing testes, there is no child-producing capacity.

From a psychological point of view, the intriguing question is: How do such individuals view their own psychosexuality? According to investigators familiar with such individuals, the answer is, "Psychosexual differentiation is invariably feminine, with a strong degree of maternalism which makes for a very good adoptive motherhood" (Money, Ehrhardt, & Masica, 1968). We can conclude that in most respects the psychosexual development of these genetic males has followed a basically female course. But what were the relative contributions of the biological fault which caused the androgen insensitivity and what was the contribution of the environment (family, society) which classified the individual as a girl? Both must be important and obviously must interact with each other. To ask the question in this way is like asking how much of the area of a field is contributed by its length and how much by its width. Social forces within the family and from society in general are powerful and must be considered in any comprehensive analysis of psychosexual development. But it is also becoming clear that these important social forces are only part of the story and that the development of psychosexuality is biased by the presence or absence of androgens during the embryonic and fetal periods. Let us look at another example.

Female pseudohermaphrodism

In the androgen-insensitivity syndrome, the individuals are genetic males who develop psychosexually as females owing, in part, to the lack of effect of androgens on the cells of their body. There is another syndrome in which the abnormal presence of androgens or related compounds in genetic females leads to a masculinized psychosexual development. This condition is called *female pseudohermaphrodism*. These individuals have the normal XX female chromosome pattern with Barr bodies, but are masculinized, which results in hermaphrodism. The prefix pseudo is attached to distinguish these individuals from *true* hermaphrodites— individuals possessing both male and female gonads and genitals (an extremely rare condition indeed).

What is the precipitating cause of female pseudohermaphrodism? The answer seems to be the presence of androgens (or some chemically related hormone) in the bloodstream of the fetus during some sensitive period of time. This sensitive period may start as early as the fifth or sixth week of pregnancy. In some women, the adrenal cortex secretes abnormally large amounts of androgens into the mother's bloodstream. Since the mother and fetus share a more or less common bloodstream, some androgens get into the fetal bloodstream, where they come into contact with various developing tissues. Still another suspected cause of female pseudohermaphrodism is the result of a side effect from the injection of some synthetic *steroid* hormones. Testosterone, estrogen, progesterone, and a variety of hormones from the adrenal cortex belong to a family of hormones, the *steroids,* which have been used by doctors to prevent miscarriage in women who have difficulty in this regard. Whatever the reason for the excess steroid, if the woman is carrying an XX fetus, the external genitals may become masculinized. At birth the child may be actually identified as a boy and raised as such until the misassignment is discovered. Quite often, the discovery that there has been a misassignment is delayed until the onset of puberty. At that point, the gonads, because they are ovaries, begin to secrete sufficient estrogen to produce menstruation, breast development, and other evidence that the individual is not a normal male. As can be imagined, these occurrences are met with dismay by the individual, who has up until this point followed a reasonably normal masculine course of psychosexual development. What is imperative to the individual is to have the bleeding stopped, and the breast development reduced—to erase the physical signs that are incompatible with his masculine self-image. With appropriate surgery and hormonal therapy, many such individuals can be "corrected" and continue their lives as males. In general, however, psychosexual development is not easily reversible, and a less-stable female psychosexual orientation is possible in these situations. In female pseudohermaphrodism, then, the individual is a genetic female possessing ovaries which secrete a reasonably normal pattern of female hormones, but such people are masculinized, both with respect to the external genitals and in the individual's own mind.

The fact that there are such incongruities in these seven variables of sex determination, as in the androgen-insensitivity syndrome and female pseudohermaphrodism, emphasizes the contribution of both biological and social forces in the development of psychosexuality. The situations are not "experiments," however, so that adequate control groups are not readily available. We cannot tell for sure whether the presence or absence of androgens in the embryonic or fetal period by itself could produce these incongruities, since the cultural forces are also present. We can state with some assurance that as far as the *physical* factors of sexuality are concerned, in the absence of effective levels of androgens, the development will be basically female, whereas in the presence of sufficient levels of androgens at the critical period of development, the development will be basically male. This will be generally true despite the genetic (XX or XY) sex determination. But we cannot easily determine the role of androgen in the determination of the psychological aspects of psychosexuality—how the individual perceives his or her own gender role. It is not ethical, of course, to conduct experiments on this question with human beings, but experiments directly relevant to this question have been conducted with another primate in which there are easily discriminable behavioral differences between males and females—the rhesus monkey (*Macaca mulatta*).

The experimental control of psychosexuality

It is possible to alter hormonal levels in experimental animals at virtually any stage of development by injecting either hormones or chemical substances which diminish the effectiveness of naturally present hormones, such as the so-called antiandrogens (Neuman & Elger, 1966). A variety of animal species have been examined following hormone manipulations of this sort, but since the monkey displays more behaviors similar to our own, it is research with monkeys that is perhaps most directly relevant to a consideration of the development of human psychosexuality.

A major research program in the experimental control of psychosexuality has been conducted at the Oregon Regional Primate Research Center. This research, directed by Robert W. Goy and Charles H. Phoenix, has provided us with information on the behavior and physical characteristics of genetic female (XX) monkeys which have been masculinized by the injection of testosterone into the mother's bloodstream during the fetal period (Goy, 1970). The situation, as you will recognize, is a direct experimental parallel to the syndrome of female pseudohermaphrodism in human beings. In the experimental work with monkeys, however, it is possible to control the hormonal levels, time of treatment, and environment in which the young monkey develops. By trial and error, Goy and Phoenix have determined that testosterone injections can be done without aborting the fetus only after the fortieth day of pregnancy. The gestational period (time from conception to birth) is about 168 days in this species of monkey. Testosterone injections have been continued for varying periods of time in different female monkeys, the longest period being to day 134 of pregnancy. No further testosterone injections are given after this point (roughly 5 weeks prior to birth), nor is there any manipulation of the hormonal state of the infant after birth. Whatever effects result from testosterone injections, they are due to the effects during the period from day 40 to day 134 (or less) of pregnancy. The total amount of testosterone injected into a single female over the entire treatment period is in the range of 650 to 750 milligrams. It is not known how much of that amount actually got to the fetus unaltered, since testosterone can be biochemically changed to other hormones (including estrogen) inside the female's body. The assumption is that since obvious masculinizing effects developed from such treatments, and not from any control substances injected (into other females), some testosterone did reach the fetus. The offspring of these females, of which there have been nine so far, have been examined for alterations in physiology, physical appearance, and behavioral changes. In particular, the research has been directed at an analysis of the nonsexual social behavior of these pseudohermaphroditic monkeys.

PHYSICAL APPEARANCE

The pseudohermaphroditic offspring of the testosterone-treated females have partially masculinized external genitals. Typically they possess a well-developed (but empty) scrotum and a small but well-formed penis. The urethral orifice is located at the tip of the penis, in normal male fashion. The fact that these monkeys later menstruate (although the onset of the first menstruation is delayed several months from normal) is presumptive evidence that the internal organs are ovaries and are functional. The degree to which the external genitals are masculinized appears to be related to the amount and timing of the testosterone. In the animals so far studied, although all have been masculinized, no actual reversal of the physiology has occurred, so that from a strictly reproductive standpoint, these animals are still fundamentally female.

SOCIAL BEHAVIOR IN SEXUALLY IMMATURE MONKEYS

Infant rhesus monkeys, like infant human beings, are dependent upon some adult care for an extended period of time if they are to survive. Monkey mothers are quite protective of their infants, and typically nurse them for a year or more. During this time, as is well known from the work of Harry Harlow and others, the mother has a significant influence on the later behavior of the infant. However, there has been no clear evidence that monkey mothers treat male infants differently from female infants, although we should keep the possibility that they might in mind. In the Oregon studies, the first two pseudohermaphroditic monkeys were taken from their mothers at birth, but all subsequent monkeys studied, both pseudohermaphroditic and normal (control) animals, were allowed to remain with the mother for the first 3 months. After that time, they lived in individual cages, but were placed together in groups of four to six for daily play and observation sessions. Observations were made on the behavior of the young monkeys in these groups for several years. Also, pairs of animals were tested for social and (later) sexual behavior.

There are fundamental and clear-cut differences in the social play behavior of young, sexually immature rhesus monkeys. This was discovered by Rosenblum (1961), working in Harlow's primate laboratory at the University of Wisconsin. These same differences were also observed with other young rhesus monkeys in the Oregon studies. Female rhesus monkeys raised in the laboratory do not become sexually active until about 2½ years, and males slightly later. (It is assumed that the same is true for wild rhesus monkeys, but less data are available.) This period of monkey childhood is one of gonadal quiescence; there is now evidence that normal males secrete virtually no testosterone during this period. The behavioral differences between normal males and females during this time cannot be due to differential amounts of testosterone. These behavioral differences can be readily observed and recorded for such play activities as initiation of play, rough-and-tumble play, chasing play, and threat gestures used in play. Most observers of infant monkeys are impressed by the fundamental similarities of much of human and monkey infant play behavior. Male monkeys show more of all these behaviors than females, although the differences diminish somewhat after the first year of life. Figure 41 is a graph which shows the frequency of rough-and-tumble play during the period from 3 months to about 2½ years of age for normal male monkeys, normal female monkeys, and the pseudohermaphroditic monkeys. The results are clear: normal male behavior is different from normal female behavior. The social

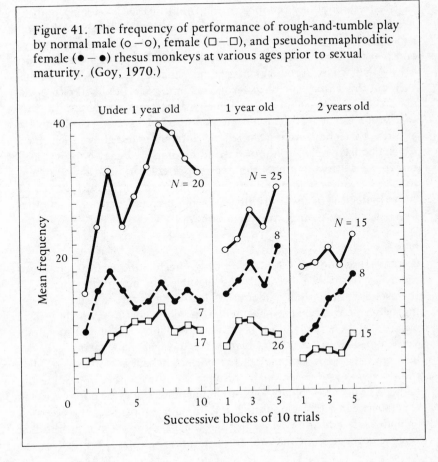

Figure 41. The frequency of performance of rough-and-tumble play by normal male (o −o), female (□−□), and pseudohermaphroditic female (●−●) rhesus monkeys at various ages prior to sexual maturity. (Goy, 1970.)

behavior of the female pseudohermaphroditic monkeys is intermediate—not identical to male behavior but definitely masculinized. These
masculinizing effects must be due entirely to the testosterone injections
administered during the embryonic or fetal period. The testes themselves are not necessary for the appearance of normal male play behavior. If normal male monkeys are castrated at birth, an operation which
removes the testes entirely, they are indistinguishable from normal male
monkeys in the social play behavior during the first 2½ years. Likewise, removing the ovaries from normal female monkeys at birth does
not alter their typical play pattern during the first 2½ years. The
male-female differences in the social play patterns of sexually immature
rhesus monkeys must be due to differences in the behavioral disposition
with which they are born, differences which these experiments indicate
are due in part to the presence or absence of testosterone in the bloodstream of the developing embryo. The male-female differences are almost certainly reflected by differences in the brains of these individuals.
At the present time, we can only speculate about the actual changes
that testosterone may produce in the brain of the developing embryo.
We must also assume that in the normal male, the embryonic gonads
produce sufficient testosterone to masculinize the developing embryo,
and that this masculinization acts on the central nervous system in such
a way that it later produces masculine behavior in the young animal.
Without this embryonic testosterone (as in the female), the brain develops in the nonmasculinized, or female, direction. It is becoming clear
that primates such as man and monkey are not psychosexually neutral
at birth, but demonstrate male-female differences in behavior which are
not due to the presence of hormones at the time the behavior is displayed
but as a result of hormonal differences present earlier in development.
In man, of course, family influences and other social forces interact with
these biological factors, resulting in a more complex determination of
psychosexuality than is true for monkeys.

SEXUAL BEHAVIOR

Another indication of the masculinizing effect of the testosterone treatment has been observed in the development of mounting behavior in
the pseudohermaphroditic monkeys. It is not accurate to equate mounting behavior with sexual behavior in monkeys, because mounting can
occur in other behavioral contexts as well (Hanby, 1972); but mounting
does represent an important element in normal male sexual behavior
in monkeys and is also part of the normal behavior of females. Male
rhesus monkeys only gradually display the adult type of mounting behavior as they grow older. Figure 42 illustrates the great difference that
exists between mature mounting and immature mounting characteristic
of both male and (to a lesser degree) female monkeys during the first
year or so of life. In the immature mounting posture, the feet of the

mounting monkey remain on the ground and the hands usually grip the back or hips of the other monkey (which may be male or female). In normal males, however, this immature mounting posture gives way to the more adult posture as can be seen in Figure 42. In the adult

Figure 42. Top: Immature mounting posture displayed by normal male, female, and pseudohermaphroditic rhesus monkeys. (Goy, 1970.) Bottom: Normal adult male double-foot clasp mount. (Photograph courtesy of H. Wohlsein, Oregon Regional Primate Center.)

male mount, the feet are not on the ground but instead tightly grasped around the rear legs of the other monkey. The hands grasp the rump. Normal male monkeys begin to show the more mature form of mount at about age 1, and by 2½, this posture has supplanted the more immature mounts in most cases. Normal females, on the other hand, rarely if ever show the normal adult male mount, retaining the more immature postures with various modifications as an occasional but normal element in their sexual behavior. What do the pseudohermaphroditic monkeys do? They follow the male pattern of development, demonstrating that their behavior (and by inference their brain) has been partially masculinized.

PHYSIOLOGY OF THE PSEUDOHERMAPHRODITIC MONKEYS

The behavior of the pseudohermaphroditic monkeys is clearly masculinized, both in the nonsexual play behavior and the more frankly sexual mounting behavior. But this does not mean that these monkeys are in fact malelike in their reproductive physiology. Although the onset of puberty as indicated by the first menses in these monkeys is delayed from the normal 2½ years to about 3 years, they do begin to menstruate and have so far shown more or less normal menstrual cycles. Most of them are probably capable of ovulating. But whether these pseudohermaphroditic monkeys will become mothers themselves, or whether any of the male monkeys will cooperate in this venture, remains to be seen. All indications so far are that they are perceived by other monkeys as male; and inasmuch as their behavior is masculinized, there seems little chance that they will become voluntarily pregnant, even though it is quite possible that they are biologically capable of being so. It would of course be of great interest to observe the maternal behavior of these pseudohermaphroditic monkeys.

We can interpret discussion of the existing evidence to indicate that the primate infant is not psychosexually neutral at birth but biased toward the behaviors and gender identity of the male (even if genetically female) if sufficient androgen has been present in the critical period. Likewise, if the androgen is absent during this critical time, the development and the initial bias is female, even in a genetic male. In humans, this initial bias is, of course, overlaid with the potent influences of family and society. We will make more substantial progress in understanding human psychosexuality by trying to discover how the biological bias and the forces of society interact to produce psychosexuality than by deemphasizing the role of either.

Activational effect of hormones: the female rat

Hormones also have definite effects on adult animals. For example, about every fifth day, a dramatic change occurs in the behavior of the normal female laboratory rat. On these occasions, the female not only proves to be receptive to the male's sexual advances (nuzzling and licking) but displays some characteristic behaviors that can best be described as enticing. For example, she runs in small hopping, darting steps for a short distance from the male, wiggles her ears, and looks back at the male. When the male follows her and begins to nuzzle her flanks and genital area, she typically darts off again, perhaps a shorter distance, and wiggles her ears again. Before too long, if the male is persistent (as most of them seem to be), the female, instead of hopping off and wiggling her ears, assumes a position in which her back is arched belly downward and her tail is held to the side. This body position is called *lordosis*, which in rats is a behavioral sign that the female is ready for copulation. When the female rat assumes the appropriate posture, the male mounts her and inserts his penis into her vagina. This is called *intromission*. After a few quick thrusts, the male may dismount for a short time and then mount again. This sequence of mounting and intromission by the male is repeated several times until the male ejaculates. Ejaculation can rarely be directly observed, of course, but it can be inferred from a long, sustained pelvic thrust of the male and a characteristically different dismounting maneuver. Following an *intercopulatory interval* of several seconds to several minutes, another bout of copulation takes place, until the entire period of sexual behavior is completed. During this time, it is not unusual for the male to ejaculate four to ten times; and the female will accept repeated males if they are available. This sexual receptivity, which occurs on a cyclic basis in the female laboratory rat, is called *estrus*.

What if the same two rats encounter one another just 24 hours earlier (or later)? Then the behavior displayed by the female is likely to be quite different indeed. Although the male's behavior may still be obviously amorous in intent (to the human observer, anyway) the female, if she is not in estrus, is no longer coquettish and cooperative. She is, in fact, downright hostile. Instead of darting off and wiggling her ears in a provocative manner, the female typically turns, faces the male, and chatters her teeth, which is a form of rodent hostility. If the male does not get the point and continues to attempt to mount or nuzzle the female, she may kick at him with her hind legs or attempt to bite him. She will not assume the posture of lordosis; and as a consequence of her noncooperative behavior, copulation will not occur (until her next period of estrus). How can we account for this profound difference in behavior in the same animals in the same environment, 24 hours apart? One factor in particular can be singled out in this case: *the hormonal state of the female*. The sexual receptivity of the female rat depends on the level of particular hormones circulating in her bloodstream. The behavioral receptivity of the female is a result of an alteration in the bias of her nervous system. We can account for these changes only if we can take the fluctuations of the hormonal state of the animal into account. Sexual behavior presents some good examples of how hormones influence behavior. Aggressive behavior in some species is also related to fluctuations in hormonal state.

What are the factors that account for these hormonal and behavioral cycles? To understand the effect of hormones on behavior, we must consider the interaction of the brain and the endocrine system.

THE BRAIN AND THE PITUITARY GLAND

In a consideration of the function of the pituitary gland, it is best to begin with the most important influence on this system, the brain itself. For it is the brain which determines the flow of hormones from the pituitary gland, and it is toward the brain, not the pituitary, that we must look for the explanation of the fundamental difference in the hormonal release pattern in male and female animals. Figure 43 shows the anatomical relationship between the hypothalamus of the brain and the pituitary gland.

In humans, as in all vertebrates, the pituitary gland is located at the

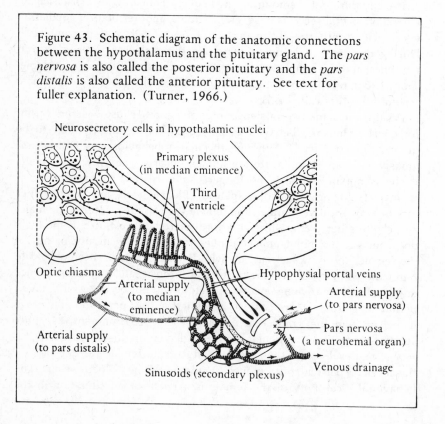

Figure 43. Schematic diagram of the anatomic connections between the hypothalamus and the pituitary gland. The *pars nervosa* is also called the posterior pituitary and the *pars distalis* is also called the anterior pituitary. See text for fuller explanation. (Turner, 1966.)

Neurosecretory cells in hypothalamic nuclei

Primary plexus (in median eminence)

Third Ventricle

Optic chiasma

Arterial supply (to median eminence)

Arterial supply (to pars distalis)

Hypophysial portal veins

Arterial supply (to pars nervosa)

Pars nervosa (a neurohemal organ)

Venous drainage

Sinusoids (secondary plexus)

base of the brain. In humans, the pituitary is attached to the hypothalamus by a slender stem of tissue known as the *infundibular stalk*. The infundibular stalk, which is actually an extension of the brain, connects the brain with the small pituitary gland, which is snugly encased in its own pocket of bone, well-protected from mechanical shock. There are two major divisions of the pituitary gland: an *anterior* lobe (also called *adenohypophysis*) and a *posterior* lobe (also called *neurohypophysis*). (There is also in many species an *intermediate* lobe, but it need not concern us here.) These two divisions operate on quite different functional principles, although the activities of both are controlled by the nervous system.

THE POSTERIOR LOBE OF THE PITUITARY

There are neurons in the hypothalamus of the brain which send long axons down the infundibular stalk to end in the posterior lobe of the pituitary gland. These axons do not form normal synapses. Their end feet come into close proximity with tiny blood vessels which are part of the general circulatory system of the body. These hypothalamic neurons are *neurosecretory* neurons, and hormones are secreted from their end feet. The posterior lobe is in many ways an extension of the brain; it serves as a point of contact between these hypothalamic neurosecretory cells and the general circulation. The hormones of the posterior lobe are made by the hypothalamic neurosecretory neurons and transported down the axon into the posterior lobe and stored there to be released under the appropriate conditions. There are two main hormones of the posterior pituitary: *oxytocin* and *vasopressin*. Vasopressin is also called *antidiuretic hormone*, or simply ADH. These substances are closely related chemically and to a limited degree can produce the same physiologic effects; but the major effects of these hormones are quite different.

Oxytocin and vasopressin are *polypeptides*. That is, they are composed of several amino acids (eight in both cases) in a particular configuration. Oxytocin is known to have two major physiologic effects in female mammals, both of which are essential for the survival of the species: stimulation of muscular contractions by the smooth muscle of the uterus during the birth of young; and ejection of milk from the breasts. Both birth and suckling are dependent upon a surge of oxytocin at the right time. Timing is critical, of course, since contraction of the uterus prior to the time when the young should be born would endanger the fetus. Males also secrete oxytocin from their posterior pituitaries, but the function of this secretion in males is still somewhat obscure. Some experiments performed with rams and male rabbits suggest that oxytocin may facilitate the ejaculation of sperm, perhaps by increasing the amount of seminal fluid in the ejaculate or by facilitating the movement of sperm from the storage points in the testes to the penis for release during ejaculation.

The milk-ejection reflex   Nursing of the young mammal is an interesting and important behavior, both from a physiological and a psychological point of view. In psychology, intense controversies have been generated regarding the importance of breast feeding to the human infant's well-being and later personality development. There seems to be little question in primates about the importance of the *body contact* (see Fig. 44) between mother and infant during the typical nursing situation for the later development of the psychological capacity to form normal love bonds (Harlow, 1971).

The milk-ejection reflex is an excellent example of the interaction of neural and hormonal factors in the production of behavior. In nursing, there are actually two distinguishable processes: the *secretion* of milk into

Figure 44. Mother and child. (Courtesy of Eugene, Oregon Register-Guard).

the *alveoli* (ducts surrounding the nipple) of the breasts; and the removal or *ejection* of the milk from these alveoli into the mouth of the young infant. Nursing is a cooperative venture, in which the active participation of the mother is required. Only a very small amount of milk, an amount insufficient for adequate nourishment, can be forcibly *sucked* from the breast. For adequate amounts of milk to be ejected, a reflex in the mother must be operative as well. For example, if a lactating (milk-producing) female rat is anesthetized so that the brain is not operating in a normal fashion, the *milk ejection reflex* is blocked and rat pups can obtain only a small amount of milk by vigorous sucking at the larger ducts.

In the normal lactating mammal, steady sucking of the breast is followed within about a minute by a steady flow of milk from the breast. This milk flow in response to breast stimulation constitutes the milk-ejection reflex, which is dependent upon the release of sufficient amounts of oxytocin into the bloodstream. The outlines of this reflex are known from a variety of experiments. Figure 45 illustrates the probable neural and hormonal events of the milk-ejection reflex. Prolactin is the hormone necessary for milk *secretion* into the alveoli. If secretion is adequate,

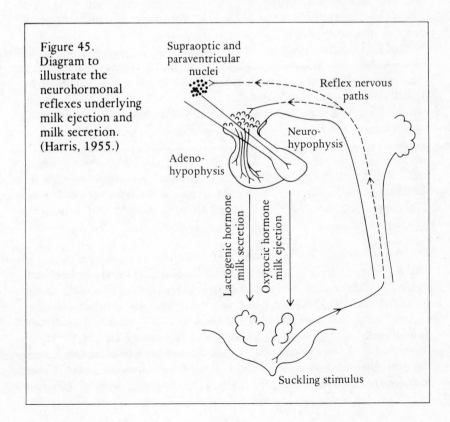

Figure 45. Diagram to illustrate the neurohormonal reflexes underlying milk ejection and milk secretion. (Harris, 1955.)

Supraoptic and paraventricular nuclei

Reflex nervous paths

Neuro-hypophysis

Adeno-hypophysis

Lactogenic hormone milk secretion

Oxytocic hormone milk ejection

Suckling stimulus

then sucking constitutes the critical sensory input into the brain such that the oxytocin-secreting neurons are stimulated and oxytocin is released into the general circulation. When a sufficient amount of oxytocin has reached the breasts, contractile cells surrounding the alveoli, called *myoepithelial* cells, respond to the presence of oxytocin by contracting, thereby squeezing or ejecting the milk which has accumulated in the alveoli out through the nipple. The reflex is completed, the infant sighs and swallows, the mother smiles, and contentment reigns. In this particular reflex, the input is carried to the brain via the sensory nerves supplying the breast, but the output is carried in the bloodstream by oxytocin to the responding myoepithelial cells of the breast.

The fact that milk ejection is a reflex has several implications. Since it is a reflex, it should be possible to condition it. For anyone who has observed the milking of cows for any period of time, this will not be news, as it is well known that the milk-ejection reflex (or milk letdown as it is often called in cattle) can be triggered by the sights and sounds (and smells?) associated with milking, such as the clanking of milk pails or the sight of the person who does the milking. This is, of course, a conditioned reflex. Surprisingly little experimental work has been done on the subject.

With human mothers, another factor of considerable significance can arise, namely, the *inhibition* of the milk-ejection reflex due to various psychological factors such as worry or anxiety. It is not at all clear how the reflex is blocked by such factors, but presumably there is a reduction or abolition of the release of oxytocin by the responsible hypothalamic neurons. The details of how psychological factors such as worry or apprehension can affect nursing should prove of fundamental importance to the psychology of motherhood.

Just a word or two about vasopressin, the other posterior lobe hormone. It also has two major physiological effects which are the same for males and females: it causes contraction of the small muscles in the blood vessel walls and acts on cells in the kidney to prevent excessive fluid from being excreted; that is, it acts to make the urine more concentrated.

THE ANTERIOR LOBE OF THE PITUITARY

Unlike the posterior lobe, there are no direct neural connections between the brain and the anterior lobe of the pituitary gland. This fact, which is of considerable importance in understanding the functions of the anterior lobe, is based on many experiments in various laboratories around the world. Perhaps the person most responsible for documenting the absence of any direct neural connections between the brain and the anterior lobe was G. W. Harris, at Oxford University. Harris and his coworkers, using careful microsurgical techniques and much imaginative experimentation, demonstrated that whereas the hypothalamic area of the brain did in fact regulate hormonal secretion from the anterior lobe, it did so in a very special way (Harris, 1955). Hypothalamic neurons do not send axons into the anterior pituitary in the fashion of the posterior lobe. Instead, there are specialized neurons in the hypothalamus which secrete chemical substances called *releasing factors* from their end feet. These end feet do not penetrate directly into the tissues of the anterior lobe. Rather, the releasing factors enter a special circulatory system in which they are transported directly to the anterior pituitary. Here, releasing factors affect cells which then secrete the various anterior pituitary hormones into the general circulation. Once into the general circulation, the hormones are widely distributed and can produce a wide variety of effects. It is often convenient to consider various organs of the body as "target" organs for particular anterior lobe hormones. For example, the ovary can be considered as the target organ for at least three different anterior lobe hormones: the follicle stimulating hormone (FSH), the lutenizing hormone (LH), and the luteotrophic hormone (LTH). LTH is more commonly referred to as prolactin. But the notion of specific target organs may obscure an important fact about hormones; since they are in the general circulation, hormones are capable of widespread physiologic effects on a wide range of tissues in the body, including the brain.

The hormones of the anterior lobe   There are six hormones which are known to be secreted by the anterior lobe: FSH; LH (which in the male is usually called interstitial cell stimulating hormone, or ICSH); prolactin; somatotrophic hormone ("growth" hormone, or STH); adrenocorticotrophic hormone (ACTH); and thyrotrophic hormone (TSH). The first two—FSH and LH—are referred to collectively as gonadatropins because of their special relevance for gonadal function.

In vertebrate sexual behavior, a basic fact to consider is that the behavior of males is different from the behavior of females. In an earlier section of this chapter, we considered how the brains of males and females come to be different. At this point, we will consider some differences in the behavior of adult male and female animals. For purposes of illustration, we will discuss the laboratory rat. The sexual behavior of many other mammals below the level of primates shows many of the same characteristics, although there are many species differences.

THE HORMONAL AND BEHAVIORAL CYCLICITY OF THE FEMALE RAT
The sexual receptivity of the female rat is cyclic, reaching a peak of receptivity about every fifth day. A variety of hormones are involved in this cyclic effect. There are four hormones, two from the anterior lobe and two from the ovaries, which are important in the production

of estrus in the female rat. The two anterior lobe hormones are FSH and LH, and the two ovarian hormones are estrogen and progesterone.

In an environment in which there is sufficient fluctuation in the level of illumination, the anterior lobe of the pituitary will secrete both FSH and LH into the bloodstream of a female rat on a *cyclic* basis. But it is the brain, not the pituitary, which is responsible for the cyclicity of the hormonal secretions in the female. This was shown by G. W. Harris and Dora Jacobsohn (1952). They dissected out the pituitary gland from a male rat and transplanted it under the hypothalamus of a female rat that had already had its pituitary gland removed. The male pituitary gland in the female rat began to secrete FSH and LH in the typical *female* fashion (cyclically) rather than at the lower steady rate characteristic of the male. Whether a pituitary gland secretes its products in the cyclic fashion of the female or the noncyclic fashion of the male *depends on the sex of the brain controlling it.* The signals for secretion, as we know, come in the form of chemical releasing factors, which come from hypo-thalamic neurons. Thus, it is the brain itself which is "sexed," male or female, and which thus determines whether the secretion of FSH and LH will be steady or cyclical.

The duration of estrus in the rat is about 16 hours. The profound change in the behavior of the female rat is regulated by hormonal changes in the following way. When the female is not in estrus, there is a relatively low level of secretion of FSH and LH. FSH stimulates the ovarian *follicles* (the small "pockets" in the ovary in which the egg is developing) to mature. When mature, the follicle will burst, releasing the egg from the ovary. This is ovulation. Figure 46 shows the various stages of follicle development in the ovary. In most mammals, FSH alone is insufficient for ovulation to occur; a surge of LH is also neces-sary. The effects of the raised levels of FSH and a rapid rise of LH combine to produce ovulation, which occurs at estrus when the female is sexually receptive. Many species have a similar arrangement, whereby the sexual receptivity of the female and the production of a ripe egg ready for fertilization are timed to occur at the same time. The behavioral receptivity is produced by the action of ovarian hormones on certain neurons in the brain. These ovarian hormones are, in turn, produced by the ovary in response to the cyclic increases in the levels of FSH and LH. The cyclic increases in FSH and LH are in turn controlled by the brain. Consequently, it is the brain itself which sets into motion those hormonal events which will result in its own alteration, producing sexual receptivity in the female and a mature egg more or less simulta-neously.

The ovarian hormones responsible for the changes in brain state which cause estrus are estrogen and progesterone. As the ovarian follicle is

Figure 46. A drawing of a composite mammalian ovary, showing progressive stages in the growth and differentiation of the Graafian follicle from a primary follicle to ovulation to its subsequent transition into a corpus luteum. This progression can be seen by reading the diagram clockwise. The mature follicle may become atretic (degenerate) or ovulate and undergo luteinization.(as seen in the ruptured follicle on right). (Turner & Bagnara, 1971.)

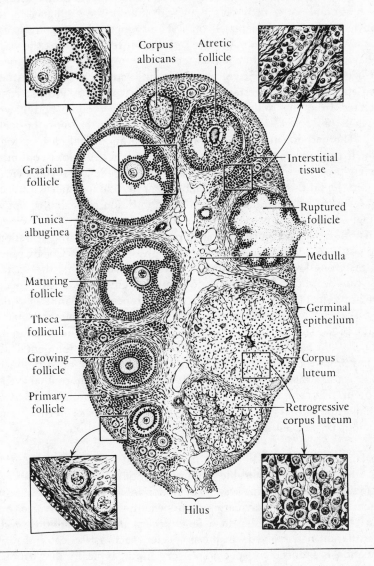

Corpus albicans

Atretic follicle

Interstitial tissue

Graafian follicle

Ruptured follicle

Tunica albuginea

Medulla

Maturing follicle

Germinal epithelium

Theca folliculi

Growing follicle

Corpus luteum

Primary follicle

Retrogressive corpus luteum

Hilus

maturing under stimulation by FSH, it begins to secrete more estrogen. Estrogen has a wide range of physiologic effects, from effects on the uterus and vagina to effects on the brain. In the brain, estrogen seems to have at least two different but functionally related effects. One is that of reducing the levels of FSH-releasing factor from those hypothalamic neurons responsible and thereby slowing the rate of FSH secretion from the anterior lobe of the pituitary. Estrogen thus acts in a *negative feedback* fashion with respect to FSH secretion. It does so by acting on the brain and not directly on the anterior lobe of the pituitary. In addition to the negative feedback on FSH production, estrogen also acts on the neurons in the brain that are responsible for generating the various behaviors which constitute sexual receptivity. Actually, in most species, estrogen alone is insufficient to trigger full estrous behavior. Another ovarian hormone, progesterone, must also be present. Progesterone is secreted from the follicle and the *corpus luteum* (yellow body), which is what the "spent" follicle is called after it has discharged the mature egg. The corpora lutea which are present in an animal such as the rat (which produces more than one egg with each ovulation) continue to secrete progesterone for some period of time. There is growing evidence that in the rat the maintained level of progesterone together with declining levels of estrogen contribute to the inhibition of sexual receptivity, bringing the period of estrus to an end.

If the female becomes pregnant, prolactin facilitates the secretion of progesterone by the corpora lutea. The physiologic effect of this higher progesterone level prepares the wall of the uterus so that the fertilized egg can be implanted and develop into an embryo. If the female is not impregnated, the whole cycle will be repeated in another 5 days, in a rhythm dependent upon the interaction of environmental factors, brain processes, anterior lobe hormonal secretions, and ovarian hormones. We have not stressed the importance of environmental input in the production of estrus cycles in the rat, but there must be fluctuations in the available levels of illumination for normal hormonal cyclicity to occur. Housing rats in either continuous light or continuous darkness will disrupt normal estrus cycles. There are other species in which sensory input plays even a more significant role in ovulation.

Ovulation as a reflex   The cycle of events that has been described for the rat is generally applicable (with some modifications) to many other mammalian species. This type of ovulation is known as *spontaneous* ovulation. In such species, ovulation occurs whether or not the female comes into contact with a male. In a few species, however, another system of ovulation has evolved. In these species, such as the cat and rabbit, ovulation is induced by specific sensory input, typically that produced by copulation. These species are termed *reflex ovulators*. The stimulation provided during copulation excites the LH-releasing factor neurons in the hypothalamus, and the consequent surge of LH causes the ripe follicle to burst and eject the egg a few hours later. Copulation with intact but sterile males is just as effective as copulation with fertile males in inducing ovulation, and even artificial procedures such as stimulating the cervix with a glass rod will trigger ovulation in female cats in estrus. Direct, brief, electric stimulation of restricted regions of the hypothalamus (presumably those containing the LH-releasing factor secreting neurons) can also produce ovulation. However, prolonged electric stimulation of the anterior lobe of the pituitary itself for as long as 7 hours is ineffective in producing significant LH secretion or ovulation. These results support the conclusion that it is the brain, not the anterior lobe of the pituitary itself, which controls the flow of hormones.

Estrogen is also important in activating (or releasing from chronic inhibition?) the neurons which produce behavioral estrus. We do not yet know just where in the brain all of these estrogen-sensitive neurons are located. Some of them are certainly in the hypothalamus. Small lesions in some areas of the hypothalamus reduce or eliminate sexual receptivity in the animal and render it insensitive to subsequent changes in estrogen and progesterone levels. The interpretation of this finding is that the neurons which trigger the behaviors of estrus have been destroyed, even though the neurons secreting the FSH-releasing factor and LH-releasing factor are still intact. Another line of evidence shows that minute amounts of estrogen implanted directly into these areas of the undamaged hypothalamus can bring about an increase in the spontaneous firing rate of neurons in this area, which in turn produces behavioral estrus. From a large number of different studies, we can conclude that there are two separable areas in the hypothalamus of mammals: a *hormone regulating* region, and a *behavior regulating* region. These two regions are functionally related but not identical.

THE HORMONE REGULATING AREA   The hormone regulating area of the hypothalamus contains the neurons which secrete the FSH-releasing factor, the LH-releasing factor, and the factor responsible for the *inhibition* of prolactin secretion. Prolactin, alone of all the anterior lobe hormones, is not released by a factor from the hypothalamus but is instead disinhibited from a tonic inhibition under the appropriate conditions by shutting off the secretion of a *prolactin inhibitory factor* (abbreviated PIF). In the nonpregnant female, PIF is secreted steadily, thereby tonically inhibiting the secretion of prolactin. During pregnancy, this inhibition is lifted by stopping the release of hypothalamic PIF. Electric stimulation of the hormone regulating area of the hypothalamus can induce ovulation in a reflex ovulator such as the rabbit (Sawyer, 1959). If estrogen is implanted into this area, the secretion of FSH is drastically reduced, and the gonads of the animal grow smaller or *atrophy*

(Lisk, 1960). In this case, the implanted estrogen serves as a false off signal for the neurons producing the FSH- and LH-releasing factor. The situation is analogous to placing a match directly under a thermostat in a cold room.

HOW THE PILL WORKS

The contraceptive pill works primarily by providing a hormonal off signal to prevent the further release of FSH and LH. The pill actually comes in twenty or more different varieties, but all contain both estrogen and a synthetic form of progesterone called *progestin*. The amounts of these two components vary slightly from one brand of pill to another, but all contain enough of these substances, particularly progestin, to block the ovulatory surge of LH. As a result, ovulation does not occur. The follicles develop somewhat but do not ovulate. Even in the extremely rare event of a mature egg that does escape from the ovaries of a woman taking the pill, two other effects of the pill diminish the chances that conception will take place to the vanishing point. In addition to blocking ovulation, progestin alters the nature of the wall of the uterus so that implantation of the fertilized egg cannot take place, and it is thereby lost. Finally, progestin also alters the plug of mucous of the cervix, so that sperm have a more difficult time penetrating the cervical mucous and entering the uterus (Kistner, 1968).

THE BEHAVIOR REGULATING AREA OF THE HYPOTHALAMUS   There is another region of the hypothalamus which contains neurons sensitive to estrogen and progesterone. Its exact location varies from species to species, but it is separate from the hormone regulating region. Lesions in this region eliminate sexual behavior, even though the hormonal state of the animal is normal. Additional hormone treatments are ineffective. This effect has been observed in both male and female animals. Implantation of estrogen in the behavior regulating region has the opposite effect from a lesion. If a minute amount of estrogen is implanted in this region, it serves as a false on signal and the animal becomes sexually active within minutes. Rats can also be "turned on" in this region by electric stimulation (Vaughn & Fisher, 1962; Caggiula & Hoebel, 1966). Stimulation of the behavior regulating region of the hypothalamus with low-level electric current can evoke quite remarkable sexual performances if a receptive female is present. In one case, a rat ejaculated 45 times in one 7½-hour session of such brain stimulation, a level of sexual vigor far beyond the normal range of rats.

Rats will also self-stimulate their own brains electrically by pressing a lever, thereby delivering an electric stimulus via a thin-wire electrode implanted so that the electric current affects neurons in this area of the hypothalamus. This is one of the parts of the brain which has been termed a "pleasure area" because rats (and other animals) will seek out the means to deliver electric current here (Olds & Milner, 1954; Olds, 1956). Since rats cannot talk in a language that we can understand, we do not really know what the stimulation feels like to the rats. However, there are a few reports from human neurological patients which indicate that stimulation of this region of the hypothalamus can indeed produce erotic, or sexy, feelings. Human patients suffering from various neurological disorders have had thin-wire electrodes permanently implanted into their brains. Low levels of electric current can then be passed through these electrodes into the brain while the patients are fully conscious and can report any sensations referable to the electric stimulation. Such reports are infrequent, but a few do exist. Patients have reported that the electric stimulation "feels good," and expressed a willingness to be stimulated again (Sem-Jacobsen, 1968). José Delgado reports on the effects of stimulating the brains of schizophrenic patients. One individual reported that electric stimulation of the septal area (a few millimeters away from the hypothalamus) made him feel as if he were "building up" to an orgasm, but he was unable to actually reach orgasm. Electric stimulation of the brain in other patients evoked behaviors that would seem out of context unless some erotic overtones were produced by the stimulation. For example, a female epileptic patient, not schizophrenic, became extremely friendly and "expressed her fondness for the therapist (who was new to her), kissed his hands, and talked about her immense gratitude for what was being done for her" (Delgado, 1969). There are a few other similar reports and the evidence is consistent but so far only suggestive. It should be added that most electric stimulation of the human brain has been in regions other than the hypothalamus, primarily in parts of the brain belonging to the limbic system.

Other reports from neurological patients provide evidence that damage in the hypothalamic area of humans can lead to quite dramatic changes in sexual behavior. Extreme sexual desire, bordering on nymphomania, as well as abrupt cessation of interest in sexual behavior have been reported for patients suffering from brain tumors or other disturbances of the hypothalamic areas and related brain tissue. This is not surprising. Such diseases can cause either the destruction of tissue or an abnormal increase in spontaneous firing rates (focal seizure). There is every reason to believe that the hypothalamus of humans, like that of other vertebrates, is critically important for the production of sexual behavior. It is tempting to hope that someday our knowledge of brain function will allow us to understand the varieties of sexual behavior which are so characteristic of human behavior. As we gain further understanding of the neural and hormonal factors in the development and operation of the brain, we will certainly penetrate more deeply into an understanding of the causes of human sexuality. Human sexual behavior, of course, like most other human behavior, is also determined by families and societies as well as by nerves and hormones.

HOW DO HORMONES WORK ON NEURONS?

We know that hormones such as estrogen, progesterone, and others can either activate or inhibit neurons in the brain. But we do not know how. There are several possibilities, and all, some, or none of them may be true. The three most likely possibilities are: (1) Hormones may operate on the neuronal membrane, somehow making it more or less responsive to input. This idea, of course, merely rephrases the question. It would not explain *how* such a change in the membrane occurred. (2) Hormones may operate by penetrating the nucleus of neurons and altering the genes that are activated. It is known that DNA can be "derepressed" in certain circumstances such that proteins not normally synthesized by that cell are produced. There is also evidence that hormones can be derepressing agents, at least in invertebrates. For example, in the small flying insect *Chironomus*, a hormone known as ecdysone (important in the molting process of this little creature) causes the chromosomes in the animal to "puff," or grow larger. The interpretation is that the chromosomal swelling is related to a genetic derepression in this region of the chromosomes. This is an important possibility, but it must be remembered that at the present, there is not much evidence that would suggest that such genetic derepression plays an important part in the way vertebrate hormones change the function of brain cells. (3) Hormones may serve as either specific or general metabolic activators or inhibitors. It is possible that hormones may work by allowing the cell to take in more products necessary for growth and development, or vice versa. A variety of metabolic effects are possible. No one effect of hormones on neurons is likely. It is more probable that a particular hormone may have several different effects.

SUGGESTIONS FOR FURTHER READING

Broderick, C. B., & Bernard, J. (Eds.) *The individual, sex, and society.* Baltimore: Johns Hopkins, 1969.

Diamond, M. (Ed.) *Perspectives in reproduction and sexual behavior.* Bloomington, Ind.: Indiana University Press, 1968.

Chapter 6

THE REGULATION OF FOOD AND WATER CONSUMPTION

Mammals regulate their food and water intake, although some species, such as man, often do so imperfectly. The behaviors associated with food-seeking, the discrimination between edible and nonedible foods, and the cessation of feeding before the available food supply is exhausted are but a few of the behaviors which have attracted the interest of behavioral scientists.

REGULATION OF FOOD CONSUMPTION

Most animals grow restless when they have not eaten recently. Even a caged rat will become more active with food deprivation, until actual physical weakness begins to occur. This increase in locomotion is a response which has obvious survival value for species that must seek out their food. Exploring the environment increases the chances of finding food.

Most animals also have a daily activity rhythm; that is, they become more active at about the same time each day. These *circadian* (from the Latin for "about a day") activity rhythms are not exactly at 24-hour intervals, but seem to be controlled by some sort of biological clock in the animal, presumably somewhere in the brain. There are many circadian rhythms, controlling such processes as body temperature, urine production, hormonal secretion, and other functions. Circadian rhythms may vary over years by as little as a few minutes each day (Aschoff, 1965). The circadian rhythms, which may influence our behavior a good deal more than is presently recognized, are poorly understood; although the general public has become more aware recently of the disturbance to the normal rhythms of life caused by flying from one time zone to another.

WHY DO ANIMALS STOP EATING?

Although there are hundreds of questions that can be raised about eating behaviors, the one which has attracted the most research interest is why animals stop eating. Most species (with some exceptions, such as man) do not chronically overeat even when food is abundant. The way in which animals regulate their food intake is not fully understood, but in general, it appears that the brain monitors some factor associated with food intake and shuts off feeding behavior when a certain set point is achieved. The analogy of a thermostat is often used to describe this kind of physiologic process. In fact, there is one theory (Brobeck, 1948) which proposes that it is the temperature of the body which is being monitored. According to this concept, when the body temperature drops, eating is stimulated; and when the body temperature rises, eating is inhibited. There is, in fact, a rise in body temperature following food intake that is known as the *specific dynamic action* of food. Although there is some supporting evidence that the temperature of the body (or of the blood?) is a partial factor affecting food intake, it is probably not the main regulating factor (Deutsch, 1971).

The level of blood sugar or glucose has also been proposed as a factor that regulates eating. There are findings that support the "glucostatic" theory (Mayer, 1953) and findings that suggest that blood glucose is not the critical factor. One big problem with respect to the glucostatic theory is that in diabetes, blood sugar level is high but so is hunger. It has been found in some studies that injections of glucose can indeed inhibit feeding, as would be predicted; but in other studies, no inhibition of feeding was observed. Thus, although blood glucose, like temperature, may be a factor regulating eating, it is almost certainly not the only one. It has also been suggested by several investigators that it is the rate of glucose utilization by the brain that is a key signal in the control of food intake. Actual levels of glucose in the blood would thus constitute only an indirect signal.

Still another factor implicated in the control of eating is a body factor associated with body fat. There are several lines of evidence which lend support to the notion that some substance (not identified as yet) which accumulates along with body fat helps to regulate eating.

The importance of the hypothalamus in the regulation of eating

Regardless of just what the signals are that regulate eating, they must be affecting brain cells somewhere. There must also be brain cells controlling the movements that constitute food-seeking and eating. The search for these brain cells has been concentrated on the hypothalamus. Input from virtually all parts of the brain converge onto hypothalamic neurons, as does sensory input from a variety of sources, including the stomach and other organs in the digestive system. Not surprisingly, the hypothalamus has been found to be involved in the regulation of eating.

A SATIETY CENTER IN THE VMH?

It has been known since the latter part of the nineteenth century that damage to the base of the brain occasionally produces obesity. But it was not until an experiment by Hetherington and Ranson in 1942 that experimental obesity was understood to be caused by bilateral lesions to the ventromedial region of the hypothalamus (VMH). If rats are given bilateral lesions of the VMH, they begin to eat voraciously (even before they are completely recovered from the anesthetic) and continue to overeat, if palatable food is available, until they are grossly obese. They often double their preoperative weight in a few weeks. However, once their weight has reached a new, greater level, their food consumption returns to a much lower level, and they do not gain weight at the same rate, but maintain a plateau at the new, obese level. Thus, there are two recognized states in the *hypothalamic hyperphagia* (overeating) caused by VMH lesions: a *dynamic phase* of several months in which the animals eat voraciously and gain weight rapidly; and a *static phase,* in which they return to near-normal levels of food intake. The animals are very fat, with as much as 74 percent of their total body weight being made up of fat (Grossman, 1967). The two main symptoms of VMH damage are overeating and obesity, and it is not surprising that many investigators have concluded that the overeating is responsible for the obesity. And to date, it appears that the main cause of the obesity in animals with VMH lesions is that they overeat. Obviously it is an important factor, but it is not necessarily the *only* physiologic effect which occurs as a result of damage to this part of the brain.

VMH ANIMALS ARE NOT SIMPLY MORE HUNGRY

One cannot conclude from the discussion above, however, that VMH animals are necessarily *hungrier.* While this may sound paradoxical at first, there is quite convincing evidence that while VMH rats will drastically overeat if the food available to them is palatable, they will eat *less* than normal rats if it is adulterated so that it does not taste as good. If, on the other hand, their food is sweetened with sugar, they will overeat even more than with normal food. The conclusion is that the lesion has somehow made the animals more sensitive to the taste of the food. If they were simply hungrier, one would expect them to eat more even if the food did not taste as good as usual. Another indication that simple hunger is an inadequate explanation for the overeating displayed by the VMH animals is that they will not work as hard to get food as will normal rats. If placed in a situation where they must press a lever to get food pellets, they do not respond with nearly as much effort as do normal rats (Miller et al., 1950; Teitelbaum, 1957).

DO VMH LESIONS BLOCK THE NORMAL OFF SIGNALS FOR EATING?

One interpretation of the effects of VMH lesions is that the operation has destroyed neurons necessary for shutting off eating behavior. Thus, although the animals do not necessarily feel hungry, they do not stop eating as do normal animals. This may be because the (unknown) signals which cause a normal animal to stop eating and thereby regulate its weight are blocked by the lesion. There is evidence to indicate that animals may monitor some substance related to the amount of fat deposits in their bodies as a means of regulating body weight. Consequently, whereas a normal animal may eat a great deal one day, over a long time span it will eat only about enough to maintain a normal body weight. In the VMH animals with hypothalamic hyperphagia, it is possible that the lesion has impaired the animal's ability to regulate its body weight at the normal levels and that it is not until a new obese set point is reached that the signals of body fat deposits are strong enough to reduce food intake. This would constitute the dynamic phase of the syndrome. Once the new weight is reached, food intake returns to near-normal levels. This would constitute the static phase of the condition. The possibility that VMH lesions interrupt the normal signaling of level of fat deposition is supported by an imaginative study by Hervey (1959) in which he experimentally produced parabiotic, or "Siamese twin," animal preparations.

PARABIOTIC RATS AND THE VMH SYNDROME

G. R. Hervey used a surgical technique, known as *parabiosis*, of uniting the bloodstreams of two animals in order to study some aspects of the VMH syndrome. In making parabiotic pairs, two animals are operated on to produce a common circulatory system. It was accomplished by Hervey in rats either by opening each member of the pair in the abdominal area and then suturing the two rats together in a Siamese twin fashion or by similarly joining them at the thigh. In such pairs, about 1 percent of one rat's plasma volume is exchanged with that of the other every minute.

Hervey then made VMH lesions in only one member of each parabiotic pair. His results, based on sixteen parabiotic pairs, confirm that VMH lesions produced voracious eating and rapid weight gain over several weeks in the lesioned rat. The unlesioned rats, on the other hand, became quite obviously thin and appeared to be eating much less than before the operation to their partner. (Direct measurements of how much food each member of a pair consumed were not taken.) The unoperated rat took no interest in food held under its nose, whereas the VMH-lesioned partner would take the food and eat it. In three parabiotic pairs, the previously unoperated rat was also given VMH lesions several weeks after the other member of the pair had been operated. Only one such double-operated pair survived, however. In that pair, both animals overate and became obese.

Does fat provide feedback?   The main finding of Hervey's experiment was that the VMH-lesioned member of the parabiotic pair ate voraciously and grew fat while the nonoperated member ate less than before and grew thin. A most reasonable interpretation is offered by Hervey to account for these results. He suggests that the nonoperated partners ate less than normal amounts because some signal in the common blood-stream indicated increasing deposits of fat. This signal was presumably coming from the hyperphagic partner whose own hypothalamus was incapable of responding appropriately to the fat-feedback signals. Thus, like a match under a thermostat in a cold room, the normal hypothalamus in the nonoperated partner received a false off signal and diminished its food intake. The hypothalamus in the VMH-lesioned partner was no longer able to respond appropriately to the fat-feedback signals and thus food intake continued in a full-steam-ahead fashion. Eventually, such VMH-lesioned animals do reach sufficient levels of obesity so that food intake is diminished, thus entering the static phase of hypothalamic hyperphagia. If this interpretation is correct, it suggests that the ventromedial region of the hypothalamus normally responds to some metabolite which is in equilibrium with stored body fat. This substance turns off eating in normal brains but is unable to shut off feeding in VMH-lesioned brains, at least when the available food is palatable. This feedback system may be one of the main ways in which the VMH controls food intake and thus helps to regulate body weight.

THE LATERAL HYPOTHALAMIC SYNDROME

Following the discovery that VMH lesions could unleash voracious eating in rats, it was found that lesions in the nearby *lateral hypothalamus* (LH) produced essentially opposite effects (Anand & Brobeck, 1951). Bilateral lesions in this area of the hypothalamus produce in rats (and some other species) an immediate and total cessation of eating (termed *aphagia*) and drinking (termed *adipsia*). The rats die in the midst of available food and water if they are not artificially fed and given water. If LH animals are kept alive for a sufficient period of time (several days), most of them will begin to eat extremely palatable foods, such as sweet chocolate. Eventually, most of them will recover to the point where they can survive on dry food and water, although they never become totally normal. Alan Epstein (1971) has carefully described the lateral hypothalamic syndrome and the various stages in the recovery process. As he points out, *the inability to regulate water balance is a permanent feature in the behavior of the animals.* Various experiments have demonstrated that the "recovery" of the drinking seen in these LH rats is strictly *prandial drinking.* Prandial drinking (from the Latin *prandium,* "meal") is the drinking of water in small sips in order to lubricate the mouth and throat sufficiently for the swallowing of dry food. Rats, like other animals, cannot swallow dry food without some moisture in their mouths. Normal rats salivate enough so that prandial drinking is extremely rare. As a matter of fact, a normal rat segregates its eating and drinking behavior rather sharply, usually drinking most of its daily water in large drafts immediately before or after dry-food meals. The lesions in the lateral hypothalamus impair the salivation process in rats, and LH-lesioned rats become prandial drinkers upon recovery if given only dry food. If LH rats are given a wet-food diet, they do not drink. Thus a prandial drinker will take a little sip of water with almost every bite of dry food, 400 to 600 sips each day. The LH animals manage to survive by such prandial drinking. Normal rats who have had their salivary glands removed quickly become prandial drinkers also, behaving in this respect much like LH rats. If LH animals are deprived of what salivation they have left by subsequent removal of their salivary glands, they increase their prandial drinking even more. The apparent recovery of drinking in such animals is tied directly to their dry mouth and does not mean that they have regained the ability to regulate their body-water supply. They have not. If they are deprived of water, they will not drink more to make up for the loss, nor will they respond to other maneuvers which cause increased drinking in normal rats or rats with only their salivary glands removed. As well as can be determined at this time, these rats have lost the urge to drink, and manage to survive only by the prandial drinking that they do in conjunction with the eating of dry food.

The urge to eat is also weakened in LH animals. They will eat enough to survive after the initial aphagic period, but only if the food is palatable. They remain quite finicky about the taste of food and water throughout the postoperative period. If their food is adulterated with quinine or some other bad-tasting substance, they will not eat to the extent that normal rats will. Even changing the food from pellet form to powder will often cause the recovered LH rats to stop eating again. Their finickiness about food and water does not change. Nor do they respond normally to artificially produced changes in glucose levels in the body. Normal rats will eat more in response to insulin injections, which lower the level of glucose in the blood. LH-lesioned rats will not. In the early postoperative stages there is even an apparent aversion to food. The LH rats will push food away or make other movements that can be interpreted as a rejection of food, even if they have not eaten for days. Their aversion gradually disappears, but the finickiness remains.

The discovery that lesions in these two anatomically adjacent regions of the hypothalamus—the ventromedial region and the lateral hypothalamic area—produce nearly opposite effects has—inspired a number of similar theories. The theories have proposed that the VMH operates as a satiety mechanism that is responsible for inhibiting the feeding and drinking mechanisms disrupted by the lateral hypothalamic lesions. If destroyed, the VMH can no longer turn off the eating mechanism, and the hyperphagic syndrome is seen. Although VMH-lesioned rats eat more and become obese, they are not hungry in the normal sense of the word; they work less for food and are more sensitive to changes in the taste of their food. VMH-lesioned rats overeat until they reach a level of obesity at which some signal (from the greatly increased fat deposits?) manages to inhibit eating, which returns to near normal levels, just enough to maintain the new, obese body weight.

The theory proposes, on the other hand, that if the lateral hypothalamic area is damaged, the urge to eat is weakened, the urge to drink is abolished, and the lateral hypothalamic syndrome occurs. Recovery occurs to a certain extent, but the nature of this process is not known, although it seems to follow rather closely the sequence of events in the development of eating and drinking in the infant rat (Teitelbaum et al., 1969).

Human obesity

If one compares the behavior of rats with VMH lesions and obese humans (15 to 75 percent overweight) as Stanley Schachter has done (1971), a surprising similarity is seen. Obese humans in general eat more good-tasting food than do normal human beings (less than 8 percent overweight) and *less* bad-tasting food, exactly like VMH-lesioned rats. There are also parallels between VMH rats and obese humans in the amount of food eaten (slightly higher than normals, not surprisingly), the number of meals per day (slightly *fewer* than normals), the speed of eating (considerably faster than normals), the willingness to work for food (less by VMH rats and obese humans), and other measures. Schachter offers an overall hypothesis to account for these and other facts that obese humans (and VMH rats) are more controlled by external stimulus conditions, such as the cues provided by food and related objects, than are normals. The overeating of obese humans is assumed to be derived from a basic perceptual difference. If such is the case, and if the ventromedial hypothalamus is involved, it would certainly bring about a whole new set of research programs on the functions of the hypothalamus. This would not be too surprising a development in the history of science, where one set of facts provides the questions for the generation of a new set of facts.

REGULATION OF WATER INTAKE

One of the most compelling sensations known to man is thirst. Most of us rarely experience real, excruciating thirst, as is reported by individuals who have been cut off from all sources of liquid. Humans (and in fact virtually all organisms) seem to anticipate their fluid needs, typically drinking long before any real thirst is experienced. Of course, a fast set of tennis in the hot sun or a long, dusty walk produces noticeable thirst, but it is not like the maddening, panic-producing agony of the castaway. Most organisms have evolved circadian rhythms of eating and drinking which allow them to avoid hunger and thirst crises. Therefore, if we wish to understand why animals drink, to say that it is because they are thirsty just won't do. Such an answer would obviously be empty, no more an explanation than the statement that animals sleep because they are sleepy. But even more than this, it appears that the sensations which we associate with thirst, such as a dry mouth and throat, do not satisfactorily account for normal drinking behavior. Another problem which complicates the study of thirst in animals other than man is that it is, like pain, a sensation. Consequently, we cannot study thirst directly in animals because they cannot tell us that they are thirsty. What can only actually be measured is drinking; and although it makes good common sense to use drinking as a measure of thirst, the two are really somewhat different. For example, animals and men do sometimes drink when there is no reason to believe they are experiencing thirst.

James T. Fitzsimons has written a thoughtful essay on drinking behavior (1971) in which he distinguishes between *primary drinking* and *secondary drinking*. Among the causes of primary drinking are water deprivation, hemorrhage, exercise, and the injection of various substances, such as salt solutions, which are more concentrated (more salty, or *hypertonic*) than the blood. Secondary drinking can be produced in an animal not suffering any imbalance in its body fluids by direct electric stimulation of the hypothalamus, or in animals in which a dry mouth is produced by removing or blocking the function of the salivary glands. Prandial drinking is also considered as a form of secondary drinking. There are also recorded cases of pathological, or psychogenic, drinking of water, where large amounts of water are drunk by individuals for reasons not related to fluid imbalance, but such behavior is poorly understood. Examples of this behavior are, of course, rare, but they serve to remind us that valid distinctions can be made between primary and secondary drinking and that explanations for one type of drinking may not apply to the other.

There are at least two basic questions we can ask about primary drinking: What starts it? What stops it? Since there are different conditions which can cause primary drinking, we must allow for the possibility of different answers for different cases.

What starts drinking?

There is a growing consensus that dryness of the mouth and throat does not fully explain drinking. It is true that virtually all conditions which produce thirst, such as water deprivation, eating of dry foods, hemorrhage, injection of hypertonic solutions, also reduce the amount of salivary flow, and therefore help create a dryness of the mouth and throat. Also, it is obvious from our own experiences and reports of others that dryness of the mouth and throat is unpleasant and that drinking usually relieves the unpleasant sensation. Thus, need for water (and drinking, if water is available) is correlated with reduced salivation. But correlation is not causality. Direct tests of the dry-mouth theory have seriously weakened the notion that the sensations arising from dry mouth and throat are major factors regulating the amount of water animals drink. Interruption of salivary flow by removal of the salivary glands causes dogs to drink more often, but these animals do not drink more water under normal conditions (Montgomery, 1931). Other experiments support this basic negative finding (Grossman, 1967). Thus, although a dry mouth certainly can make us feel thirsty, it is not the significant factor in regulating primary drinking. The important stimuli for regulating the amount of water an animal drinks must be sought elsewhere. At the present time there are two leading hypotheses.

1   The increase in the concentration of the dissolved salts in the extracellular fluid in the body *relative to* the concentration inside the cells, which would result in an increase in the effective *osmotic pressure* of cells in the body
2   The reduced volume of the fluids in the extracellular compartment of the body

It is probable that both factors contribute to the production of drinking.

Molecules of a dissolved substance which cannot flow freely through the cell membrane exert an osmotic pressure on that side of the membrane. Water from the other side of the membrane (which can flow readily through) is attracted to the side of the greater concentration of dissolved substance. If the concentration of dissolved substances inside the cell is greater than the concentration of dissolved substances in the extracellular fluid outside the cell, water will flow into the cell and the cell will expand. One version of the osmotic pressure theory of thirst contends that there are *osmoreceptors* located in the hypothalamus which are sensitive to changes in osmotic pressure. The osmotic changes would thus set into motion the complex circuitry of the brain which leads to a search for water and drinking. There is strong evidence, dating from the now-classic work of Verney (1947), that there are cells in the hypothalamus which respond to the injection of solutions that vary in osmotic pressure from either the intra- or extracellular fluid. Verney made his injections into the carotid arteries that supply the hypothalamic area. Subsequent research has confirmed Verney's original observations. Recently, Vincent and Hayward (1970) have recorded from neurons in the supraoptic nucleus and immediately surrounding region of the hypothalamus which respond rather specifically to changes in osmotic pressure brought about by techniques similar to Verney's. There are almost certainly osmoreceptors in the hypothalamus. More recent evidence has also demonstrated that there are osmoreceptors in the adjacent lateral preoptic area of the hypothalamus (Blass & Epstein, 1971). There are experiments which show that injection of tiny amounts of hypertonic saline into the supraoptic region of the hypothalamus of goats produces almost immediate drinking of large amounts of water (Andersson, 1953; Andersson & McCann, 1955). Similar injections in nearby regions of the hypothalamus had no effect on drinking. Andersson was also able to demonstrate that the osmoreceptors involved in drinking were anatomically distinct from those involved in the secretion of ADH. Andersson's's results provide strong evidence that activity in osmoreceptors in the hypothalamus does contribute to the initiation of drinking.

Hypovolemia

It has also been suggested that another factor, called *hypovolemia* (decreased volume of the extracellular fluid compartment of the body) is a trigger stimulus for primary drinking. The strongest evidence for this comes from the work of Fitzsimons and his coworkers (Fitzsimons, 1971). In these experiments, the volume of the extracellular fluid was reduced by various techniques. The procedures produced considerable drinking in rats without great changes in osmotic pressure in the cells. Fitzsimons and Simons (1969) have provided evidence that a product of the kidney, called *angiotensin*, may be responsible for triggering the drinking caused by reduced extracellular volume. Injection of this substance into the hypothalamus also causes drinking in rats.

Thus, there may be two (or more) critical stimuli for primary drinking: osmotic changes, which are monitored by osmoreceptors located in the hypothalamus; and reduction of the volume of the extracellular fluid (perhaps mediated by angiotensin). On the basis of present incomplete knowledge, it does seem likely that there will be many further developments in our understanding of the causes of thirst.

What stops drinking?

It would be very tidy if a simple reversal of the stimulus conditions which triggers drinking stopped drinking. But the basic experimental finding is that animals stop drinking long before the fluid drunk can reverse the cellular or extracellular conditions which presumably triggered the drinking in the first place.

There is as yet no satisfactory answer to the question: What stops drinking? Many animals, including ourselves, are rather good at drinking just about the right amount to make up for fluid needs after a period of deprivation. This drinking is usually done in a matter of minutes, which is too short a period of time to allow for the water to correct the fluid imbalances. For example, dogs that are deprived of water for several hours can drink almost exactly what they need in a few minutes. Bellows (1939) studied drinking in dogs with *esophageal fistulas* (in which the esophagus was severed and the cut ends brought through the skin to the outside). In these animals, the water (and food) that they ingested did not reach the stomach but was diverted back to the outside of their neck. They had to be fed and watered through the esophageal opening which goes directly to the stomach. These dogs drank about twice the normal amounts when there was not any water actually getting to the stomach, but they did not do it all at once. They drank, stopped, and then returned to drink again. If, however, the amount of water needed was put directly into the stomach through the fistula, and at least 20 minutes was allowed to elapse, then the dogs did not drink. Somehow the water in the stomach inhibited drinking. Temporary satiety is probably related to some signal from the stomach to the brain, but whether this is produced by the distension of the stomach or the release of some chemical messenger released by the stomach in response to the water load is not entirely clear. Whatever the physiological explanation, it is clear that there are short-term satiety mechanisms at work which speed up the process whereby animals can regain an optimal fluid balance. Actual complete restoration of balance in the various fluid compartments can then proceed at a more leisurely rate while the animal goes about his business. The adaptive value of such a system is considerable, inasmuch as it relieves the animal from staying near sources of water for long periods of time.

RELATION OF HUNGER AND THIRST TO ACTIVITY

Life is more than just eating and drinking, of course. Mammals are complex organisms, and motives other than hunger and thirst influence their behavior. We have already discussed sexual behavior. Although eating, drinking, and sex do account for a considerable proportion of the drives in many mammals, it would be wrong to think of mammals as being active only when in search of food, water, or sex. Even well-fed, nonthirsty, and sexually aroused mammals do not simply sit still, waiting to become hungry again. On the other hand, there is a fairly good correlation between drive levels and activity levels in most mammals. Animals who have been without food or water for several hours become more active. Activity levels in female rats vary in close correspondence to their estrus cycle, peaking at the time of behavioral estrus. Many species do become quiet and sleep after heavy meals or prolonged bouts of sexual activity. It seems reasonable that states of the nervous system which are associated with food or water deprivation should also be associated with a more active state of the nervous system. The probability of finding food or water would generally be improved as an organism became more active and explored more of its environment. How deeply embedded into the behavioral repertoire of mammals is this correlation between states of deprivation and activity levels is not known. Even caged animals begin to pace at a greater intensity as the time since the last feeding increases (and as the time of the next feeding grows closer).

As is discussed in Chapter 10, we are beginning to understand something about the parts of the mammalian brain that seem responsible for general arousal. But we have no good understanding of how these arousal systems might be interfaced with hunger or thirst systems in the brain. We can anticipate that much of the brain will be involved in the regulation of behaviors associated with hunger. The hypothalamus is certainly a key element in such drive systems.

Much of human behavior, as well as that of other primates, is not very directly tied to the satisfaction of basic biological needs such as food, water, oxygen, etc. With the evolution of the brain, curiosity becomes an increasingly dominant motive. It is interesting to speculate that human intellectual curiosity may be the evolutionary result of the restlessness that accompanies food or water deprivation in lower mammals. Thus the metaphor "a thirst for knowledge" may not be so far off. However, when a biological scientist begins to speculate and particularly when he resorts to metaphors, you can be reasonably sure that he has very few genuine facts to offer.

SUGGESTIONS FOR FURTHER READING

Stellar, E., & Sprague, J. M. (Eds.) *Progress in physiological psychology.* Vol. 4. New York: Academic, 1971.

Chapter 7

OUR CHANGING BRAINS

The brain is alive and subject to change; and the list of such changes is long. It includes both normal changes that occur with growth and aging and abnormal changes that result from disease, injury, or poisoning. Some of the changes can be observed by a careful examination of brain tissue; whereas others may be happening even though we cannot prove it. One of the changes which we believe to happen in the brain is called *learning*. We cannot, of course, observe learning directly; we can only observe changes in the behavior of ourselves and others. But it is widely assumed that some change in the nervous system must occur to explain the observed changes in behavior. Brain scientists generally agree that there are probably changes in the microstructure of some neurons during learning, but the identification of these changes has not yet been accomplished.

In this chapter we will consider some of the major types of changes known to occur in nervous systems. The first is the normal *developmental changes* that occur as the brain is being formed and matures. These developmental changes can be classified into four critical cell processes: division, migration, specification, and death.

CELL DIVISION

Until quite recently, it has been widely believed that most mammals, including man, are born with all the central nervous system neurons they are ever going to have. This conclusion is based primarily on the fact that neuroanatomists have been unable to "catch" neurons from the brains of mammals after birth in *mitosis* (the act of dividing to form two cells). The examination of the brains of adult mammals reveals no evidence of mitosis, and thus the conclusion has been reached that there is no further addition to the number of neurons in the brain after birth in mammals. However, this conclusion appears to need revision in light of some recent experiments by Joseph Altman (1967).

Altman and his coworkers have published several articles which demonstrate that in rats and cats, there are undifferentiated cells in the brain—called *neuroblasts*—which do multiply in the brain after birth. These neuroblasts then differentiate and form new neurons. The neurons migrate through the brain, often for long distances, and insert themselves into the developing circuitry of the growing brain for several weeks or even longer following birth. In order to detect this division of differentiation and migration, Altman used an experimental technique called *autoradiography*. In this technique, young animals are injected with thymidine, a chemical substance used by cells to make DNA. This injected thymidine is made radioactive, or is "tagged," before it is injected. Cells apparently use thymidine only in very large amounts when they are making DNA, which they do when they are undergoing mitosis. If a cell incorporates a relatively large amount of thymidine, this is presumptive evidence that the cell is active and making new DNA in preparation for cell division. Since the injected thymidine is radioactive, it gives off enough energy to "expose" a photographic film, making a dark spot or grain for each radioactive molecule present. Thus, when Altman later made microscopic slides of the brains of these young rats, he was able to "take a picture" of those areas of the brain where the radioactive thymidine had been incorporated and concentrated by brain cells. These were the areas of the brain in which active cell division had recently taken place.

In the rat, new neurons are formed quite vigorously for 2 to 3 weeks after birth. This process, termed *neurogenesis,* then tapers off in the young adult rat. However, in some areas of the brain, such as the hippocampus, there is evidence that although neurogenesis slows down in the adult rat, it never actually ceases, thus indicating that new neurons are being added to the rat hippocampus throughout life. We do not yet know the significance of this continued neurogenesis. It is possible, however, that the process is related to the behavioral changes in the rat that are apparently not due to any "training." They are called developmental changes, that is, changes that happen at quite predictable ages, given a normal environment.

The most characteristic type of neuron formed by postnatal neurogenesis is what Altman refers to as *microneurons,* because of their small size and short axons. The short axon reflects the common functional property of all microneurons; they have a restricted, local sphere of synaptic output. Microneurons can be contrasted with sensory neurons, which must bring information from the body surface, often over long distances, into the central nervous system. These neurons have in many cases evolved extremely long axons. Likewise, many motor neurons in mammals have evolved long axons to enable them to reach cells in the spinal cord before synapsing. If long axons have evolved to perform long-distance communication, then the short-axoned microneurons may have evolved to perform local "switching" functions. Altman has speculated that these neurons are primarily concerned with the modulation and refinement of the information coming to and going from brain regions such as the hippocampus; and this functional role for the microneurons would be increasingly important as the animal reached various developmental stages in which its behavior became more "mature."

One obvious example of increasing behavioral capacity with biological maturation is the ability of mammals to make smooth, coordinated movements. The cerebellum is an organ of the brain which is involved in the coordination of movement and postural adjustments. There is a very striking relationship in several different species between the ages at which adultlike movements are first observed and the age at which neurogenesis ends in the cerebellum. Guinea pigs, unlike many other mammals, can move about quite effectively shortly after they are born but show little further improvement in movement capacity. This coincides in time with the end of neurogenesis in the cerebellum of the little guinea pigs, which occurs within a few days after birth. Rats, on the other hand, cannot stand or walk for several days after they are born, but their movement capacity improves gradually over the first few weeks. By the end of three weeks, rats display almost adultlike movements. In the rat cerebellum, neurogenesis does not become complete until just this time—3 weeks. Kittens are even slower than rats to achieve the quick, coordinated movements of the adult cat, taking about 6 weeks to reach this stage. Cerebellar neurogenesis is not completed in cats until the end of about 2 months. In man, the ability to stand erect, walk readily, and use the fingers reasonably well takes about 2 years. This coincides in time with the disappearance in the cerebellum of the external granular layer, a sign which Altman uses to indicate the end of cerebellar neurogenesis. *Thus, in every species so far studied, there is a correlation in time between the attainment of an advanced maturational level of motor coordination and the end of postnatal neurogenesis of microneurons in the cerebellum.* Although the correlation is very suggestive, there is as yet no evidence that the relationship between postnatal neurogenesis in the cerebellum and the maturation of motor skills is necessarily a *causal* one.

The cerebellum is only one of several regions of the mammalian brain to show active postnatal neurogenesis. The hippocampus is another site of active postnatal neurogenesis. The differentiation of new neurons in the hippocampus of both the rat and cat brain occurs at a high rate for several weeks following birth. The general function of the hippocampus is less clear than that of the cerebellum. We cannot readily identify the behavioral changes in maturation that might be associated with the postnatal neurogenesis in the hippocampus. I have theorized (Kimble, 1968) that the hippocampus in the rat is important for the *inhibition of maladaptive behaviors.* It may be that as the hippocampus in the rat develops, its adult behavioral capacity increases as a result of the addition of microneurons to the hippocampal circuitry after birth. This hippocampal maturation may increase the capacity of the young rat to inhibit behaviors which are maladaptive, and thus increase the flexibility of its behavior.

CELL MIGRATION

The fetal brain grows by cell division, a process that tends to take place in particular areas of the developing brain. One major area is along the walls of the ventricles. Following division, the neuroblasts must migrate from the region of differentiation and division to their final destination in the brain. Once they have reached this destination, they undergo the final specification into a particular sort of neuron. Very little is known about how the neurons know where to go or how they move through the brain, although it is known that such movements can be very complex (Sidman, 1970).

CELL SPECIFICATION

We do not know how one cell comes to develop differently from another. Even among neurons, there is great diversity in such characteristics as the extent of dendritic branching, the size, the length of axon, the number of axon branches, the transmitter agent released from the end feet, the amount of myelination around the axon, etc. The different types of neurons in the mammalian brain all develop from neuroblasts which appear to be virtually identical, each possessing all the genetic information available to other body cells. Just how cell specification occurs is a fundamental and unresolved problem.

In considering the specification of neurons, we must account not only for the diversity of structure but also for the specificity with which neurons make synaptic contacts. This is not a random, or chance, process—the right neurons must make synaptic contacts with the right muscles if proper movement is to take place. Also, in sensory systems, the synaptic connections must be made in a precise way if normal function is to follow.

How are sensory neurons "labeled"?

In vertebrates, the sensory neurons from the body surface provide a quite orderly point-to-point representation of the sense organ surface by their connections in the brain. Neurons in the lateral geniculate are responsive to only certain portions of the visual field. The orderly projection of the sensory surface into the brain produces spatial representations, or "maps," in both thalamic and cortical areas. The maps are found for all the senses that have the property of spatial localization (thus excluding taste and smell). The precise and orderly relation between the receptor surface and the receptive areas in the brain raises a fundamental question of brain organization. How do the ingrowing sensory nerves from the sensory surface make the proper synaptic connections with neurons in the central nervous system? In turn, what guides the neurons in developing the correct connections at the next level of sensory processing? Many individuals have conducted experiments which have been directed at gaining information about these questions. Some of the most valuable experiments have come from the laboratory of Roger W. Sperry.

NANCY MINER'S EXPERIMENTS

Nancy Miner, in a series of doctoral studies in Sperry's laboratory at the University of Chicago, demonstrated some basic facts about the development of sensory nerve connections in vertebrates (Miner, 1956). In one of her experiments, Miner cut a rectangular strip of skin (extending from the middle of the back to the middle of the belly) from a number of tadpoles (Rana pipiens). When the strip of skin was gently freed from the underlying tissue, it was immediately replaced on the skinless area, but rotated 180 degrees so that it was replaced in a reversed position from normal. The portion of the skin strip that had been taken from the back of the tadpole was now on the belly of the tadpole, and vice versa. The operation itself was quite successful, and the skin grafted nicely in its new orientation. As the tadpoles grew and developed into frogs, the skin underwent a process of differentiation which was dictated by the original position on the tadpole. That is, the tadpole belly skin that had been rotated to the back side of the animal differentiated into the ivory color of normal frog belly skin. Likewise, the tadpole back skin that had been rotated and grafted onto the belly surface of the animal differentiated into the green-and-black-spotted pattern typical of frog back skin, despite its new location on the belly of the frog. Miner then stimulated various parts of the skin (both normal and grafted) of these frogs with a fine copper wire. Such stimulation evokes specific reflexes in normal frogs. For example, when the back skin of a normal frog is touched with the wire, it will reflexively brush that spot of skin with one hind foot. If the belly skin of a normal frog is touched, one of the forelimbs will rub the stimulated area. These reflexes are not dependent on an intact brain for their execution. Like the scratch reflex in dogs, and other spinal reflexes (see Chapter 9 for more details), these reflexes can be elicited in the frog even after the spinal cord is severed. In fact (perhaps not surprisingly), these reflex movements are even more consistent, reliable, and automatic after the spinal cord has been severed from any communication with the brain. The responses are "wired in" to the frog's nervous system.

In frogs with the back-belly-skin reversals, when the back skin (now on the belly) was stimulated, the frogs brushed their back. When the belly skin now located on the back was stimulated, the frogs wiped their bellies. The misplaced skin had somehow retained its "local sign" with respect to these reflex wiping responses, even though the sensory nerves that grew out to supply the misplaced skin would, in a normal frog, have supplied skin of the opposite sign.

What is the explanation of these findings? Miner offered the following hypothesis. First, it is assumed that the sensory neurons grow out to supply the skin in an essentially random fashion, simply growing into the nearest skin area without taking into account whether that patch of skin is in its correct position or not. At that point in development, *the skin must somehow instruct the nerve about what "kind" of skin it is and what sort of synaptic connections the axon of that sensory neuron must make in the spinal cord in order to produce the appropriate reflex movements when that area of skin is stimulated.*

In the experimental tadpoles with the skin in reversed positions, the neuron which grew into the back skin on the belly must, theoretically, have been instructed by the skin: "I am back-skin; make the appropriate back-skin reflex connections in the spinal cord." In the normal tadpole, of course, this neuron would have invaded normal belly skin. Apparently, then, a developing neuron is open to different commands from the skin at this stage of development of the tadpole. This "plasticity" is lost at later stages of development of this animal. It is not known, however, whether the skin loses its ability to instruct the outgrowing sensory neuron or if the ability of the neuron to alter its central connections is lost or both. In any case, skin grafts made *after* this plastic period in tadpole development always give rise to normally directed wiping reflexes, unlike those described by Miner for the earlier period (Jacobson, 1970).

These experiments tell us something about the way in which sensory neurons make their central connections, but they also raise a number of other questions, as good research always does. One question which comes to mind is: What is the mechanism by which the skin instructs the neuron growing into it about the kind of skin it is? We are accustomed to neurons instructing other cells by the release of chemicals, as at synapses. In this case, however, the transfer of information is the other way around—from a peripheral cell *to* the neuron. It is usually called *retrograde transfer of information*, although the term retrograde only indicates our biases about which way information ought to go. There is no doubt, however, that such peripheral-to-central transfer of information is a reality. There are other indications that such information transfer must occur, including experiments that demonstrate that there are changes in the metabolism of the motor neurons which supply a muscle when the condition of the muscle is changed (Prestige, 1970). The nature of the messenger (presumably some chemical substance going from muscle to neuron) that instructs the developing neuron is not known.

Another question is: Do sensory neurons which enter the brain directly also know with which central neurons they are to form synaptic contact? The answer seems to be yes. There is now considerable evidence that the synaptic connections made by the ganglion cells of the optic nerve are programmed to form very precise central synapses, presumably by genetic instructions.

Sperry has provided much of the evidence that in amphibians, optic nerve axons make specific connections with cells in the *optic tectum* (the amphibian equivalent of the LGN). His experiments were conducted on amphibians because of the remarkable ability of these species to regenerate nervous tissue that has been damaged. Mammals do not possess this ability to any significant extent, particularly with respect to the optic nerve. If the optic nerve in a mammal is cut, it does not regrow; the animal is totally and permanently blind in that eye. However, in fish and amphibians, if the optic nerve is cut and the animal is kept healthy, the nerve regrows and the animal can see again. This process takes about a month in frogs. Not only can the frog see again, but as far as can be determined, its vision is as good as it was prior to the operation.

If one examines the optic nerve and brain of these experimental animals, it becomes very clear that the cut ends of the optic nerve axons have regenerated new endings and have made their way back into the brain and reestablished synaptic connections with neurons of the optic tectum. If the operation is a simple section of the optic nerve, the vision of the frog is normal. The fact that vision is normal does not in itself prove that the regenerating optic nerve fibers grew back and made selective synaptic connections. It might be possible to conclude that the regenerating axons had made "random" synaptic connections in the optic tectum and that the frog's nervous system had then learned to respond to the visual world in a normal fashion. However other experiments by Sperry (1951) have ruled out the learning hypothesis.

It is also possible to rotate the eyeball in a frog, leaving the optic nerve intact. The eye heals in this new position, and thus the eye can be rotated 180 degrees front to back as is shown in Figure 47A. (It is necessary to remember that frogs' eyes are on the sides of their heads.) What about the frog's behavior with respect to objects in its visual field on that side. *Vision is reversed front to back.* As Figure 47 shows, if a fly is presented above and behind the frog, the frog's tongue strikes down and in front of its head, 180 degrees off target. There is no improvement in the frog's strike accuracy with further experience.

A frog's eyes can also be cut out and transplanted to the eye orbit on the other side of its head. By combining right-left transplantation of the eyes along with inversion, Sperry was able to demonstrate further

Figure 47. (*A*) With eye rotated 180°, the frog's strike is directed at a point in the visual field diametrically opposite to the fly. (*B*) After right-left transplantation and dorsoventral inversion of the eye, the frog strikes correctly with reference to the nasotemporal dimensions of the visual field, but inversely with reference to the dorsoventral dimensions. (*C*) After right-left transplantation and nasotemporal inversion of the eye, the frog strikes correctly with reference to the dorsoventral dimensions of the visual field, but inversely with reference to the nasotemporal dimensions. (Sperry, 1951.)

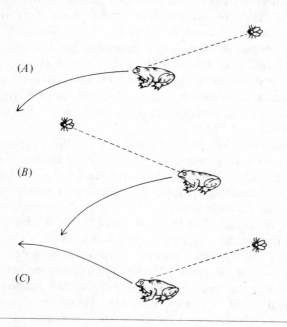

(*A*)

(*B*)

(*C*)

changes in the frog's vision. After the eyes are cut out, transplanted, and rotated, the regenerating optic nerve, apparently undismayed by such treatment, dutifully grows back through the massive scar tissue caused by the operation, threads its way to the optic tectum, grows new end feet, and reestablishes synaptic connections with the neurons of the optic tectum. In every case, the frog persistently behaves in a manner that can only be interpreted to mean that the regenerating optic nerve fibers made synaptic connections with their original termination sites in the optic tectum—the neurons in the optic tectum with which they had synapsed prior to the surgical rearrangement. Similiar experiments with amphibians and fish lend more support to the basic principle: *The regenerating axons of the optic nerve grow back into the brain, seek out and find particular neurons in the optic tectum, and only then reestablish synaptic connections with the right neurons.*

Although these experiments deal with the manner in which ingrowing optic nerve axons form synaptic connections in regeneration, they would appear to provide a good clue to the sort of process that occurs during the original development of these connections. The factors which guide the regenerating axons to their right place in the optic tectum are not known. Presumably these factors are chemical; somehow the developing or regenerating axons must "sniff out" the correct cells with which to form synapses. Or perhaps only the correct cells in the optic tectum will accept the advances of the end feet as they seek to establish "relations." Perhaps both processes take place. The process is obviously one of profound importance, and forms a major research area in modern science. Simple mechanical guidance for the regenerating optic nerve seems unable to account for the capacity of the axons to make the appropriate connections as they twist and thread their way through the scar tissue. Sperry has marshalled the evidence in favor of chemical selectivity in this situation (Sperry, 1965) and there seems no doubt that he is correct. The details of *how* the recognition of one cell by another occurs, however, remain largely unknown.

CELL DEATH

It may seem strange to discuss the death of cells in the context of the early development of an animal. Nevertheless, many more cells are formed in developing embryos than are actually used, and cell death is a common event in the development of complex organisms. Cell death is a useful mechanism for keeping the number of cells to an optimal level. Cell death is also common in adult animals. In most tissues, cells which die are replaced by new ones produced by cell division of the surviving cells. This is almost certainly not the case in the brain of adult mammals. Neuronal death in the brains of adult mammals is not balanced by the production of new neurons. Cell death may then play a more important role in "molding" circuits in the brain by the dropping out of certain elements. Although there is as yet no good evidence linking such selective cell death with changes in behavior, it is a possibility.

Cell division, cell migration, cell specification, and cell death: these processes are some of the most important events that underlie the growth and development of the central nervous system and its peripheral connections. Birth does not mark the end of these processes: developmental changes in the brain continue for a considerable period of time. It is almost certain that many of the developmental changes in behavior which we observe in young mammals, including our own children, are in part the result of biological changes going on in the nervous system. These changes, of course, can be and almost certainly are modified by events in the environment. Some of these environmental conditions may be quite constant for most of the individuals of a particular species, thus reinforcing homogeneity in the behavior of that species. Other conditions may be unique for that individual, contributing to individual differences among members of that species. The relative contributions of the environmental factors may vary considerably for different behaviors. Such environmental factors do not have their effect on a blank slate, however. The developing organism is already genetically biased to behave, *in general*, like other members of its species. This biasing can also allow for considerable individual variations in addition to more general species-specific features. The more complicated the brain, the more we can anticipate individual variations.

REORGANIZATION OF SYNAPTIC CONNECTIONS IN ADULT MAMMALS

Until very recently, it was not known if there was any appreciable regrowth of synaptic connections in the adult mammalian brain after injury. Experiments by Geoffrey Raisman (1969) have provided some interesting information on this subject. These experiments may be relevant not only with regard to the response of the brain to injury but also with regard to the general question of how plastic, or malleable, the mammalian brain may be in general.

The electron microscope was a necessary tool in these experiments. Raisman was able to investigate changes at the synaptic level in the brains of adult rats which had one or two specific nerve tracts destroyed. The particular area of the brain examined by Raisman was a narrow strip of brain tissue called the *septal area*, so-called because it forms a "septum," or dividing wall, for a short distance down the middle of the brain. In the rat, as in most mammals, the septal area can be subdivided into several different clusters of cell bodies, called *nuclei*. Two of the more prominent pairs of septal nuclei are the *medial septal nuclei* and the *lateral septal nuclei*. The medial septal nuclei lie next to one another across the midline of the brain, separating the two lateral nuclei. A major reason for examining this area of the brain is that there are only two principal nerve tracts which enter these two nuclei. These two tracts enter from opposite directions and can be selectively destroyed. Figure 48 illustrates this anatomical situation schematically. One of the two major nerve tracts entering the septal area is the *medial forebrain bundle* (MFB), which contains axons from neurons whose cell bodies are in the hypothalamus, as well as septal axons headed toward the hypothalamus. The other major tract is the *fimbria*, which contains axons going between the septal nuclei and the hippocampus.

A few general points about how nervous tissue responds to injury are in order. If the brain is examined within 2 or 3 days following the operation in which a nerve tract is destroyed, the degenerating remnants of the axonal end feet are still approximately in place near the postsynaptic site of termination. These degenerating end feet can be readily identified because they react to tissue stains differently than do living end feet. However, if several weeks are allowed to elapse before the animal is killed and its brain examined, all traces of the axonal end feet which were cut off from their cell bodies will have degenerated, and their remnants cleared away by scavenger glial cells.

Using these well-known facts, Raisman was able to plot the *pattern of distribution* of the synaptic endings on neurons in the septal area coming from each of the two major input tracts, the fimbria and the medial forebrain bundle. This was done by cutting one of the nerve tracts, waiting a few days, and then plotting the pattern of distribution of the degenerating terminals in the electron micrographs he made of thin sections through the septal area. At this level of magnification, he was able to determine whether the end feet were making synaptic contact on the dendrites of the septal neurons or directly on the cell body. As it turned out, the axons from the fimbria (from hippocampal neurons) ended predominantly out on the dendrites of the septal neurons, while axons coming up from hypothalamic neurons (via the medial forebrain bundle) ended both on the dendrites and on the cell body of septal neurons. In other animals, he destroyed first one of the nerve tracts and then, several weeks later, the other one. (Incidentally, such brain lesions do not impair the general health of the rats.) The brains were then examined within 2 to 3 days after the second tract was cut, in order to determine the pattern of distribution of axonal end feet from the second tract after the first tract's end feet had degenerated and disappeared. These were lengthy experiments, in which Raisman analyzed over 50,000 synapses. Summarizing his results, Raisman concluded

Figure 48. (*A*) In the normal rat brain, axons from the medial
forebrain bundle (MFB) end on both the cell body or soma (S)
as well as further out on the dendrites. The axons from the
hippocampus running in the fimbria are restricted in termination
to the dendrites. (*B*) Several weeks after a lesion of the fimbria,
the medial forebrain bundle endings extend across from their own
termination sites to occupy vacated sites left by degenerating
fimbrial end feet. The degenerated connections are indicated by
the dashed line, the presumed plastic changes by the heavy black
line. (*C*) Several weeks after a lesion of the medial forebrain bundle,
the fimbrial axons now give rise to end feet occupying termination
sites on the cell body, presumably those sites vacated as a result of
the MFB lesion. (Raisman, 1969.)

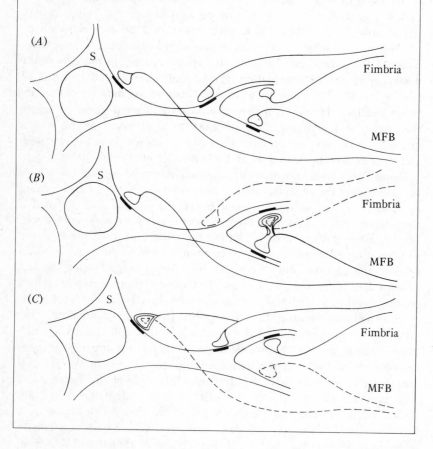

that following the destruction of one of the two major tracts into the
septal area, and the subsequent degeneration of those end feet, *the synaptic*

sites on the septal cell bodies and dendrites which were vacated by the degenerating end feet from the first tract cut were reoccupied by the new growth of end feet from the nearest available axon.

Raisman's interpretation of these results is that when one set of synaptic connections degenerates, the postsynaptic sites do not simply remain vacant but somehow act as a stimulus for the growth of new end feet from surviving axons in their general vicinity. These new end feet then occupy the vacated postsynaptic sites. If this interpretation is correct, it would indicate a greater degree of plasticity in the synaptic connections of the adult mammalian brain than has been generally thought possible.

One implication of these experiments is that the brain, although perhaps not able to grow entirely new neurons, is capable of responding to injury by sprouting new end feet from surviving axons. Whether or not these new end feet make *functional* synaptic connections is not yet known. The electron microscope cannot reveal, at least with present techniques, whether a synapse is actually working as a synapse or is making physical contact only. It is possible that the new synaptic connections which are formed are capable of functioning as normal synapses. If so, in this particular case, the overall function of the septal neurons affected would be changed. The new end feet are not from axons in the tract that normally go to the septal sites, since that tract had been cut. The new end feet are probably sprouts from axons which make up the other tract and, thus, provide a totally different kind of input from that coming to the septal neurons before surgery. Thus, while the brain may respond to injury with compensatory sprouting of new end feet, the function of the brain may be altered, both as a consequence of the loss of the old synaptic connections and as a consequence of the occupation of the vacated postsynaptic sites by end feet from a totally different nerve tract. This synaptic reshuffling could constitute a considerable reorganization of that part of the brain.

LEARNING AS A CHANGE IN BRAIN FUNCTION

One characteristic of human behavior is that we can learn. So can other animals: flatworms, sea slugs, rats, chimpanzees, dolphins. All it takes, it seems, is enough of the right assortment of neurons, connected in the proper way. It is not possible to observe learning directly; we can only infer learning from a change in an animal's behavior. It is easy to see how a great many arguments have been initiated regarding the nature of learning. Even satisfactory definitions of learning are difficult to devise. Neal Miller has publicly wrestled with the definitional problem on more than one occasion. He has contributed both wisdom and humor (and both are helpful) to a definition of what he terms "Grade-A certified learning": "learning is a relatively permanent increase in response strength that is based on previous reinforcement and that can be made specific to one out of two or more arbitrarily selected stimulus situations" (Miller, 1967).

While it is possible to take issue with this definition, and the assumptions which underlie it, it is a useful working definition. The fact that a completely satisfactory definition of learning is very difficult to produce is due to a number of factors. One factor is that there are a great number of diverse phenomena which all share some characteristics that encourage us to think of them as a kind of learning. The imprinting (following response) of a baby duckling onto the first large moving object it sees (normally the mother duck, but humans or moving dummies will substitute) during a sensitive period following hatching, the waning of the closing response of a sea anemone to repeated touching, the ability of some individuals to mentally photograph images (so-called eidetic imagers), a child's learning to talk: all of these have been offered as examples of learning. Yet it is apparent that we may be dealing with quite different biological mechanisms in these different situations. There seems to be a stage in the investigation of some phenomena where overly rigid definitions may be more of a hindrance than a help, particularly if by defining a phenomenon, we define relevant problems out of consideration. We do not have to worry too much, however. Investigators in this area seem to be a hardy lot and not overly inhibited by other scientists' definitions.

Habituation: A simple kind of learning?

Sitting in your room, studying *Psychology as a biological science*, you are probably not aware of the ticking of your alarm clock across the room. But as soon as you read this, you suddenly notice it again. Likewise, you are probably unaware of the slight sensation of the collar of your shirt or sweater on the back of your neck. But now you are, at least for a short while. All organisms display decreased responding to repeated stimulation provided the stimulation is relatively mild and does not signal some other event (for example, one does not cease responding to the ticking of a time bomb). This decreased response to repeated stimulation is called *habituation.* It is a pervasive and widespread phenomenon. Habituation can be observed in the withdrawal response of the sea anemone tentacle and in the gradual waning of awareness to the ticking clock.

A repeated stimulus can also produce an increase in responding, particularly if it is intense or occurs in the context of an arousing situation. This phenomenon is generally termed response *sensitization,* and is less well studied than habituation.

Habituation is widely regarded as a simple form of learning. Some experience with the previous stimuli seems to be a requisite for the waning of response to repeated stimulation. Habituation has been observed in a variety of experimental situations; and in some situations, it has been possible to monitor the activity of a single neuron in the stimulus-response pathway. The most compelling work to date in mammals uses the surgically isolated spinal cord of the cat as the experimental system (Spencer et al., 1966a, 1966b, 1966c; Groves & Thompson, 1970). In such preparations, it is possible to record not only the muscle-twitch response to stimulation of the skin or cutaneous nerves, but also the response of internuncial neurons which lie between the incoming sensory neurons and the motorneurons of the ventral root (Chapter 9 discusses these reflex arrangements in greater detail). In these experiments, three different kinds of internuncial cells have been discovered: *nonplastic* cells, which do not change in their response to repeated stimulation; *habituating* neurons, which show a steady decline in their response rate to repeated stimulation; and *sensitization* cells, a more complex type of neuron which at first increases and then decreases in its response rate. This latter type of cell follows the same course as does the muscle response, which first increases and then decreases. Even in the isolated spinal cord, however, the situation is quite complicated, and it is not possible to conclude that the similarity in response pattern between the sensitization cells and the muscle cells is more than an interesting parallel. It does appear that this approach is likely to yield even more information about habituation. The evidence gathered so far indicates that the change which underlies the waning of the response occurs somewhere in the internuncial neurons, and not in either the incoming sensory neuron or the motorneuron which supplies the muscle.

It is important to distinguish habituation from fatigue. The repetition rate in habituation experiments is typically far below that which would bring about a failure of response due to fatigue (which is not very well understood either). A simple test to differentiate between habituation and fatigue is to change the nature of the stimulus slightly, for example, from one tone to another. If the waning of the response has been due to habituation, the response will reoccur to the altered stimulus. In fact, one interesting aspect of the habituation phenomenon is the missing stimulus effect. If in a series of regularly sequenced repeated stimuli, a stimulus is *not* presented in its normal spot, an increase in response will often be observed "to" the missing stimulus. Clearly, no fatigue process can be an appropriate explanation for this phenomenon.

Classical conditioning and instrumental learning

Two basic types of learning procedures are generally recognized: classical (or Pavlovian) conditioning; and instrumental (or operant) learning situations. Although valid distinction can be made between these two techniques, it is not necessary to conclude that there are two (or more) different kinds of learning. The study of learning is complex and in a highly active state, so that we should not be overly committed to any theoretical distinctions at the present.

CLASSICAL CONDITIONING

The basic phenomena associated with classical conditioning were made known by Ivan Pavlov, the Russian physiologist. (Further discussion of Pavlov's work is discussed in the next chapter.) In classical conditioning, an *unconditioned stimulus* (UCS) such as meat powder is administered to an animal (Pavlov used dogs) in a tightly controlled laboratory environment, where distracting stimulation can be held to a minimum. The stimulus evokes an *unconditioned response* (UCR); in this example, salivation. Actually, the unconditioned stimulus may evoke a variety of responses at first, such as changes in heart rate and respiration, but the experimenter typically ignores all but the response he is interested in. Conditioning takes place by pairing the presentation of the unconditioned stimulus in time with the presentation of a neutral or "to-be" *conditioned stimulus* (CS) such as a tone or light that does not initally evoke the unconditioned stimulus. Here too, life is not really that simple. No stimulus is really neutral in all respects. Although a novel tone may not evoke any salivation, it will evoke responses such as ear movements, autonomic responses, etc. However, these responses can be habituated (see above) prior to the first conditioning session so that the to-be conditioned stimulus can be regarded as neutral with respect to that animal in that setting.

As the unconditioned and conditioned stimulus are presented together, or with the UCS presented shortly after the CS, a new response, a *conditioned response* (CR), begins to occur in response to the CS. This conditioned response is the learned element of behavior in the classical conditioning situation. Now it is entirely possible that the animal is learning a good deal more about the situation, but for the most part, any other aspects of the situation are ignored. It is important to point out that the CR is not usually *exactly* identical with the UCR. That is, both may be salivation but differ in viscosity or other properties.

Pavlov and his many students and colleagues discovered several fundamental conditioning phenomena (Pavlov, 1927) in the years 1902–1936. Some of these phenomena are worthy of mention. *Extinction* is the dropping off of the response in frequency and/or intensity if the CS is presented alone, without the "reinforcing" UCS. Following a rest period of several hours or days, the extinguished response can often show a *spontaneous recovery,* such that the effects of the extinction procedure are *partly* diminished.

Another conditioning phenomena worth mentioning is *generalization.* If an animal is conditioned to respond to a particular stimulus, for example, a tone of 1,000 cycles, it will show some response to stimuli which are similar to the CS. For example, a tone of 1,050 cycles will elicit more of a response than will a tone of 1,500 cycles. Generalization is a powerful theoretical tool, because it can account for (at least in theory) a variety of otherwise puzzling behavior. For example, a child who has been badly frightened by a large white dog might generalize his fear (CR) to Santa Claus's whiskers, white horses, and other dogs. Such a child would not, presumably, show any noticeable fear response to a white rose, however, since the similarity with the original CS (the white dog) would be too remote. It is likely that much of our behavior is the result of generalization from other learning situations, although not usually classical conditioning situations, of course.

INSTRUMENTAL LEARNING

Another major learning situation is that in which rewards and punishments increase and decrease the likelihood of a response reoccurring. Instrumental learning (or *operant conditioning*) has been most associated recently in this country with the name of B. F. Skinner, although the basic ideas have been known for a much longer time. The American psychologist E. L. Thorndike studied the behavior of animals in laboratory settings during the early part of the twentieth century; and in the 1930s, Skinner developed his now-famous Skinner boxes in which animals can press a lever or perform some other simple act in order to obtain a reward. The principle of operant conditioning is that the likelihood of a particular response will be increased if it is followed by a reward or reinforcer and decreased if it is not. From this innocuous-seeming notion has developed an extensive behavioral technology which has been applied to a variety of problem areas, from training animals to perform circus acts to the rehabilitation of the mentally retarded. Even plans for Utopian societies have been predicated on the principles of behavioral modification as outlined by Skinner (1948).

It should be emphasized that different techniques of training do not necessarily imply that the brain's response to these different procedures is fundamentally different. In the search for how learning might affect the brain, of these techniques classical conditioning and instrumental learning have been used.

What then is the question?

You are probably familiar with the famous death-bed interchange between Gertrude Stein and her faithful friend Alice B. Toklas. As Gertrude Stein was dying, she asked: "What is the answer?" Alice replied softly that there was no answer. To which Gertrude Stein responded: "Well, then, what is the question?" Not knowing the answer to how the brain changes when learning occurs, we must settle for trying to frame questions which are of some possible value. There are several questions which have attracted the attention of scientists. We can place them in one of two general categories: *molecular* questions or *organizational* questions.

The basic molecular question can be phrased: Is there a detectable change in the nervous system that can be reliably related to a learned response which has been observed in the owner of that particular nervous system? Over the past years, there have been numerous theories regarding possible changes in, for example, synaptic efficiency, which would be related to learning. Many of these theories, however, were not testable (and some remain so) because of the technical difficulties involved in actually evaluating synaptic efficiency at a particular synapse that can also be demonstrated to have been involved in some learned response.

It might appear at a first glance that it should be possible to train a rat to perform some new task (for example, to traverse a maze) and then to examine its brain tissue, slice by slice, using an electron microscope. Thus, one might argue, changes in synaptic structure would be evidence for a change in synaptic efficiency. One might suppose, for example, that it should be possible to compare electron micrographs of synaptic connections from "trained" brains with similar electron micrographs from "naïve" or "untrained" brains and look for systematic differences. A few moments thought should reveal some of the difficulties with such an experiment. First of all, the number of synapses in a rat brain is virtually incalculable, but would certainly be in the billions. Even if one were to use but a small sample of neurons, getting any significant fraction would be unmanageable. Also, unlike a needle in a haystack, it would not be obvious just what one was looking for. Would the presynaptic end feet be larger at certain synapses? Larger than what? One cannot compare the same cell before and after learning in such a situation, nor can one identify particular neurons from brain to brain in a complex brain such as that of a rat. (This identification is actually possible in "simpler" organisms such as many marine invertebrates.) Also, in this particular hypothetical experiment, the neurons under consideration would be dead. It is very possible that some small shrinkage or swelling of the tiny synaptic endings might take place after death, and thus their appearance would be altered. These are only a few of the problems one would encounter in such an experiment; you can probably think of several others. An experimental approach that may appear straightforward and reasonable on first examination may therefore turn out to be considerably more difficult, if not impossible, on closer examination.

If central brain neurons are capable of sprouting new end feet and occupying different synaptic sites, however, perhaps some similar type of growth could be involved in less traumatic brain changes, such as learning. This is, at the present, just speculation, and does not necessarily follow from these experiments, although the plasticity shown by Raisman lends new encouragement to such speculation.

Learning at the single neuron level

In the laboratory of James Olds at the California Institute of Technology, some recent studies have shown that it is possible to map out areas of the brain of the unanesthetized rat which contain neurons that change their firing rate while the animal learns a simple association between a tone and the presentation of food (Olds et al., 1972). In these experiments, rats are equipped with from six to nine electrodes chronically implanted in various areas of their brains. The activity of individual neurons can then be recorded from the animals as they walk about the experimental cage. After pairing the presentation of a tone stimulus with the delivery of a food pellet, Olds and his colleagues were able to show that neurons at various levels of the brain responded to the conditioned stimulus (tone) with accelerations or decelerations that were significantly different from the spontaneous base rate discharge obtained prior to presentation of the tone-food pairing. A criterion was used such that only short-latency (10 to 20 milliseconds from stimulus onset) responses were eligible as learned responses. In analyzing their results, they found that while these short-latency learned responses could be found in widespread areas of the brain, only 7 percent (31 out of 443 of the neurons tested) displayed these learned responses. The responses appeared in the brainstem, thalamus, restricted portions of the hippocampus, and cortex. The largest proportion of them were found in the posterior nucleus of the thalamus, part of the brain's auditory system. The tentative localizations found in the study should not be interpreted to mean that only these areas of the rat brain are involved in this sort of learning; the sample was too small and too preliminary for any final conclusions on that basis. However, the exciting possibility exists that units can be identified as either learning or nonlearning on the basis of this kind of experiment. If future results follow the lines sketched out in this experiment, it would appear that while learning neurons may be located in widespread areas of the brain, they are probably localized into clusters or related to systems of neurons in the brain. Such a result would not be surprising, but it would be of great help in pursuing the elusive site of learning in the brain.

Does learning change the metabolic machinery of brain cells?

Since the late 1950s, an increasing number and variety of experiments have been performed in an attempt to investigate possible relations between learning and altered metabolic activity in brain cells. Certain themes or basic assumptions seem to be widespread among scientists in this area. One of the most persistent ideas is that during learning, there are unique molecules of RNA and/or protein molecules manufactured by the cells involved in the learning—that these RNA or protein molecules are then the structural correlates of the learned behavior. At the time this book is being written, however, there is no conclusive evidence that this is true, although several suggestive findings do exist. A related assumption, often not made explicit, is that these unique RNA and/or protein molecules are also involved in *producing* the learned response on later occasions—serving as the biological link between past and present (Gaito & Bonnet, 1971).

Let us briefly review the relationship between the genetic material, DNA, and the molecules which translate the genetic code during protein synthesis. In addition to DNA, there are various types of RNA and *polypeptides*, which are chains of amino acids but smaller than proteins. The polypeptides and proteins form virtually all the important biological catalysts, or *enzymes*, which trigger the various biochemical processes of life. Polypeptides and proteins are themselves constructed from twenty different amino acids. The order and three-dimensional pattern in which the amino acids are put together determines which polypeptide or protein will be formed. This biochemical construction is regulated by RNA, on instructions from the chromosomal DNA. The chromosomes contain all the necessary information for the construction of all the substances which that cell is capable of producing. Not all the DNA is active in any cell at any one time. Much of the chromosome is "repressed," and not active in RNA-protein production. This repression need not be permanent, and various events may derepress that portion of the chromosome, resulting in the subsequent production of different proteins.

There are several types of RNA. Messenger RNA (*mRNA*) appears to be responsible for reading off the genetic instructions from DNA as the mRNA is formed in the nucleus. The mRNA then moves from the nucleus to the cytoplasm where, together with at least two other types of RNA, *transfer RNA* and *ribosomal RNA*, it helps in the putting together of the various amino acids into polypeptides and proteins. The rapidity of some protein synthesis may be critically important for theories of learning based on the production of unique polypeptides or proteins, for it is well known that some forms of learning can take place in very short periods of time.

It is not hard to see how people became attracted to the possibility that unique RNA and/or proteins might somehow serve to code for the memories that are built up in an organism by experience. DNA is known to code for the hereditary, genetic "memories" expressed in the physical structure of the organism. There is an attraction in the possibility that RNA and/or protein production might provide a complementary code for the memories of the individual organism.

Are there unique brain proteins produced during learning?

Holger Hydén and P. W. Lange at the Institute of Neurobiology, University of Göteborg, in Sweden, have published several reports in which they report that there is a brain-specific protein, called S100, which is produced during the training of a "handedness" task in rats (Hydén & Lange, 1970).

There are several proteins which are apparently found only in brain tissue. Some have no names, just numbers such as 14-3-2, while others have names such as "antigen α." S100 is one of these brain-specific proteins. Its structure, as is the case for most proteins, is not known. It has a molecular weight of about 21,000 and is acidic, having a high content of glutamic and aspartic acid. It makes up about 0.2 percent of the total of brain proteins and is found in neurons and, even more so, in glial cells.

The training situation used by Hydén and Lange was as follows: Rats were placed in an apparatus which contained a glass tube, slightly larger than a rat's forelimb, through which the rats could retrieve small food pellets. Untrained rats in this situation show "handedness"—they consistently use one paw much more than the other. The learning task which Hydén and Lange arranged was to force the rats to use their nonpreferred paw in order to obtain the food pellets by placing a wall parallel and close to the tube on the side opposite the preferred paw. The rats readily learned, over a period of a week or so, to use their nonpreferred paw.

Biochemical analysis was made on a sample of pyramidal cells (neurons whose cell bodies are pyramidal in shape) from a particular region of the hippocampus in these "trained" rats. The hippocampus was chosen because of previous evidence suggesting that this part of the brain may be involved in learning new responses. Fresh pyramidal cells from the hippocampus were removed with microdissection techniques and analyzed for protein content. The results of the biochemical analysis indicated that the amount of S100 brain protein increased in the sample of neurons taken from the brains of trained rats but not in the sample of neurons taken from the control rats who were not trained to switch paws.

In further experiments designed to test the importance of the S100 protein for this handedness learning, Hydén and Lange injected small amounts (60 micrograms) of S100 *antiserum* into the lateral ventricles of some rats. This antiserum reacts with and presumably destroys S100 specifically, without any great impact on brain protein in general. Six rats were injected after 3 days of handedness training, and were continued in the experiment for 3 additional days. Although their performance had improved normally for the first 3 days, no further improvement was seen following the antiserum injection. There was no general motor or sensory effect observed in the animals. Injections of control substances (antiserum mixed with S100 to absorb the antiserum) did not block further improvement in a group of eight control rats. An analysis of the brains of the experimental animals injected with unabsorbed antiserum revealed that the antiserum had penetrated into the hippocampal pyramidal cells where it presumably had interfered with the synthesis of S100 in these animals. Although this may not be the only brain protein produced during this situation, injection of the antiserum specific to S100 was sufficient to prevent further increase in performance.

Other experiments (i.e., Beach et al., 1969) have also found evidence for increased production of RNA and protein metabolism in the hippocampus (but not in other areas of the brain) during the learning of an avoidance response in rats.

Organizational questions about learning

One of the questions which has interested scientists is: What are the smallest fragments of nervous tissue which can be shown to produce systematic changes that might be considered examples of simple learning? One of the reasons for asking this sort of question is the recognition that the entire mammalian brain is simply too complex to analyze in its entirety with present techniques. The hope is that if a smaller chunk of nervous tissue can be demonstrated to learn, then present analytical tools might be more effective on the smaller fragment. Although as yet even the smaller fragments have also proved too difficult for useful analysis, many of these experiments have enlarged our view of learning and the various combinations of neurons which can potentially produce it.

Investigators have carefully isolated and studied the electrical properties of "slabs" of cerebral cortex in experimental animals. They have conditioned reflexes in the spinal cord which has been severed from the brain. They have conditioned flatworms, cut them in half, and demonstrated "savings" of the conditioning in the regenerated worms. In one experiment it has been demonstrated that the headless ventral nerve cord in large insects such as the cockroach or locust can learn to associate electric shock with the position of its leg at the time the shock is received.

Learning in the isolated thoracic ganglia of insects

G. Adrian Horridge performed a series of experiments which demonstrate a type of postural learning that occurs in headless insects such as cockroaches or locusts. These animals have had their anterior nervous tissue removed (including the cerebral ganglion, or "brain," as well as the subesophageal ganglia) and then are pared down to the thoracic ganglia and as few as two legs. This insect fragment remains apparently quite healthy and vigorous for several hours. During this time, Horridge studied the ability of these headless insects to learn an avoidance response (Horridge, 1962).

The basic experimental setup is illustrated in Figure 49. The isolated thoracic ganglion, together with two of the animal's legs (one leg is not pictured), is suspended over a bowl of saline, and fine silver wires are attached to the leg such that when the leg position is lowered, the P (for positional) preparation receives an electric shock to the leg via the silver wire. The R (for random) preparation is rigged up in parallel so that it receives a shock each time the P preparation does. However, there is no necessary association between the leg position of the R preparation and the reception of shock, as is true of the P preparation, in which leg position and occurrence of shock is associated. The R preparation thus serves as a shock control, such that any changes due simply to repeated shock on the mechanical properties of the muscles will be the same in the two preparations, and any differences should be due to the associative factor present in the P preparation. This sort of experimental control is referred to as a *yoked* control. While the rate of learning by the R animals is either indistinguishable from or slightly poorer than naïve animals, the P animals display a much lower level of shocks right from the beginning of the retest situation. In other words, the P preparations which have experienced electric shock associated with a particular postural position of their legs appear to remember that critical position. But the R preparations which have experienced an equal number of shocks, distributed across time in the same fashion (but not in association with any particular leg position), do not show any significant adaptive change. This plasticity, or learning, by headless insect fragments illustrates the potential which may exist in even relatively small portions of nervous tissue.

Two (or more) memory processes

There is now considerable evidence that when an organism learns something, there may be at least two different memory processes which are involved [see McGaugh (1969) for a representative review of this subject]. These two memory processes are generally spoken of as short-term and long-term memory. According to such notions, short-term memory would account for such phenomena as the learning and rapid forgetting of a telephone number infrequently used. It seems intuitively the case that we do not really store much of what we experience in any long-term

Figure 49. Postural learning of leg position by the metathoracic ventral ganglion of a headless locust. (A) Training situation. In the initial training situation, both the P (paired) animal and the R (random) animal receive shocks when the P animal lowers its leg below the critical level. (B) Testing situation. Subsequent to training, the P and R animals are separated and now each receives a shock when it lowers its leg below the critical level. (C) Results from an experiment in which right metathoracic legs of locusts were trained and tested on the same leg. The numbers of shock for twenty P and twenty R animals are plotted for each minute interval following the start of the testing situation. The corresponding numbers of shocks received by the naive P animals when first trained, shown by thicker lines, are similar to those made by the R animals on retest. (Horridge, 1968.)

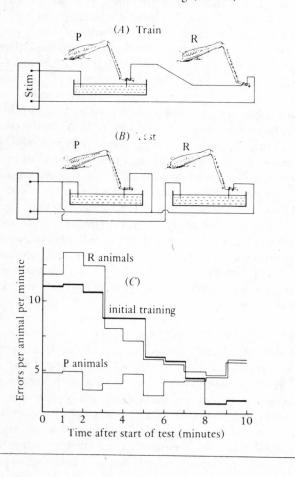

memory, which suggests that one characteristic of short-term memory might be that items in it do not invariably then proceed to long-term memory.

Closely related to the notion that there may be two or more different memory processes is the concept of the consolidation of memories, which proposes that a memory becomes more firmly established with the passage of time following the learning experience. Müller and Pilzecker are generally credited with the early development of the concept of consolidation to account for the fact that human subjects were better at remembering one list of items if they learned a second list two days after learning the first list than if they learned the second list on the same day as list 1. They suggested that the memory for list 1 somehow grew stronger, or became "consolidated," during the 2-day period, becoming less vulnerable to the interfering effects of list 2 than it was immediately after the initial learning (Müller & Pilzecker, 1900). Support for the concept of consolidation also comes from studies of retrograde amnesia caused in many (but not all) cases of head injury and/or brain concussion (Russell & Nathan, 1946). Although retrograde amnesia is not always caused by head injury, it is a frequent consequence, which is often permanent. One interpretation of this amnesia is that the injury disrupts the normal brain processes in a vulnerable period, while the memory for the events are being consolidated into a more permanent, long-term memory. Extended discussion of these concepts can be found elsewhere (Kimble, 1965, 1967).

Experimental research designed to produce more systematic interference with the (unknown) brain processes which are inferred to underlie consolidation have included heating and cooling the animal, administering depressant and convulsant drugs, giving electroconvulsive shock, and using several other techniques. It turns out to be fairly easy to disrupt memory with these treatments, and the degree of disruption is typically related to the delay between initial experience and treatment. In general, the sooner the disruptive treatment is given after training, the more severe the retrograde amnesia for the events of training. There is no "magic" length of time, however. Consolidation periods vary from seconds to days, depending upon task, subjects, treatment, and other experimental variables, some of which are as yet unknown.

There is also evidence that certain treatments such as injection of excitant drugs may serve to facilitate learning, and the degree of facilitation is also related to the time of treatment following training (McGaugh, 1969). Presumably these facilitative effects are also related to brain processes underlying consolidation, but interpretations in this area of research are particularly difficult. Whatever the processes which may be affected by these treatments, both disruptive and facilitative, there is one brain structure in particular that is consistently implicated as playing an important role—the hippocampus.

THE HIPPOCAMPUS AND CONSOLIDATION IN THE HUMAN BRAIN

Although it is extremely rare, there are a few cases in which for treatment of severe epilepsy, surgery was performed on humans involving extensive removal of part of the brain along the medial surface of the temporal lobe. This surgery generally removes parts of the cortex of the temporal lobe, amygdala, and the hippocampus, but there is evidence that it is the hippocampus which is the critical structure in producing the memory defects. In these patients, there appears to be a deficit in the process of consolidation whereby recent experiences are somehow "committed" to long-term memory. Much of our knowledge of this temporal lobe amnesic syndrome comes from the extensive study, over a period of many years, of a single individual, whose initials are H. M.:

> This young man, a motor-winder by trade, had had generalized seizures since the age of 16, which, despite heavy medication had increased in frequency and severity until, by the age of 27, he was no longer able to work. Because of his desperate condition, Dr. W. B. Scoville carried out a radical bilateral medial temporal-lobe resection on August 25, 1953. The patient was drowsy for the first few days, but then, as he became more alert, a severe memory impairment became apparent, which has persisted with only slight improvement to the present day. (Milner, 1970.)

These are the words of Brenda Milner, who has studied the psychological capacity of this man since his operation and has described the persistent memory deficit which he displays. If H. M's memory problem were only part of a general mental deterioration as a result of the radical brain excision, his case would be of only mild interest. But H. M.'s general intelligence was measured at 117 on the Wechsler IQ scale in 1962, whereas it had been 104 before surgery in 1953. There was no impairment in general intelligence. (The increased score may reflect the relative absence of seizure incidence following surgery.) H. M. shows no amnesia for events from his early life, but he fails almost completely in retaining any memory for events which have occurred since his operation in 1953. The memory failure is profound. Six years after H. M.'s family moved, he was unsure of his "new" address, he worked and reworked the same jigsaw puzzles, and read and reread the same magazines over and over without any apparent recollection of their contents. He still fails to recognize faces of individuals he has met since his operation, despite repeated encounters. He is capable of remembering simple items for a few minutes, only if he is not distracted.

Thus, he was able to retain the number 584 for at least 15 minutes, by continuously working out elaborate mnemonic schemes. When asked how he had been able to retain the number for so long, he replied: "It's easy. You just remember 8. You see, 5, 8, and 4 add to 17. You remember 8, subtract it from 17 and it leaves 9. Divide 9 in half and you get 5 and 4, and there you are: 584. Easy!" A minute or so later, H. M. was unable to recall either the number 584 or any of the associated complex train of thought; in fact, he did not know that he had been given a number to remember because, in the meantime, the examiner had introduced a new topic. (Milner, 1970.)

There is some residual memory capacity left to H. M. It appears to be nonverbal. For example, he shows normal improvement in learning to trace around the outline of a five-pointed star while looking in a mirror (a standard laboratory motor learning task). Like a normal subject, he makes very few errors after a 3-day learning period, although he is totally unaware that he has seen the task before; in other words, he displays a normal reduction of errors in the motor task but without the normal conscious memory that usually accompanies such learning in humans! H. M. is also capable of showing progressive improvement in the recognition of incomplete pictures (sketches of boats, airplanes, etc.), but again, this improvement, or memory, is without any awareness on H. M.'s part that he has seen the pictures before. Memory without awareness for both perceptual and motor learning stands in sharp contrast to H. M.'s chronic inability to form conscious long-term memories of the events in his life.

There is no compelling explanation of these results. We do not know the exact extent of the tissue removal in this case, nor was H. M.'s brain perfectly normal to begin with, since he suffered from severe and frequent epileptic seizures prior to his operation. Nevertheless, the dramatic effect on the formation of new memories, while leaving older memories and immediate attention-span memory intact, may indicate that the hippocampus in man has some rather critical function in the consolidation process. Whatever the explanation as to how the hippocampus might be involved in such a process, the existence of quite adequate short-term memory (given minimal distraction) and the almost total lack of long-term memory as exhibited by the same individual is a strong argument that at least two dissociable memory processes exist in man.

The effect of hippocampal lesions in experimental animals

Since the discovery of the amnesic syndrome in H. M. and some similar cases, no further radical ablations such as these have been carried out.

Experimenters have turned to other mammals in an effort to produce and study this amnesic syndrome in experimental animals with hippocampal lesions. Surprisingly, the overwhelming result is that the memory deficit is not as great. It must be remembered that in the animal experiments, the tasks are all either motor or perceptual, since we cannot readily ask the animals whether things "seem familiar" to them. It is relevant to remember at this point that H. M. could also learn motor and perceptual tasks, but without awareness. Several theories of just what the hippocampus does contribute to mammalian behavior have been published (for example, see Douglas, 1967; Kimble, 1968). One theory holds that the hippocampus acts to modulate other brain regions, particularly the hypothalamus and brainstem reticular formation, to act as an inhibitory factor, or "brake," on behaviors which are no longer adaptive to the animal (Kimble, 1968; Isaacson & Kimble, 1972).

What can we teach our hearts?

In Western culture, it has been generally assumed that some of our bodily responses are beyond our voluntary control. For example, we are not accustomed to thinking that we can, by sheer will power or other voluntary means, alter such things as heart rate, intestinal contractions, kidney function, etc. These sorts of responses are mediated by the autonomic nervous system. The very name autonomic implies that this is a portion of our nervous apparatus which operates automatically, or autonomously. This view has been put forth not only in the general culture but also in the scientific literature.

Recently, however, Neal E. Miller and several of his students at Rockefeller University have shown that the view of the autonomic nervous system may be erroneous (Miller, 1969). In a series of ingenious experiments, Miller and his students have shown that laboratory rats can learn to control autonomic responses such as heart rate, gastrointestinal activity, and blood flow in various portions of the body. It is possible that human beings can be similarly trained, and some preliminary experimentation in this direction has already been accomplished.

It has been known since Pavlov, of course, that autonomic nervous system responses can be *conditioned*. The classical response in Pavlov's experiments was salivation by dogs, an autonomic nervous system response. Also, heart rate, blood pressure, and many other autonomic responses have been conditioned in several species, including man, using Pavlovian conditioning techniques. But there has been a strong belief that while such responses can be conditioned in this fashion, animals cannot learn to exert any significant *voluntary* control over such responses, that is, these responses are not subject to *instrumental learning*. Instrumental learning, in which the subject learns to perform a response that is rewarded or cease to perform a response that is punished, had been thought only possible with skeletal muscle responses. In the Rockefeller experiments, it has now been shown that the control of autonomic responses can also be learned in instrumental learning situations.

One of the major difficulties encountered in this research is that autonomic responses such as heart-rate and blood-flow changes, or *vasomotor* responses, can be altered by skeletal muscle responses which are already known to be under voluntary control. These potentially interfering responses include tensing certain muscles and holding the breath. Unless these responses are eliminated as possible explanations, it is extremely difficult to demonstrate direct voluntary control over the autonomic responses without an intermediary skeletal muscle response. To avoid this difficulty, Miller and his students paralyzed all skeletal muscles by administering curare, a drug which selectively blocks synaptic transmission at the motor end plate of the muscle (the postsynaptic surface) without affecting either consciousness or autonomic nervous system responses. Humans paralyzed with curare report that they are perfectly aware of the environment and fully conscious. Of course, under curare, the subject must be artificially respirated, because the skeletal muscles involved in breathing are paralyzed.

In one such experiment (DiCara & Miller, 1968) rats were paralyzed with curare, placed under artificial respiration, and trained to either increase or decrease their heart rate. The reinforcing situation in this experiment was an electric shock to the rat's tail. A 10-second preshock period allowed the animal time to try to avoid the tail shock by either increasing its heart rate (if it was assigned to that experimental group) or decreasing its heart rate, if that was *its* assigned response. If the rat did not make the required change, the tail shocks began and continued until the rat did make the correct heart-rate change, which turned off the shock and the shock signal. Other trials were "safe," or nonshock, trials, in which no shock was administered. These trials were signaled by a steady tone. Finally, in order to compare the results with and without a specific signal, blank trials were inserted during the training. These blank trials lasted 5 seconds, during which the heart rate was recorded, but nothing else was done.

The results are shown in Figure 50. As training went on, all twelve rats in the experiment had heart-rate changes in the direction which allowed them to avoid tail shock. The most dramatic changes were those in the 10-second period preceded by the shock signal, but the overall heart rate also went in the same direction. These results show that rats can learn to control their heart rate in order to escape or avoid a mild shock to the tail. Since these are animals completely paralyzed by curare, it is not possible that some skeletal muscle response was responsible for mediating the heart-rate changes. In Figure 50, there is a noticeable difference in the heart rate during the safe signal trials, indicating that

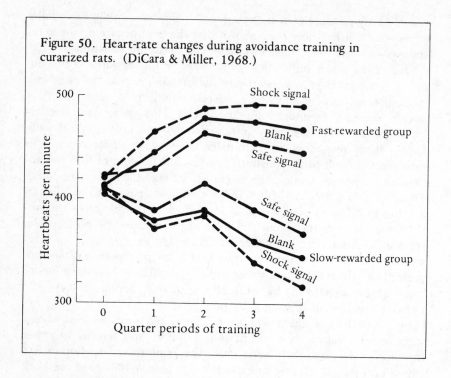

Figure 50. Heart-rate changes during avoidance training in curarized rats. (DiCara & Miller, 1968.)

the rats were able to tell whether the coming trial was to be a shock trial or not. There seems to have been some inhibitory or suppressing effect of the nonshock trials on the heart-rate change, as seen during either the blank or shock trials.

In other experiments, Miller and his students have extended these findings. They have been able to train animals to either increase or decrease their intestinal contractions, alter the rate of urine formation by increasing or decreasing the blood flow through the kidney, increase or decrease stomach contractions, and increase the blood flow in only one ear at a time (Miller, 1969).

Are men as smart as rats?

Although these experiments have not as yet been repeated with human subjects, as Miller aptly points out, men probably are as smart as rats. The possibility that such important bodily responses as heart rate, intestinal contractions, and blood flow may possibly be brought under voluntary control has stimulated a number of research projects with human beings, and the results are encouraging so far. For example, various individuals have been able to train patients with irregular heartbeat patterns (cardiac arrhythmias) and patients with too-rapid heartbeat (tachycardia) to partially improve their heart-rate abnormalities. It is too early to tell whether or not such learning therapy will become a regular part of medical treatment, but the implications of such research are far reaching indeed.

Karl Lashley's search for the "engram"

Karl Spencer Lashley (1890–1958) was one of the pioneers of modern physiological psychology. In 1950, at a scientific conference, Lashley reviewed some of his thinking of the previous 30 or so years in a rather famous article called "In search of the engram" (Lashley, 1950). The article summarizes many experimental findings on the effects of cortical destruction on learning and memory. The summary of this article begins:

> This series of experiments has yielded a good bit of information about what and where the memory trace is not. It has discovered nothing directly of the real nature of the engram. I sometimes feel, in reviewing the evidence on the localization of the memory trace, that the necessary conclusion is that learning just is not possible.

(One is reminded of Don Marquis, creator of *Archy and Mehitabel*, who once described his life as "searching for something I cannot name.") Things aren't quite that bad. Since Lashley wrote the article, a considerable amount of information has accumulated, and Lashley's (somewhat tongue-in-cheek) pessimism about the reality of learning is no longer quite so necessary. It is useful, however, to review Lashley's general findings and the implications of these findings for theories of cortical function.

MASS ACTION?

If rats are trained to run a complex maze without error, and are then subjected to damage or removal of portions of their cerebral cortex, the degree to which the rats lose the maze habit seems to depend primarily upon the *amount* of cortex that has been destroyed rather than the location of the tissue that had been lost. Lashley also found that the relationship between the amount of cortical tissue damaged and the degree of impairment of the maze habit increased if the rats were trained in more complex mazes. Similar data were gathered on rats trained to solve a latch-box type of problem.

Figure 51 illustrates the floor plan of the most complex of the three mazes which Lashley used, the Lashley III maze, which contains eight cul-de-sacs. Rats are naturally rather quick at learning such mazes. Although they may make many errors (arbitrarily defined as cul-de-sac entries) in their initial explorations, normal rats can readily master this

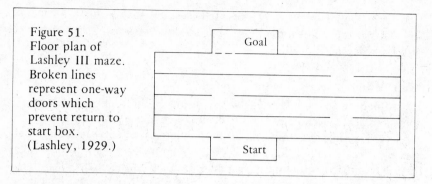

Figure 51.
Floor plan of
Lashley III maze.
Broken lines
represent one-way
doors which
prevent return to
start box.
(Lashley, 1929.)

maze and make repeated errorless runs. A critical question for Lashley's results is: What sensory modalities do rats rely on for guidance in a maze? Several experiments have yielded the conclusion that rats probably use vision, olfaction, kinesthesis, perhaps audition, and the sense of touch, particularly via their whiskers, or *vibressae*. It seems probable that individual animals may rely more heavily on one or another sensory modality, but that most rats use more than one modality for navigating in complex mazes such as the Lashley III. One implication of this reliance on more than one sense is that by increasing the extent of cortical destruction, Lashley necessarily reduced the overall capacity of the animal to respond accurately to sensory input. The greater the extent of the damage, the more likely that more than one sensory modality would be affected. Could it be that since rats learn mazes on a basis of a variety of sensory cues, the increasing sensory deficit with larger and larger cortical lesions is the main explanation for the increasing loss of memory for the maze with increasing cortical destruction? It is quite probable that this is part of the explanation, as Lashley finally conceded it to be: "the most reasonable explanation of the quantitative relation between habit loss and extent of lesion" (Lashley, 1950). However, he was unwilling to accept a sensory deficit explanation as the *only* factor. He and some of his students (particularly Yü-Chüan Tsang) performed some ingenious experiments which demonstrated (to Lashley's satisfaction at least) that the destruction of the cortical sensory area for a particular sensory modality produces *more* of a deficit in maze habit or latch-box performance than does loss of the relevant peripheral sense organ. For example, in a series of experiments that provoked considerable controversy, Lashley and Tsang investigated the effects of lesions of primary visual cortex on rats that had previously been blinded by surgical removal of the eyes, either at birth or as adults. When the peripherally blinded animals were trained in the maze, damage to the cortex produced a serious impairment in the maze performance of these animals, despite the fact that these rats could not possibly have been making use of visual cues in learning the maze in the first place. Lashley interpreted these results as demonstrating a nonvisual learning function for the primary visual cortex (Lashley, 1929, 1931; Tsang, 1934).

One of the persons who took issue with Lashley was Cecile Bolton Finley, who pointed out some serious inadequacies in Lashley's interpretations (Finley, 1941). Lashley had based part of his conclusions on the results of a small number of animals with quite variable scores. For example, in an experiment in which Lashley measured the loss of a brightness discrimination habit in rats with cortical lesions in primary visual cortex, he used only seven rats. These seven rats committed 0, 2, 8, 13, 574, 689, and 1,191 errors, respectively. Lashley reported the mean, 353, rather than the median, 13, which would have been more representative of such a small and variable group of scores.

Another problem arises in defining just how much of a rat's cortex is in fact primary visual cortex. One standard way of defining primary visual cortex is as that area which receives direct synaptic input from neurons whose cell bodies are in the lateral geniculate nucleus. After destroying parts of this cortical area and severing the axons which are coming from the lateral geniculate nucleus, the cell bodies in the LGN will degenerate and die. This process is termed *retrograde degeneration.* With appropriate tissue stains, it is possible to estimate rather accurately how much of the visual projection fibers from the LGN have been destroyed, that is, how much of the primary visual cortex had been ablated. But Lashley's earlier reports had left room for doubt that the lesions in his rats had been confined to this region of the primary visual cortex. Finley challenged Lashley with some experiments of her own. She prepared two different groups of brain-lesioned rats, trained in both light and dark, and her results led her to conclude that when the area of cortex destroyed was confined to that producing retrograde degeneration only in the lateral geniculate nucleus, there was no evidence of any nonvisual function for this cortex.

Lashley did not allow Cecile Finley the last word on this matter. Almost certainly stung by her criticisms, Lashley repeated some of his earlier experiments, using more rats and being more careful in his procedures (Lashley, 1943, 1950). He used three basic experimental groups in his later experiments:

I.   Rats blinded by removal of the eyes (enucleation) and then trained to traverse a Lashley III maze without error ($N = 23$)

II. Normal rats trained to run the maze, then enucleated and retrained to errorless performance ($N = 19$)

III. Normal rats trained to run the maze, then operated upon to destroy the optic radiations, the axons of the lateral geniculate nucleus headed for the primary visual cortex, but without any actual direct cortical damage ($N = 11$).

In addition to evaluating the maze learning of the above three groups of rats, Lashley also took seventeen rats from Group I and another twelve rats from Group II after they had learned the maze and subjected them to primary visual cortex lesions. However, these lesions did invade some of the cortex surrounding the primary visual cortex as well as some of the brain structures underlying the cortex, particularly the dorsal part of the hippocampus.

From the performance of these various groups, Lashley found several relevant facts:

Peripheral blinding, not surprisingly, increases the number of *errors* that rats commit in learning the maze (from an average 50 to 116). However, the number of *trials* necessary is not dramatically greater than for normals (24 rather than 17). Lashley interpreted this fact as meaning that while blinded rats do experience more difficulty than normals in getting oriented in the maze, once a blind rat learns the correct path, it has no particular difficulty in remembering how to maneuver in the maze, using cues from other sensory modalities.

Peripheral blinding also impairs the retention of the maze habit by rats that had learned the maze with their vision intact. Although the variability among the scores was rather great, the rats blinded *after* learning the maze relearned the maze in an average of 12 trials, 46 errors, as compared with 17 trials, 50 errors, which they took to learn the maze in the first place. Therefore, although it was clear that many of the rats did rely heavily on the sense of vision in learning the maze initially, they could relearn the same maze without vision in about the same number of trials.

Cutting the optic radiations also produced an impairment in the retention of the maze habit, but considerably less so than peripheral blinding. These animals needed only 7 trials and 43 errors to relearn the maze. Thus, "central blinding" (as Lashley referred to this operation) was no more devastating to the memory for the maze habit than was peripheral blinding. There are some objections possible here. If only a small number of optic radiations were spared, some vision would be left to the animal, perhaps enough to recognize major landmarks in the maze. It is also possible, although somewhat unlikely, that subcortical visual centers such as the superior colliculus or tectal area might have been operative in the learning of the maze habit. While these possibilities are unlikely, they have not yet been satisfactorily disproven.

Finally, damage to the primary visual cortex produced the most profound disturbances in maze habit retention. "Only one of the 29 animals reached the criterion of five consecutive errorless trials within fifty trials of retraining. The others were all making numerous errors at the end of fifty trials, when the experiment had to be discontinued" (Lashley, 1943). At this point, the cortically damaged rats had made an average of 416 errors and were still obviously far from relearning the maze.

Since the rats which had undergone cortical removal had also suffered inadvertent damage to other brain structures, such as the hippocampus, Lashley analyzed the error scores to determine if there was any systematic relationship between such inadvertent brain damage and the number of errors made. There was no reliable relationship:

> In view of this evidence, the conclusion is justified that the severe effects of the cerebral lesions of Groups I and II were not due to invasion of nonvisual structures, but to the extensive destruction of the cerebral visual areas themselves. Destruction of the visual cortex in animals which have learned the maze without visual cues results in a total disorganization of the habit and a retardation in relearning greatly exceeding that produced by peripheral blinding. . . . (Lashley, 1943.)

Although Lashley did not find that damage to the hippocampus significantly increased the error scores for the cortically lesioned animals, most of these rats did suffer hippocampal damage. In more recent experiments, Birger Kaada and his colleagues in Oslo, Norway have found that hippocampal lesions do impair the maze retention of rats (Kaada et al., 1961). There were several differences between Lashley's experiments and the Norwegian experiments, including strain of rat used, exact location of the lesion, and type of maze used, so direct comparison is somewhat difficult. Perhaps the biggest procedural difference is that while Lashley's rats were trained to run the maze *without error* before surgery, Kaada's rats were only incompletely trained preoperatively. It is very possible that the importance of the hippocampus to the rat's maze-solving ability may be greater during the early or middle stages of learning than for the retention of an already well-learned habit. Hippocampal lesions greatly increase the number of errors made by rats as they first learn the Lashley III (Madsen & Kimble, 1965; Jarrard & Lewis, 1967). Moreover, Thomas (1971) has provided good evidence that hippocampal lesions do impair the retention of a well-learned maze habit in rats.

In discussing his own findings as well as those of Cecile Finley, Lashley pointed out that the complete removal of just the primary visual cortex, without any damage to adjacent cortex, is technically impossible. Also, he argued that Finley's lesions were incomplete and did not remove the entire primary visual cortex. In this way, Lashley reversed the criticism that his lesions were too big and invaded cortex adjacent to the primary visual cortex, thus involving other sensory modalities. While these results might have created an impasse, Lashley made several points which strengthened his argument that neurons in the primary visual cortex are responsible for more than just the analysis of visual input. In particular, damage to the visual cortex produced at least ten times greater behavioral deficit in the peripherally blinded animals that had (necessarily) learned the maze without visual cues as compared with the deficit caused by the peripheral blinding of rats that had learned the maze with their vision intact. Also, damage to the optic radiations plus damage to nonvisual brain structures results in a comparatively mild deficit, much less severe than destruction of the visual cortex itself combined with damage to nonvisual structures.

As Lashley concluded, his experiments did not reveal the locus or the nature of the maze habit engram. Nor have any subsequent studies. Nevertheless, Lashley's research has still provided the most substantial base of experimental results in this area, and has served to sweep away previous and inadequate theories of brain function.

SUGGESTIONS FOR FURTHER READING

Altman, J. Postnatal growth and differentiation of the mammalian brain, with implications for a morphological theory of memory. In G. C. Quarton, T. Melnechuk, & F. O. Schmitt (Eds.) *The neurosciences: A study program.* New York: Rockefeller University Press, 1967. Pp. 723–743.

DiCara, L. V. Learning in the autonomic nervous system. *Scientific American,* 1970, **222**, 30–39.

Gaze, R. M. *The formation of nerve connections.* New York: Academic, 1970.

Kimble, D. P. (Ed.) *The anatomy of memory.* Palo Alto, Calif.: Science and Behavior Books, 1965.

Sperry, R. W. The growth of nerve circuits. *Scientific American,* 201, November 1959.

Chapter 8

SPECIAL PROPERTIES OF THE HUMAN BRAIN

Are there "special" properties of the human brain which account for the differences in behavioral capacity between humans and other primates? This, of course, is a loaded question, for it implies that the differences we perceive between our own behavior and that of other "lower" primates, such as the great apes and chimpanzee, call for some special functional capacities of the human brain. Perhaps. It is possible to point out two features of the human brain which appear to distinguish it from that of other primates:

1   The human brain is both functionally and anatomically asymmetrical.
2   The human brain seems to have a great (unique?) capacity to produce language and manipulate abstract symbols.

THE ASYMMETRY OF THE HUMAN BRAIN

If you were to examine the superficial anatomy of the human brain, you would first notice the two large cerebral hemispheres which dominate the entire brain in size. With a knife blade, you could easily cut a large band of white, myelinated fibers that forms the major commissure, the *corpus callosum*, which connects the two hemispheres. If you were to continue slicing down the middle of the brain, you would cut through other connecting tracts such as the anterior, posterior, and hippocampal commissures. Eventually, you would sever the *massa intermedia* in the middle of the thalamus and you would have two pieces of brain instead of one. You would then have divided the human brain into what appear to be two mirror-image halves. That is, after a cursory examination, the chances are very good that you would conclude that although there are some slight differences, in general the two halves are quite similar to each other. Yet if careful measurements are made, as has been done by Geschwind and Levitsky (1968), the chances are approximately 2:1 that an area of cortex on the upper surface of the temporal lobe *in the left* cerebral hemisphere would be about 1 centimeter (or 33 percent) longer than the corresponding area in the right hemisphere. In about one brain in ten the opposite is true, with the larger area being in the right hemisphere. In only one brain in four are the two hemispheres approximately equal. Moreover, this structural asymmetry has been observed in the brains of stillborn infants by J. Wada (Geschwind, 1970). While a centimeter of brain tissue may contain several million neurons, it is reasonable to ask if "merely millions" is significant in the context of billions of brain neurons. In this particular case, however, the asymmetry is in a cortical area thought to be critical for the understanding of both spoken and written language. This part of the brain is the posterior portion of the temporal lobe, in the superior temporal gyrus. It is referred to by neurologists as *Wernicke's area* after the brilliant nineteenth century neurologist Carl Wernicke (1848–1905). Among other accomplishments, Wernicke developed a theory which is still useful in accounting for the effects of brain damage on speech and language comprehension.

Whether or not the *anatomical* asymmetry between the left and right cerebral hemispheres is an important consideration, there is evidence that there are profound *functional* differences between the left and right human cerebral hemispheres. This *functional lateralization* is evident in such tasks as speaking, writing, and dealing with spatial relations. The evidence for functional lateralization has been accumulating for over a century, since Paul Broca presented some evidence linking aphasia (a disorder of language due to brain damage) with brain lesions in a specific part of the left cerebral hemisphere. Such evidence has come from observation of patients with traumatic brain injuries, epilepsy, and other neurological disorders. More recently, three different neurological techniques have greatly increased the information available from the study of brain-damaged humans:

1   The electric stimulation of the brain in wide-awake, unanesthetized human patients
2   The so-called split-brain operation, developed to counteract the spread of epileptic seizures from one side of the brain to the other

3   The *Wada* technique, in which a depressant drug (barbiturate) such as sodium amytal is injected into either the left or right carotid artery, thus rendering one half of the brain temporarily nonfunctional (Wada & Rasmussen, 1960)

On the basis of many experiments with these techniques, together with older observations by countless neurologists, several generalizations about the functional lateralization in the human brain can be made.

One of the more obvious examples of functional differences between the left and right hemispheres is that one of them, generally the left, is dominant in the control of movements of the hands and legs—which is, of course, handedness. Most of us are right-handed, which means that the opposite (left) hemisphere is dominant for control of hand and arm movements. This is because (for no obviously good reason) the motor neuron axons which travel from the cortex down to the spinal cord cross over to the opposite side of the cord before synapsing with the motor neurons that supply the muscles.

A less obvious but well-documented fact is that one hemisphere, usually the left, is dominant with respect to speech and writing. There is no necessary correspondence between the hemisphere which is dominant for controlling movement and that which is dominant for speech and writing. In most people, the left hemisphere is the dominant, or major, hemisphere for speaking, writing, and controlling movement. Special techniques are necessary to determine which hemisphere is dominant for speaking and writing. The injection of the depressant into either the left or right carotid artery (the Wada technique) causes one half of the brain to become almost instantaneously nonfunctional. If the depressed hemisphere is the one dominant for speech and writing, the patient injected becomes aphasic, that is, he cannot speak or write until the drug effect has worn off. The patient remains conscious, however. This test is applied to patients about to undergo brain surgery in order that the neurosurgeon can avoid damaging the speech areas of the dominant hemisphere if possible.

Brenda Milner and coworkers have reported on a group of 169 such patients, 95 of whom were right-handed and 74 of whom were left-handed. The group was in no way random, since all were to undergo brain surgery. In this group, 92 percent of the right-handers became aphasic when their left hemisphere was depressed, while only 7 percent of the right-handers became aphasic when the drug depressed the right hemisphere. Only 1 person of the 95 apparently had some speech functions controlled by both hemispheres, since neither left nor right hemisphere depression caused complete aphasia. Among the 74 left-handed patients, 69 percent also had their left hemisphere dominant for speech, 17 percent became aphasic on depression of the right hemisphere, and 13 percent had some speech representation in both hemispheres. In general, in both right-handed and left-handed patients alike, the left hemisphere was more likely to be dominant for speech and writing. Left-handed individuals are more likely, however, to have some bilateral speech representation than right-handed individuals. Similar information on non-patient populations is not available.

If one cerebral hemisphere is more or less in control of such advanced skills as speaking and writing, does this mean that the other "nonspeaking" hemisphere is somehow grossly inferior or subhuman in capacity? Because of some imaginative and careful observations of split-brain patients by Roger Sperry and his colleagues (Sperry, 1968; Sperry & Gazzaniga, 1967) it is now possible to answer this question. In certain cases of advanced epilepsy, in which drug therapy is no longer effective, a radical type of brain surgery has been developed and has been proven to be very beneficial in reducing or eliminating the frequency and intensity of the epileptic seizures. This operation disconnects the two cerebral hemispheres by cutting all direct nerve connections that normally allow for interhemispheric communication. The major tract severed is the corpus callosum. Other communicating tracts cut in this operation are the anterior commissure, the hippocampal commissure, and in some cases, the massa intermedia of the thalamus. It may seem surprising, but this major change in the structural connections of the brain does not result in a dramatic alteration in the behavior of the patients or, according to their own reports, in their mental life. They do report difficulty in remembering recent events, particularly during the first postoperative year. They report that they fatigue more quickly while reading. But on casual observation, they appear relatively normal after such operations. By asking the right questions, however, Sperry and his colleagues have been able to demonstrate a startling fact about these split-brain patients. After surgery, they possess *two separate "selves," or conscious awarenesses*. To quote Roger Sperry:

> Instead of the normally unified single stream of consciousness, these patients behave in many ways as if they have two independent streams of conscious awareness, one in each hemisphere, each of which is cut off from and out of contact with the mental experience of the other. In other words, each hemisphere seems to have its own separate and private sensations; its own perceptions; its own concepts; and its own impulses to act, with related volitional, cognitive and learning experiences. Following the surgery, each hemisphere also has thereafter its separate chain of memories that are rendered inaccessible to the recall processes of the other. (Sperry, 1968, p. 724.)

One of the results of the study of these patients has been that of increasing our knowledge regarding functional lateralization of the two hemispheres. The individuals no longer have the normal neural connections between the left and right hemispheres. It is thus possible to communicate with each hemisphere privately at least through the senses of vision, touch, and olfaction.

Due to the nature of the human visual system (Figure 52), stimuli presented *to the left* of a central fixation point directly in front of the nose are projected via the visual system only to the right hemisphere. Similarly, stimuli presented to the right of the middle fixation point are projected exclusively to the left hemisphere, due to the crossing over to the opposite side of half of each optic nerve at the *optic chiasm.* Of course, in order to prevent the visual stimuli from being presented to both hemispheres, it is necessary to present them at a rate fast enough so that the individual cannot move his eyes or head and bring the stimulus into the other visual field and thereby to the other hemisphere. The human brain (both hemispheres) can process simple visual signals in 0.1 second. This is a presentation rate fast enough to eliminate the possibility of rapid eye movements getting the stimulus into the other visual field. By using this technique of rapid presentation of visual stimuli, Sperry and his colleagues have discovered that the two hemispheres are quite different in their responses to visual stimuli.

In all the split-brain patients examined so far, the left hemisphere has been the dominant hemisphere for speech and writing. When visual stimuli such as words or outline figures of familiar objects are flashed rapidly into the right half of the visual field of these individuals (and therefore projected onto the left hemisphere), they can describe the stimuli in either speech or writing in a normal fashion—naming the objects or words without hesitation. The left hemisphere in these patients seems fully capable of carrying on the normal speaking and writing functions of the individual despite being totally disconnected from the right hemisphere.

On the other hand, the person cannot name, either by speech or by writing, the objects flashed into the left half of the visual field (and therefore projected onto the right hemisphere).

The *verbal* response of these patients to visual stimuli flashed into the left visual field is that they "did not see anything" or perhaps saw only "a flash of light." It is the left hemisphere which is talking, and the left hemisphere did not, in fact, see anything in its visual field. However, while it is true that the speaking hemisphere is indeed ignorant regarding the identity of visual stimuli in the left visual field, it can be readily demonstrated that the right hemisphere has perceived the stimulus and knows what it is but cannot tell about it in words. If the patient is asked to identify by touch (from a group of objects kept out of sight) an object which matches the one just presented visually in the left half of the visual field, he can, *if he uses his left hand, controlled primarily by the right hemisphere.* The right hand does no better than chance.

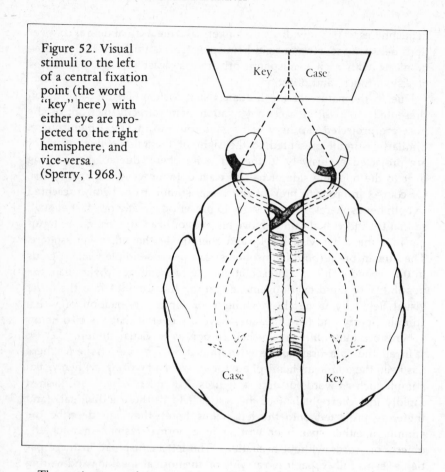

Figure 52. Visual stimuli to the left of a central fixation point (the word "key" here) with either eye are projected to the right hemisphere, and vice-versa. (Sperry, 1968.)

The patient can then simultaneously grasp and produce the correct matching object and deny, verbally, that he saw anything. Moreover, both hemispheres are answering truthfully!

Such observations are convincing evidence that the two cerebral hemispheres are specialized with respect to function. The left (in all cases so far) is dominant for speech and writing. The right hemisphere, although mute, has some language capacity. Simple words presented in the left visual field can be correctly matched by pointing with the left hand. The right hemisphere is able to read nouns, but is very poor on verbs. It can also be shown that (in four out of six patients so far tested) the right hemisphere possesses some arithmetical ability, enough to add numbers up to products of 20 or so. These are not startling mental feats by human standards, but they are beyond anything so far demonstrated in other primates. For example, these patients can follow verbal instructions which are transmitted to both hemispheres by the auditory system. If told to "find a piece of silverware" with the left hand, unaided by vision, such patients are able to select a spoon or fork from a variety of objects, both silverware and non-silverware. The fact that the left hemisphere did not participate in this identification is shown by the inability of the individual to name the object he has just correctly selected by touch. These sorts of findings have demonstrated that the ability to recognize objects by the sense of touch alone, called *stereognosis,* is also lateralized. Sensory impressions from objects touching the left hand are projected to the right hemisphere. These results also indicate that the cerebral hemispheres in these individuals can function independently, although not equally. Each hemisphere is indeed cut off from and unaware of the perceptions and memories of the other.

The right hemisphere is not inferior in all ways to the left. Sperry and his colleagues have now been able to identify a whole series of activities in which the minor hemisphere is superior. These tasks are all nonverbal, and all involve the comprehension of spatial form and spatial relations (Sperry, 1972). Figure 53 shows a schematic outline of the functional lateralization of the human brain.

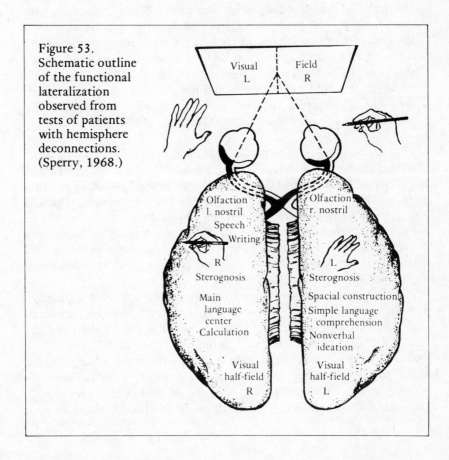

Figure 53.
Schematic outline of the functional lateralization observed from tests of patients with hemisphere deconnections. (Sperry, 1968.)

An example of this sort of skill is the drawing of a simple outline house in perspective. Even in right-handed split-brain individuals, the left hand, controlled by the right hemisphere, is much better than the right hand at such a task. The superiority of the nonspeaking right hemisphere is also seen in a task in which the subject is required to match a geometrical pattern by the manipulation of colored blocks. In some cases when the patient is attempting (and blundering badly) in such a task with his right hand, the individual's left hand can be observed to sneak out toward the blocks in an apparent attempt by the silent but frustrated right hemisphere to set things right.

Both the right and left hemisphere appear capable of characteristically human emotional responses. Gazzaniga gives a good example:

> In one of our experiments . . . we would present a series of ordinary objects and then suddenly flash a picture of a nude woman. This evoked an amused reaction regardless of whether the picture was presented to the left hemisphere or to the right. When the picture was flashed to the left hemisphere of a female patient, she laughed and verbally identified the picture as a nude. When it was later presented to the right hemisphere, she said in reply to a question that she saw nothing, but almost immediately a sly smile spread over her face and she began to chuckle. Asked what she was laughing at, she said: "I don't know . . . nothing . . . oh—that funny machine." Although the right hemisphere could not describe what it had seen, the sight nevertheless elicited an emotional response like the one evoked from the left hemisphere. (Gazzaniga, 1967.)

There is yet another way in which the right hemisphere may be functionally superior to the left. As reported by Penfield and Perot (1963), direct electric stimulation of the cerebral cortex in wide-awake, unanesthetized humans can produce a variety of mental experiences. Penfield and a series of coworkers accumulated observations on the effects of electric stimulation of the human brain in approximately 1,300 patients during the period 1934–1961. These observations were made as part of the necessary exploratory stimulation preparatory to brain surgery at the Montreal Neurological Institute.

Although their procedure may sound terrifying and even a little bizarre, it is actually quite routine and an extremely low risk technique that yields valuable medical information regarding the location and extent of damaged or diseased brain tissue. The procedure is carried out under local anesthesia (to eliminate stimulation of nerve endings in the scalp). Once the subject's brain is exposed, however, no further anesthesia is required. The cortex (and in fact most of the brain) cannot experience pain from direct electric stimulation. Such stimulation can be performed without endangering the patient in any way. Typically, such stimulation is done by placing a small silver ball electrode on the surface of the cortex and passing alternating current through the electrode. This stimulates the small region of the cortex directly under the electrode. A typical stimulus would be alternating current of 40 to 100 cycles per second, 1 to 5 volts, and a current of between 50 and 500 microamperes.

Many kinds of sensations can be elicited with this procedure. One of the most interesting results concerns what Penfield has called experiential responses. Such responses are relatively rare. They have been observed in only 40 of 1,132 (7.7 percent) patients. The experiential responses consist of a sequence of the individual's past experience—"reproductions of past experience." Most commonly they are auditory in nature, but frequently they are visual; and more rarely, they are combined auditory and visual responses. These responses have only been elicited from stimulation of the temporal lobe. Relevant to our present discussion, it has been the nonspeaking hemisphere (typically the right) which has yielded most of these experiential responses: 64 percent of the auditory experiential responses and 74 percent of the visual experiential responses were produced by stimulation of the nonspeaking minor hemisphere. If these statistics do indicate a significant trend toward lateralization in the production of experiential responses, what could we infer from this? At the present time, we can only speculate. It seems quite clear that some specialization has occurred in the evolution of the human brain, resulting in the functional lateralization we have described. It may be that the necessity to devote a substantial number of cortical neurons to the brain mechanisms underlying speech and writing has thereby reduced the number of neurons available for other functions. The neurons incorporated into circuits devoted to language function thus identify that hemisphere as the major one for speaking and writing. Except in rare individuals, there is no mirror-image speech in the opposite hemisphere. Now it is from what would be the mirror-image speech area in the right hemisphere that the majority of the experiential responses are elicited. No such responses have ever been elicited from the major speech areas in the dominant hemisphere. Perhaps as one of the hemispheres gains control of speech and writing, the mirror-image area in the other hemisphere begins to develop its own, different functional specialization. In this case it may be some interpretive or memory function. Such speculation goes beyond any available data as yet, and other questions can be raised. For example, it is not clear why the *left* hemisphere should be so much more likely to become the talking hemisphere. Could it be due to the slight but reliable size advantage that this area in the left hemisphere enjoys in most individuals?

There is further evidence that the minor hemisphere has developed some functional superiority over the major one in some other nonverbal skills. Much of this evidence has been gathered by Brenda Milner and her coworkers at the Montreal Neurological Institute. The patients were mainly undergoing treatment for severe epilepsy. In a majority of these cases, the medical procedure is the removal of the abnormal brain tissue which is responsible for the seizures. In many cases, the temporal lobes are the site of the abnormal tissue; thus many partial temporal lobectomies have been carried out. Most of these removals involve only one hemisphere, but in some cases tissue from both temporal lobes is removed. By comparing the effects of right-temporal-lobe operations with those of left-temporal-lobe operations, a rather good picture of functional lateralization has been built up. In all these cases reported by Milner (1967), the left hemisphere was dominant for speech and writing. The patients ranged in age from 14 to 54 years, the average age being 26.

There were several aspects of mental function in which removal of right temporal lobe tissue caused severe deficits in performance but removal of the similar area of the left temporal lobe did not. For example, *perception of irregular visual patterns, visual memory, tonal memory,* and *timbre discrimination* were all much poorer after right temporal lobe tissue removals than before, but these skills remained normal after left temporal lobe tissue removal.

The deficit in the visual tasks among the right temporal lobe lesioned patients was revealed in a variety of tests. These patients are not blind or impaired in tests of visual acuity. Nonetheless, they consistently show a subtle but readily detectable deficit in the perception of irregular patterns such as sketchy cartoonlike drawings or ambiguous figures. The deficit is more noticeable when there is no obvious name or other verbal label which can be attached to the stimulus. This fact almost certainly means that the intact left hemisphere is responsible for verbal labels which can serve as a crutch for the disabled right hemisphere, and that it is the right hemisphere which normally excels in making perceptual sense out of incompletely defined visual stimuli. After Brenda Milner and her colleagues had noticed this result, they designed some special visual memory tasks in which the stimuli could not be easily language-coded. An example of such a nonsense drawing is shown in Figure 54. Right-temporal-lobe patients experience more difficulty than other patients with different sorts of brain operations in recognizing whether or not they have seen a particular nonsense figure before. Similar results are found if the experiment involves the use of photographs taken from an unfamiliar school annual. To these right-temporal-lobe-lesioned patients, all the faces look just the same. They are very poor, much more so than patients with brain damage elsewhere, in determining whether or not the face presented to them is one that the experimenter has presented before.

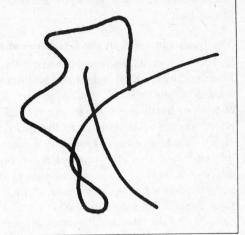

Figure 54. A nonsense figure. Patients with right-temporal-lobe damage have great difficulty in recognizing such figures. Patients with left-temporal-lobe damage have no more difficulty than normals in this sort of recognition test. (Kimura, 1963.)

In analyzing the auditory capacities of these patients, Milner used a standard musical talents test consisting of a variety of subtests of various musical abilities. Two subtests in particular proved extremely difficult for patients with right-temporal-lobe damage—the tonal memory test and the timbre discrimination tests. In the tonal memory tests, two short sequences of notes are presented. The second sequence differs from the first sequence only in that one note is changed. The task is to identify the changed note. Timbre is the characteristic quality of a sound independent of its pitch and loudness. It is through our ability to discriminate timbre, for example, that we tell the difference between middle C as played on a piano and as played on a violin. Simple pitch discrimination in these patients is normal.

It is apparent that the human brain has evolved to a stage in which the two cerebral hemispheres are differentially specialized. Although normal human behavior in advanced cultures is very dependent on language skills, we should not underestimate the degree of functional specialization that exists in the nonspeaking minor hemisphere. This hemisphere has evolved too, and in most individuals it has become important for nonverbal memory functions, visual construction tasks, auditory memory, and timbre discrimination. The minor hemisphere may also play a fundamental role in memory processes. It is possible to speculate that the long-lasting short-term-memory impairments observed in split-brain patients (Sperry, 1968) may result from disconnecting an important memory area in the right hemisphere from the talking left hemisphere. It is the left hemisphere that is necessary to make the statements by which short-term-memory performance is normally judged. Without access to the right hemisphere, the handicap will be displayed. We can regard the minor hemisphere as inferior to the major one in language function, but it is by no means generally less developed or specialized in function.

The language areas in the left hemisphere

In 1861 a French neurologist named Paul Broca reported that he had examined two patients who had lost their speech due to brain damage—a condition called *aphasia*. Broca performed autopsies on these individuals after their death (from other causes) and discovered that both had sustained severe brain damage to the posterior portion of the frontal lobe of the left hemisphere. From these two cases, Broca made the daring inference that this area of the left hemisphere was specialized for language functions. Although subsequent information has only partially supported Broca's claim, this area of the frontal lobe is generally referred to as *Broca's area* (see Figure 55).

A few years later Carl Wernicke pointed out that there were clear differences in the kinds of language disturbances which resulted from damage to Broca's area and those which resulted from damage to the temporal lobe of the left hemisphere. There is considerable disagreement and controversy regarding the exact classification of the various types of aphasia or dysphasia (an impairment but not total loss of language). We will follow the basic classification as outlined by Wernicke, a classification that has stood up quite well over the past century.

The main distinction between Broca's aphasia and Wernicke's aphasia is that in Broca's aphasia the primary difficulty is in the *production* of speech and writing. Patients with Broca's aphasia have severe difficulty in producing any intelligible speech whatsoever. The few words that may still be available to the patient are uttered with great effort. Recognition of language, however, may still be near normal. Broca's aphasics can often demonstrate that they recognize a word by pointing to a matching picture but are unable to read the word aloud or copy it in writing.

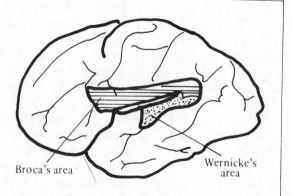

Figure 55. Lateral surface of the left hemisphere of the human brain showing Broca's area and Wernicke's area. (Modified from Geschwind, 1970.)

Broca's area

Wernicke's area

The difficulty in language output is seen both in speech and writing, although not necessarily to equal degrees. The problem is often so profound that the person is either totally without language or has a vocabulary of one or two words. Quite often when a few words are left, they are swearwords. In one famous case the entire vocabulary consisted of the word "horseradish" (Ruch & Patton, 1965). It is important to emphasize that the language output problem is not due to any paralysis or other muscular problem with the vocal cords. Dramatic illustrations of this fact are common: aphasics who can barely speak single words can, a moment later, sing a wordless melody easily and well. The difficulty is in the organization of the neural machinery that makes up the elements of language, not in the muscles of the vocal cords. Broca's aphasia, because of the difficulty in language output is often called *expressive aphasia.*

Wernicke's aphasia, on the other hand, is due primarily to difficulty in coping with language on the input side; it is often referred to as *receptive aphasia.* In Wernicke's aphasia, patients show a great loss in their ability to comprehend both speech and writing, not necessarily to equal degrees. There is no general impairment, however, in vision or hearing. Receptive aphasics show none of the difficulty or great effort in uttering words which so torments the expressive aphasic. In fact, the flow of speech may appear almost effortless and the rate of speech even more rapid than normal. The rhythm and melody of normal speech are present, but there is a profound problem—the words do not convey any real information. Nonwords, incredible circumlocutions, vague generalities, and erroneously used words dilute the meaning of the speech and render it nearly unintelligible. Some typical examples: "I was over in the other one, and then after they had been in the department, I was in this one" (Geschwind, 1970). Or, in response to the request to name a bunch of keys: "Indication of measurement of piece of apparatus or intimating the cost of apparatus in various forms" (Brain, 1961).

According to Wernicke, these two types of aphasia result from damage to different regions of the dominant hemisphere for speech, as shown in Figure 55. Many variations and combinations of these two basic types of aphasia occur in different individuals, depending upon the extent and location of the damage. There are also reports of exceptions to Wernicke's generalization, including cases in which destruction to Broca's area did not result in aphasia. Nevertheless, Wernicke's ideas are useful generalizations regarding aphasia.

It would be very satisfying to discuss now exactly *how* the human brain manages to comprehend and invent language. Unfortunately, our ignorance of this subject is almost perfect. However, it is not the nature of most brain scientists to accept lack of relevant data as sufficient reason to remain silent on an interesting subject. A discussion aptly entitled

"Lacunae [gaps in our knowledge] and research approaches to them" (Teuber, 1967) is an excellent example of careful and informed speculation. Teuber's analysis of lacunae breaks the problems of language into three subareas: input processing, central elaboration, and patterning of output.

With respect to input processing, it is in the area of how we understand language that the clearest clues may exist. The neural processing principles discovered in the cat and monkey visual systems (see Chapter 4) may be more generally used in the brain. Research indicates that increasingly complex feature analyzers can be constructed out of the synaptic communication of hierarchically arranged populations of neurons. The convergence of many lower-order analyzers onto a single neuron higher in the hierarchy allows the higher-order neuron to display more complex analyzing capacities. The billions of neurons available in the human cerebral cortex may provide just the necessary reservoir of elements for the construction of such a hierarchical feature detection system. Such a system would operate on the principle which Teuber calls "cascade specification of input." By the convergence of increasingly complex feature analyzers, neurons may be found, perhaps in Wernicke's area, which respond maximally to the visual stimulus as produced by the configuration of letters or entire words. This might allow for the rapid visual processing of language. However, in speech perception, it is the auditory system which is critical. There is as yet no information which indicates that similar principles of stimulus feature analysis are operative in the auditory system. It would be instructive to find neurons which respond maximally, for example, to phonemes (basic sound units of language).

About language output, there is not too much to be said. As Teuber points out, the problem of understanding the motor output of speech is related to the problem of understanding spontaneous, or voluntary, movement in general. Likewise, the nature of the central elaboration of language is totally obscure. These special properties of the human brain, if they are indeed special, remain mysterious.

THE ANATOMY OF THE CEREBRAL CORTEX

The cerebral cortex ("bark") is the most recent evolutionary development of the mammalian brain. Although reptiles have some rudimentary cortical tissue, true *neocortex*, vastly complicated in cellular microstructure and at least six cell layers thick, exists in mammalian brains only.

The cerebral cortex is composed of neurons, glial cells, and blood vessels. Estimates of the number of neurons in the cerebral cortex of man vary from 5 to 9 billion (Sholl, 1956). For most individuals, the number is somewhere between these two figures—in any case, a huge number of cells, well over half the total number of neurons in the entire nervous system. There are many more neurons in your cortex than there are people in the world. Because of the many folds in the cortex of the human brain, it is extremely difficult to obtain an accurate measurement of the total volume of the cortex, but it is estimated to average about 3,000 cubic millimeters. It varies in thickness from area to area (1.5 to 4.5 millimeters) but averages about 2.5 millimeters thick, from the surface of the brain to the underlying white matter.

More by general agreement and compromise than by any compelling lines of demarcation, cortex is divided into six layers (although subdivisions enlarge this number considerably). Figure 56 gives a diagram of these six layers and Figure 57, a corresponding diagram of a representative cortical neuron, both of which indicate the general relationships between various parts of cortical neurons and layers. The layers are numbered from the surface down as follows:

I   Superficial plexiform layer, containing only some superficial dendrites, and generally devoid of any cell bodies

II   The layer of small pyramidal neurons (so-named because of the shape of their cell body)

III The external layer, containing medium-sized and large pyramidal neurons

IV The granular layer, containing a mixture of small neurons, many with short branching axons

V   The inner layer of large pyramidal neurons

VI The spindle cell layer (named for the presence of neurons with elongated spindle-shaped cell bodies)

Figure 57 shows the outline of a representative neuron from the cortex of a mammal. Which mammal this neuron comes from is not particularly important, because it would appear much the same whether it were from the brain of man, a mouse, or an elephant. There are, of course, more neurons in the larger brains, but the basic design is much the same.

Although Figure 57 shows only two dimensions, the neurons actually exist, of course, in three. The dendrites typically extend out from the cell body in all directions, defining a receptive field, or sphere of influence of that neuron. If one were to look at the cell from the top or bottom, the dendrites would form a fringe around the main axis of the neuron, in a bottle-brush arrangement. Cortical neurons can thus be thought of as forming a tiny cylinder of brain space. Billions of such neuronal cylinders, packed together in overlapping fashion, constitute the total cortex. Cortical neurons range from 0.2 to 2 millimeters in length, while the diameter of the cylinder is generally about 0.1 milli-

Figure 56. A drawing to illustrate the various aspects of cortical lamination of typical six-layered cortex. The Roman numerals at the sides of the figure indicate the cortical layers. (*A*) Some of the fiber relations including the stripe of Kaes (sK), the external stripe of Baillarger (esB), and the internal stripe of Baillarger (isB). (*B*) The cytoarchitectonic pattern. (*C*) Various cell types demonstrable in Golgi preparations: H, horizontal cells; M, Martinotti cell; MP, modified pyramidal cell; P, pyramidal cell; S, stellate cell. Compiled from various sources. (Crosby, Humphrey, & Lauer, 1962)

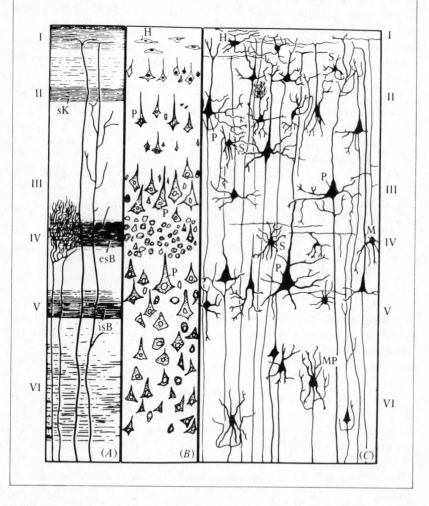

meter. For the most part, neurons are oriented perpendicular with respect to the nearest surface of the brain. Dendrites do not emerge equally

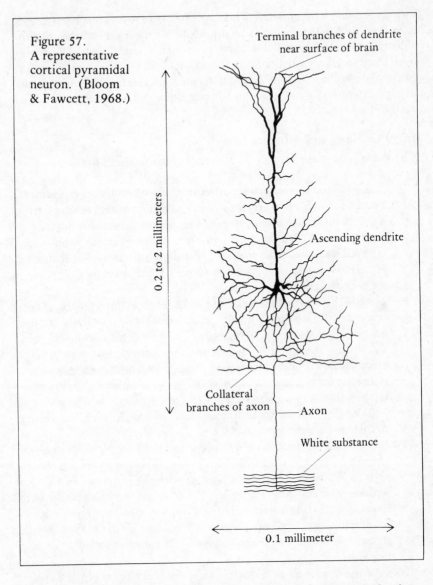

Figure 57.
A representative
cortical pyramidal
neuron. (Bloom
& Fawcett, 1968.)

Terminal branches of dendrite
near surface of brain

0.2 to 2 millimeters

Ascending dendrite

Collateral
branches of axon

Axon

White substance

0.1 millimeter

from all parts of the neuron's cell body. There are two main dendritic
concentrations on most cortical neurons, an outcropping from the base
of the cell body (the *basal dendrites*) and another set of more extensive
and longer dendrites, from the apex of the cell body, termed the *apical
dendrites*. The cell body is often quite elongated, and the distinction
between the main shaft of the apical dendrite and the cell body itself
is not always clear. The axon of the cortical neuron (in this illustration
quite thin) typically exits from the cortex by plunging directly downward

into underlying white matter. This layer of tissue just beneath the cortex is termed *white matter* because of the whitish appearance of the myelin-sheathed axons of which this layer is primarily composed. The cortex itself, composed primarily of cell bodies, dendrites, and the smaller ends of the penetrating afferent axons is termed *gray matter,* although in the living brain it has a definite pinkish color due to the presence of blood vessels.

Input channels to cortical neurons

There are four main sources of afferents to cortical neurons.

1 *Sensory-specific afferents* from particular thalamic nuclei. For example, neurons in the visual cortex receive specific afferent endings from axons whose cell bodies are in the lateral geniculate nucleus of the thalamus. Neurons in the primary auditory cortex receive specific afferents from the medial geniculate nucleus of the thalamus.

2 *Nonsensory-specific,* or *generalized, afferents* from neurons in the brain stem and thalamus.

3 *Commissural afferents* from the opposite cerebral hemisphere. These commissural afferents include axons from symmetrically located areas of the opposite hemisphere, so-called mirror-image sites. The axons from one hemisphere to the other form several large commissures (bundles of axons). The largest of these commissures is the *corpus callosum,* containing over 100 million axons in man. Other major commissures connecting the two hemispheres are the anterior and posterior commissures, although both are much smaller than the corpus callosum.

4 Intracortical afferents from other cortical neurons of the same hemisphere. These include *recurrent collaterals,* axon branches which turn back and make synaptic contact with the same cell body from which the main axon emerges. Other axons which synapse with neurons in the same hemisphere do not, typically, penetrate directly horizontally but dip downward to the white matter before branching upward again to synapse. These are termed *U fibers.*

Most of the synapses on a neuron are on the dendrites. In the cortex especially, the dendrites of many neurons have small protuberances called *spines.* These dendritic spines may account for only 5 to 10 percent of the total dendritic surface, but they are extremely important points of contact, accounting for virtually all the synapses in some neurons. There is almost certainly great variability in the number of spines from one neuron to another. As an example, however, one neuron in the cortex of a rat was carefully examined and found to have 517 spines on its dendrites (Peters & Kaiserman-Abramof, 1969). In the majority of cortical neurons, dendrites and the dendritic spines all provide postsynaptic receptive surfaces for incoming axons. Although axon-axonic synapses are known to exist, they seem to be rare.

The receptive field of the cortical neurons is defined by the cylinder formed by the dendrites. The response of the neuron is computed by the neuron as a function of all of the influences, excitatory and inhibitory, imposed upon it. As far as can be determined, these influences come to it exclusively via synaptic inputs.

EFFECT OF THE ENVIRONMENT ON THE DENDRITIC FIELD

The number and rate of growth of dendritic spines may be determined, in part, by the environment in which the animal develops. The number of spines can be decreased by depriving the neuron of its normal synaptic input. This has been accomplished by blinding an animal or by destroying the lateral geniculate nucleus. Both these maneuvers will deprive neurons in the visual cortex of normal synaptic input. As a consequence, the number of dendritic spines on neurons in this area is diminished (Globus & Scheibel, 1967).

Conversely, the rate of development of dendritic spines can be accelerated in baby rats which have been put into an intensely stimulating sensory environment a few minutes each day for a week or so during their early development (Schapiro & Vukovich, 1970). In particular, in this experiment, rats were either left untouched by the experimenters (nonstimulated control animals) or:

> were removed from the nest gently with forceps three to five times a day and subjected to a wide range of sensory stimuli for 20 to 30 minutes: they were handled and stroked, shaken on a mechanical shaker; placed in warm and cold water and on cold and then warm metal; and subjected to noise and flashing lights and to short periods of electric shock.

Following this sensory barrage all the animals, both stimulated and nonstimulated, were sacrificed (8 to 16 days later) and their brains removed for examination. The analysis of samples of cortical neurons revealed that the stimulated animals contained from 10 to 33 percent more spines per micrometer of dendrite surface than did their nonstimulated controls. There was no change in the size of the cell body or the length of the dendrites in the brains of the stimulated rats. Not all parts of the dendritic tree were equally affected; the most marked difference was seen in the number of spines present on dendrites relatively closer to the cell body than on those farther away from the cell body.

Since the brains were examined after the rats had lived only a short period, it was not possible to conclude that the total number of dendritic spines would be different in adult animals as a result of the increased sensory stimulation in infancy. Other reserach has shown that the density of the dendritic spines continues to increase in normal rats at least through the first 3 weeks of life. It is necessary to be quite cautious in inferring whether the acceleration of the rate of spine development in the Schapiro and Vukovich studies is a direct effect of sensory input via synaptic channels or the result of internal changes, hormonal or otherwise, which could have easily been produced by the intense stimulation. The responsiveness of the developing rat brain to influences from the environment is a provocative finding, however.

Experimental techniques for the analysis of living cortex

Most of the structural details of the cortex which we have discussed so far are based on studies of dead tissue. Such neuroanatomical information is indispensable and provides the base upon which functional considerations must rest. But the analysis of dead tissue cannot tell us directly how the living brain operates. In their efforts to examine the function of the living brain, experimenters have removed portions of it, heated it, frozen it, treated it with hundreds of different chemical agents, applied electric currents to it, and inserted gold pins, tantalum wires, and mica plates into it. The electrical activity of the cortex has been recorded in dozens of different species, including man. Each of these experimental techniques has its limitations, and our present knowledge of the function of the cerebral cortex, slim though it is, is based on a variety of approaches. It is certain that many approaches, including some not yet developed, will be necessary to increase our understanding.

HOLISTIC APPROACHES TO CORTICAL FUNCTION

In the primate brain, as in most mammals, the cerebral cortex is not perfectly uniform in thickness, in type of cells in various layers, and in other features. Over the years, these irregularities have stimulated a variety of investigators to propose some scheme for numbering or otherwise distinguishing among the different *cytoarchitectural* areas. The most enduring of these proposals are the *cytoarchitectural maps* developed by Brodmann (1914) and by Von Bonin and Bailey (1947). Brodmann's system, which identifies about fifty different areas of the primate brain, is useful in providing a shorthand form of communication among brain scientists. It is simpler to say "area 18" rather than "that strip of cortex which forms an elongated crescent in a dorsal-ventral orientation, having its anterior border just posterior to the lunate sulcus." There is always a certain amount of ambiguity, of course, as to exactly where area 18 merges with area 19 (for example), but Brodmann's system has proved quite useful. He based his distinctions among the various areas on differences in the appearance of the cerebral tissue in microscopic sections. It was hoped that such structural differences might prove to correlate with particular physiological or psychological functions, but this hope has so far not been well realized.

If the cerebral cortex is heterogeneous tissue, both in structure and function, is it reasonable to discuss it in holistic terms, that is, to talk about the function of the cortex? Perhaps not; but this has not prevented several theorists from doing so.

PAVLOV'S "SWITCHYARD" CONCEPTION OF THE CEREBRAL CORTEX

Ivan Petrovich Pavlov (1849–1936) devoted much of his life trying to discover the physiological rules that govern cortical function. He believed that by using conditioning techniques he would be able to infer the principles by which the cortex was analyzing and responding to signals from the environment.

For Pavlov, the overwhelming importance of conditioning was that it might reveal the workings of the brain, particularly the cortex (Pavlov, 1927). The observable facts of behavior as were revealed to him in his experiments were important, but not nearly as important as the facts of brain physiology which he ardently believed would be revealed by the behavioral observations. It is somewhat ironic that it is Pavlov's behavioral observations, techniques, and insights which have proved to be most valuable to other scientists. His theories and speculations regarding the physiology of the cortex have, for the most part, been proved wrong, or otherwise inadequate, and are now largely ignored.

It is not easy to specify exactly what Pavlov did think about how the cortex functioned. His theoretical ideas changed over the years as he and a large number of coworkers gathered masses of new data. There was never a "final statement" of his theory. He was too careful and wise a scientist to assume that he had ever arrived at any final truth. However, there are certain themes in his writings, and these form a base for his theoretical views on a wide variety of topics, including sleep, hypnosis, psychopathology, and personality types in addition to learning.

One of Pavlov's basic ideas was that the cerebral cortex was the ultimate critical component of the nervous system for the elaboration of conditioned reflexes. Early experiments by Zeliony in Pavlov's laboratory had shown (it seemed) that destroying most of the cortical tissue of a dog rendered the animal incapable of being conditioned. Later experiments (Poltyrew & Zeliony, 1930; Girden et al., 1936; Bromiley, 1948) have qualified this conclusion. Decortication certainly makes conditioning more difficult and severely limits the sensory capacities of mammals, but decorticate animals can be conditioned; the cortex is not absolutely essential for the elaboration of some conditioned responses.

One of Pavlov's difficulties in theorizing about cortical function was that very little information was available concerning the nature of the communication among nerve cells. The concept of the synapse had been proposed by Charles Sherrington late in the nineteenth century, but very little reliable information on how neurons actually communicated with each other had been discovered during Pavlov's lifetime. (Otto Loewi had discovered a chemical substance he termed "Vagusstoff," which was secreted by the vagus nerve and inhibited the contraction of frog heart muscle in 1921. Loewi later correctly identified this substance as acetylcholine, but the implication of this discovery for synaptic transmission did not significantly affect Pavlov's writings.) In the absence of any detailed physiological information, Pavlov theorized about cortical function from inferences based on behavioral observations. From these observations, he postulated a number of different processes as occurring in the cortex which could account for the behavior he observed. Irradiation was one such postulated process. In Pavlov's view, irradiation was an excitatory process which spread from a particular locus in the cortex outward, like ripples in a lake. Cortical excitation produced by neural impulses triggered by the conditioned stimulus was postulated by Pavlov to irradiate from the site of initial reception across the cortex. Conditioning was postulated to occur as the result of an interaction between the wave of irradiation from the cortical reception site of the conditioned stimulus with a similar wave from the cortical reception site of the unconditioned stimulus, although the details of how this interaction might occur were never clearly specified. There were several major flaws to this notion. One flaw was that Pavlov never attempted to directly measure anything which could be identified as irradiation. He worked at a time when the techniques now available for measuring cortical electrical activity were virtually nonexistent. It was not until the last few years of Pavlov's life that electroencephalographic techniques were developed, although for many years it had been known that brain tissue did generate electric signals.

Pavlov viewed the cerebral cortex as a complicated neural switchyard in which incoming sensory signals were analyzed in a particular area and motor commands to the muscles were issued from another distinct area of the cortex. In most of his theorizing, the concept of the *reflex arc*, based on research on the spinal cord by Sherrington and others, was used extensively as a model for cortical function. Later experiments designed to test this switchyard theory of conditioning have demonstrated that at best Pavlov's theory was oversimplified. For example, it appears that horizontal, or transcortical, connections are not important for the retention of Pavlovian conditioning, since placing cuts in the cortex at right angles to the surface does not interfere with previously conditioned reflexes very much at all. In general, Pavlov's theories of cortical function have not survived, but the techniques of classical conditioning have had long-lasting effects on experimental psychology.

Distinctions among different areas of the cerebral cortex

The cerebral cortex of an advanced mammal is the most complex and highly evolved biological structure known. Therefore, it is not surprising that neither its structure nor function is well understood. We can, however, sketch in some guidelines which should prove useful. One such set of guidelines is provided by dividing the cortex into subregions which may have specialized functions. For example, it is possible to identify sensory cortical regions from motor cortical regions on the basis of certain anatomical and physiological criteria. The distinctions are not perfect, and may or may not coincide with other criteria, but they furnish a way to begin to understand cortical function.

There are several major methods by which brain scientists have analyzed brain function; these include neuroanatomical procedures, electrophysiological recording techniques, electric- and chemical-stimulation techniques, and ablation of brain tissue combined with behavioral observations.

NEUROANATOMICAL METHODS

In determining the pattern of retrograde degeneration, the cortical tissue is stripped off by suction or some equivalent technique and the animal is allowed to recover from the operation for a sufficient period of time. After the appropriate number of days or weeks, the brain tissue is sliced, stained with tissue stain, and examined. Removal of cortical tissue, if it cuts all of the major axon branches, results in the retrograde degeneration of the cell bodies that give rise to those axons. The staining shows the degenerated cell bodies, and thus it becomes possible to trace quite accurately the pattern of these neuronal connections coming into the cortex. The thalamus is the main source of these connections, but not the only one. Enough of this research has now been accomplished to allow quite reliable maps of *thalamocortical projections* to be drawn for several different species.

Importance of the thalamus to cortical function

The thalamus must be considered together with the cerebral cortex for a more accurate perspective. The dorsal thalamus (which in most mammals constitutes the vast majority of the entire thalamus) and the neocortex have evolved together, and together form functional systems. The interdependence of these two regions of the mammalian brain is seen across several different mammalian species, allowing us to generalize somewhat regarding the mammalian plan of thalamocortical connections. There will certainly be exceptions to the basic plan; the spiny anteater (*Echidna*) has already been found to differ rather markedly from it, but the great majority of mammals seem to have evolved similar thalamocortical systems.

We can consider the thalamocortical systems as belonging to one of two basic divisions: *specific* or *generalized*. These two divisions can be defined both in terms of their neuroanatomical connections and their (proposed) functional differences. The specific thalamocortical systems are concerned primarily with a single sensory modality such as vision, audition, or somesthesis, or with the control of motor output. The generalized thalamocortical systems, on the other hand, are not exclusively concerned with a single sensory modality or with just motor output (Mountcastle, 1968). The monkey brain will serve as our example of these distinctions.

SPECIFIC THALAMOCORTICAL SYSTEM

The dorsal thalamic nuclei which are included in the specific thalamocortical system are listed in Table 1. The various nuclei are grouped according to their proposed functional role. Three different categories are used: specific sensory analysis and relay nuclei, nuclei associated with the production of motor commands, and nuclei whose function is as yet unclear. The last category will remain unsatisfactorily vague until we know considerably more about the neural events that underlie the brain activities involved in thinking, speaking, and emotional feeling.

Specific sensory analysis and relay nuclei These nuclei contain neurons whose axons typically ascend to the neocortex without synapse. There the axons divide and ramify to synapse with dozens or hundreds of cortical neurons. This ramification of the specific sensory thalamic axons occurs primarily in the fourth (and lower portion of the third) cortical

Table 1 *Thalamic nuclei belonging to specific thalamocortical system*

I Specific sensory analysis and relay nuclei
  Lateral geniculate nucleus (vision—projects to occipital lobe)
  Medial geniculate nucleus (audition—projects to temporal lobe)
  Ventral posterior nucleus (actually a collection of nuclei);
    somesthesis—projects to parietal lobes
II Nuclei associated with motor output
  Ventral anterior nucleus (projects to motor cortex)
  Ventral lateral nucleus (projects to motor cortex)
III Function unclear
  Anterior nuclei (project to cingulate cortex)
    N. anteromedialis
    N. anteroventralis
    N. anterodorsalis
  Pulvinar nucleus (projects to portions of temporal, occipital, and parietal
    lobes)
  Lateral posterior nucleus (projects to posterior portion of parietal lobes)
  Dorsal medial nucleus (projects to prefrontal area of frontal lobes)

layer. The area of the cortex to which the specific nuclei project are limited and the boundaries are rather precise. The axons of neurons in the lateral geniculate nucleus belong to this category, sending their axons in the optic radiations to synapse with neurons in the primary visual cortex. In a parallel fashion, the axons of neurons in the medial geniculate nucleus send their axons to synapse with cortical neurons in the superior gyrus and medial aspect of the temporal lobe. These cortical regions constitute the primary auditory cortex. Finally, the neurons of the ventral posterior nucleus synapse with cortical neurons in the primary somesthetic areas of the parietal and frontal lobes. The ventral posterior nucleus is actually composed of a cluster of smaller nuclei concerned with sensory messages of touch, pressure, vibration, kinesthesis, and taste.

The olfactory system in mammals is unique among the senses. It has no connections in the dorsal thalamus. Axons from olfactory neurons in relay nuclei along the base of the brain project to cortical reception areas according to a more ancient anatomical plan.

The specific thalamocortical nuclei all share certain characteristics. All have evolved comparatively recently. The axons of their cells project without synapse to rather precise, circumscribed cortical areas. These axons are of large diameter and are heavily myelinated; both factors contribute to the fast conduction velocities characteristic of these neurons. Each nucleus is concerned primarily with a specific sensory modality: vision or audition or somesthesis. [With regard to somesthesis, you may question whether it is accurate to describe somesthesis as a single sense inasmuch as this term actually includes at least four recognizably different sensations—touch-pressure, warmth, cold, and kinesthesis (the appreciation of the position and movement of the joints). However, because these senses tend to contribute jointly to our sensations of body feelings, it has seemed reasonable to physiologists and psychologists to consider them as a single integrated sensory modality.]

The specific thalamocortical systems constitute the neural networks by which information regarding the location, intensity, and specific nature of environmental events is appreciated by the brain. Clearly, normal behavior is critically dependent upon the proper functioning of these systems. Yet, although these systems are necessary for the brain to appreciate the world, they are not sufficient. In order for normal perception to occur, the generalized thalamocortical system must also be working properly. Before we consider the generalized system, however, let us complete our survey of the specific systems.

Nuclei associated with motor output   The two nuclei associated with the motor commands going out to skeletal muscles are the ventral anterior nucleus and the ventral lateral nucleus. These nuclei relay impulses from the cerebellum and basal ganglia to the motor cortex, an area of cortex located immediately anterior to the central sulcus (see Figure 24, Chapter 3).

Nuclei with unclear function   There are a number of nuclei tentatively categorized as specific whose anatomical connections are known in general but for which no clear function can be assigned.

The group of anterior nuclei receive synaptic input from two major sources outside the thalamus: the mammillary bodies of the hypothalamus and the hippocampus. The anterior nuclei project to the *cingulate area,* a strip of cortex on the medial surface of each hemisphere, just dorsal to the corpus callosum.

The *pulvinar* nucleus is present only in the brains of higher mammals, reaching its greatest size in the primate thalamus. It can be divided into clusters of smaller nuclei. It appears probable that the pulvinar receives input from the optic tract and the lateral geniculate nucleus and is therefore likely to be concerned with vision in some way. The pulvinar projects to a rather large region of the cortex, particularly the occipital lobe, immediately adjacent to the primary visual cortex (Brodmann areas 18 and 19). It also projects to portions of the temporal and parietal lobes. The *lateral posterior* nucleus projects to the posterior portion of the parietal lobe in the monkey brain.

The *dorsal medial* nucleus projects to the most anterior portion of the primate brain in the frontal lobe. It is the area of the brain (Brodmann areas 8, 9, and 10 in monkey, and simply area 10 in man) that is typically meant by "prefrontal cortex." This cortical region has been the subject of hundreds of experiments and theories concerning its possible role in thinking, feeling, and displaying emotion. It is the axons of this nucleus which are severed in the psychosurgical technique known as frontal lobotomy.

THE GENERALIZED THALAMOCORTICAL SYSTEM

Table 2 lists the major anatomical subdivisions of the generalized thalamocortical system. Our present knowledge is insufficient to make any convincing functional distinctions among these various nuclei. Taken together they help to perform a function of supreme importance: the regulation of the overall level of excitability of the brain and, as a direct result, the regulation of the level of consciousness of the individual. Without the proper functioning of the generalized thalamocortical system, behavior comes to a halt. Even if the specific sensory systems are operative, conveying nerve impulses from the sense organ to the cortex, there is no perception of, no response about, and no memory of the event by the animal unless the generalized thalamocortical system is also simultaneously active.

Table 2. *Thalamic nuclei belonging to generalized thalamacortical system*

I. Medially located nuclei
    N. reuniens
    Massa intermedia
    N. paratenialis

II. Intralaminar nuclei
    N. centrum medianum
    N. centralis medialis
    N. paracentralis
    N. centralis lateralis
    N. pararascicularis
    N. suprageniculatus
    N. limitans

The neural input into the generalized thalamocortical system comes from both the cerebral cortex and from the *brainstem reticular formation.* The axons of the neurons in these thalamic nuclei project to widespread areas of the forebrain, including not only the cerebral cortex but also the basal ganglia. In the cortex, end feet from both specific sensory neurons and from generalized thalamocortical neurons converge onto single neurons. In some cases, specific sensory neurons from a particular modality (e.g., vision) may converge with the generalized neuron's end- ings on a single cortical neuron. In other cases, axons from more than one specific sensory system, along with axons of the generalized system, may converge onto single cortical neurons. The cortical neurons that receive afferent impulses from two or more different specific sensory systems are termed *polysensory* neurons and are found in various areas throughout the brain, including the cerebral cortex.

We will have more to say about the brainstem reticular formation when we discuss sleep and other varieties of consciousness (Chapter 10). For the present, we will stress only the importance of the generalized thalamocortical system in the maintenance of consciousness so that the signals coming into the cerebral cortex via the specific thalamocortical system neurons and from other regions of the cortex can be processed so that we can react in an adaptive fashion to our environment.

SUGGESTIONS FOR FURTHER READING

Darley, F. L. (Ed.) *Brain mechanisms underlying speech and language.* New York: Grune & Stratton, 1967.

Magoun, H. W. *The waking brain.* (2nd ed.) Springfield, Ill.: Charles C Thomas, 1963.

Sholl, D. A. *The organization of the cerebral cortex.* London: Methuen, 1956.

Sperry, R. W. Hemisphere deconnection and unity in conscious awareness. *American Psychologist,* 1968, **23,** 723–733.

Chapter 9

THE CONTROL OF MOVEMENT AND POSTURE

Behavior is movement. Aphasia is a dramatic example of how helpless thought can appear when it cannot grasp the levers of language. Like most other animals, we depend on our ability to move in order to survive. We express our thoughts and our feelings with gestures as well as words; it is possible to gain insight into a person's state of mind from his posture as well as from his speech.

A large portion of our central nervous system is devoted to the initiation and control of movements and postural adjustments. Many of these adjustments occur automatically, that is, without our thinking about them. This is possible because we have neuronal reflex systems which do not require us to make second-to-second decisions. Other movements are more obviously the result of our will: we desire to move and do so. A detailed consideration of how the brain and spinal cord cooperate to produce flight or fight, the outstretched hand, or the upraised fist entails scientific problems of both complexity and subtlety. In this chapter we will try to identify some principles of the control of movements.

THE PRINCIPLE OF THE FINAL COMMON PATH

The mammalian brain is constructed to allow many different neurons to converge on the neurons which finally go to the muscles of the body. Several million neurons may participate in a relatively simple movement such as scratching one's ear. But only a small number of muscles would be necessary to scratch the itch. Somewhere in the chain of command, the influence of large numbers of neurons must be funneled down and summated by a much smaller number of neurons, those which go to the muscles directly involved in the movement. The last neurons in this process are the motor neurons of the ventral horn of the spinal cord. The axons of these ventral horn neurons emerge from the spinal cord and form neuromuscular junctions (*synapses*) with individual muscle cells. These few thousand ventral horn cells are the last pathway for movement commands from the central nervous system to the muscles. They are therefore called the *final common path* for the execution of movements. The degree of convergence of axons from other parts of the nervous system onto these ventral horn neurons is considerable. There are, on the average, 5,500 synapses on each ventral horn neuron in the human spinal cord, and some neurons may have as many as 10,000 synapses. The neural influences which impinge on these cells in the final common path come from a variety of sources, both peripheral and central.

The frequency of nerve impulses in the axon of a ventral horn cell determines the degree of contraction of the muscle cells which it supplies. There is also a feedback situation such that the frequency of firing is determined partially by the degree of contraction of the muscle it supplies and the contraction of related muscle groups. It is important to realize that even without any commands from the brain itself, the organization of the spinal cord neurons and their connections with the muscular system can reflexively produce a variety of movements and postural adjustments. These *spinal reflexes* have been studied for almost a century. Additional information has been obtained from the study of human accident victims with spinal-cord damage. Our fundamental base of information concerning the nature of the local control exerted by the spinal cord is the monumental research program of Sir Charles Sherrington and his coworkers at Oxford University, England. Although many additional details and a few corrections have been added, Sherrington's research still is the outstanding source in this area (Sherrington, 1906).

One of Sherrington's discoveries was that if the spinal cord of an experimental animal is surgically severed, muscles below the level of the cut can still respond to stimulation, via their connections with the isolated section of spinal cord to which they are still connected. If an experimental animal is prepared so that a particular muscle is cut off from all other sources of neural influences except that coming from the ventral horn cell, the result is referred to as a *nerve-muscle preparation*. If the muscle part of such a preparation is stretched slightly, the muscle responds with a rapid contraction. This is the *stretch reflex*. In the nerve-muscle preparation, the stretch reflex is abolished by cutting the axon of the motor neuron, which proves that the reflex is a true neuron-produced reflex and not simply due to the elastic propeties of the muscle. The stretch reflex can be observed in all mammalian muscles, although only those which oppose the force of gravity (called *antigravity muscles*) remain contracted for the duration of the time the muscle is stretched. The stretch reflex of a nerve-muscle preparation is the simplest element of movement which can be demonstrated in a mammal. If the fragment of nervous tissue under study is enlarged somewhat, another important functional principle can be appreciated: the integration of excitation and inhibition.

A fundamental operating principle of all nervous systems is that the two basic neural processes of excitation and inhibition must be correctly integrated to produce normal behavior. Some observations in "spinal animals" (experimental preparations in which the spinal cord is severed) illustrate this principle at the reflex level. In a spinal animal in which all of the connections between the muscles and the spinal cord are left intact, a stretch applied to a muscle will evoke a reflex contraction of that muscle. This is the stretch reflex, described above. In addition, there is a reciprocal inhibition, measured by a lessening of the degree of contraction, of muscles which are opposed in their function to the muscle which was stretched. Muscles that are opposed in function (that is, flex the leg as opposed to extending it, for example) are termed *antagonists.* The decreased contraction of antagonists as a result of stretching a muscle is called *reciprocal inhibition.* The spinal cord is organized in such a way that when one muscle is stretched, producing a reflex contraction, those muscles which if contracted would work against the resulting movement are inhibited. Reciprocal inhibition of antagonistic muscle groups is essential in allowing an animal to perform movements which require simultaneous or near-simultaneous contraction of some muscles with the relaxation of other muscles. Let us consider walking as an example. There must be a smooth coordination among those muscles which must be contracted to raise the foot from the ground and those which must relax.

There is a third reflex response to the stretching of a muscle. In addition to the reflex contraction of the muscle stretched and the reciprocal inhibition of antagonistic muscles, there is a reflex excitation of muscles that are functionally coupled so as to work together with the stretched muscle. These cooperating muscles are called *synergistic* muscles. Thus, a single stimulus—a stretch of a muscle—elicits three more or less simultaneous reflexes in the spinal cord: reflex excitation (contraction) of the muscle stretched, excitation of muscles synergistic to the stretched muscle, and a reciprocal inhibition of antagonistic muscles.

Let us consider the nature of the sensory signals that underlie these various built-in reflex movements. For the signals of muscle stretch, there are small, elongated sense organs, named *muscle-spindle organs* (because of their shape) embedded in the muscles of the body. These are stretch receptors, sensitive to the *length* of the muscle. They are excited as the muscle in which they are located is stretched. The axons from the receptor cells in the spindle organ leave the muscle and enter the spinal cord by way of the dorsal root. Once within the spinal cord, the axon branches into a number of collaterals. Some of these collaterals make local synapses at the same level of the spinal cord at which they entered. These local connections include ones made to the motor neurons that supply the muscle containing the spindle organ and its synergists. These are the synaptic connections which form the basis of the classic reflex arc. If there is only one set of synapses involved, such a reflex arc is called *monosynaptic* (one synapse). Figure 58 illustrates in a simplified form the basic elements in a monosynaptic reflex. The knee-jerk reflex is a monosynaptic reflex that is usually elicited by tapping on the patellar (kneecap) tendon. The critical stimulus, however, is actually the slight stretch that the tap causes to the muscle attached to the patellar tendon. The stretch to the muscle elongates it, activating the receptors in the muscle-spindle organ and thus delivering nerve impulses into the spinal cord. The response, or stretch reflex, is a contraction of the stretched muscle and its synergists, which causes the leg to jerk upward slightly. Since there is only one set of synapses to cross, this particular stretch reflex is very rapid.

In addition to the local synaptic contacts at the level of entry, all the sensory axons which enter the spinal cord send some collaterals up to synapse at higher levels of the spinal cord or in the brain. If these long, ascending axon collaterals are cut, the animal can still display some spinal reflexes if the portion of the spinal cord below the cut is undamaged. There is a recovery period necessary for the lower spinal

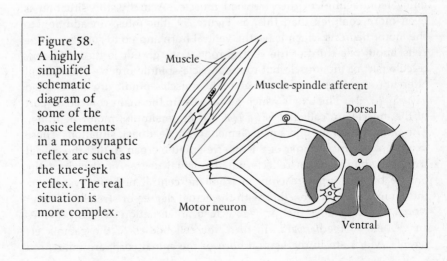

Figure 58. A highly simplified schematic diagram of some of the basic elements in a monosynaptic reflex arc such as the knee-jerk reflex. The real situation is more complex.

Muscle

Muscle-spindle afferent

Dorsal

Motor neuron

Ventral

reflexes to return after the severing of the cord. The exact length of this recovery period depends on such factors as the species, nature of the injury, and quality of the postoperative care. The depressed activity in the spinal cord below the cut during this recovery period is called *spinal shock*. As a general rule, the more advanced the mammal, the more disruptive a spinal section is and the longer the period of spinal shock. A dog or cat may show a return of spinal reflexes within hours after its spinal cord is severed; a monkey may take many days and a man weeks or months (Mountcastle, 1968).

Still other axons from the muscle-spindle organs synapse in the cord with neurons which form a link between the stimulus and response neurons. These linking neurons, termed *internuncial neurons,* are important points of integration in the operation of spinal cord reflexes. In a stretch reflex, for example, there is an inhibitory internuncial neuron in between the incoming axon from the muscle spindle and the motor neurons which supply the antagonistic muscles. There are many more internuncial neurons in the mammalian spinal cord than there are motor neurons or sensory axons. (The cell bodies of the sensory neurons lie outside the spinal cord in the dorsal root.) The ratio of internuncials to motor neurons varies from species to species and from one part of the spinal cord to another, but internuncials are everywhere the most common element. In the lumbar region of the dog's spinal cord, for example, the ratio is approximately 30:1. As a rule, even a simple spinal reflex will involve thousands of neurons from the three different functional classes: sensory, internuncial, and motor.

The stretch reflex operates as a negative-feedback device. As the length of the muscle is increased, the muscle-spindle organ is excited and sends impulses into the spinal cord which result in the reflex shortening (contracting) of the stretched muscle. Actually, the situation is even more complex than this, as Figure 59 illustrates. In addition to the motor neurons which leave the ventral horn and go to supply muscle cells, about one-third of the ventral root axons go not to the main contractile part of the muscle but to the muscle-spindle organ. These small efferent (outgoing) axons which go to the muscle-spindle organ are called *gamma efferents.* The axons which go to activate the main contractile part of the muscle are called *alpha efferents* (or more simply, motor neurons). The gamma efferents add a new element to the feedback situation. These axons provide for a *biasing* of the muscle-spindle organ so that the output from the spindle organ reflects not the actual degree of stretch of the muscle but the input reaching it from the central nervous system via the gamma efferents together with the actual degree of stretch. In other words, not only does this provide a feed*back* situation, it also provides an element of feed*forward*. In turn, the cell bodies of the gamma efferents, which are in the ventral horn of the spinal cord, are influenced

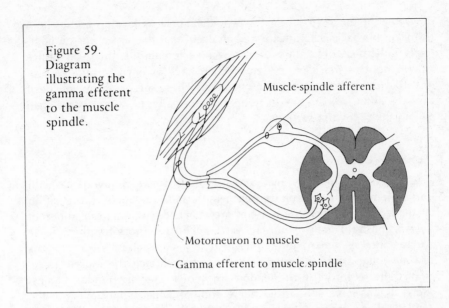

Figure 59. Diagram illustrating the gamma efferent to the muscle spindle.

Muscle-spindle afferent

Motorneuron to muscle

Gamma efferent to muscle spindle

by many neurons originating in the brain itself. The feedforward possibilities contributed by the gamma efferents mean that the brain can *anticipate* possible adjustments in the length of the muscle and thereby bias the spindle organ via the gamma efferents. Commands issued to the muscles from the brain can take advantage of this system to override the signals due to the *actual* length of the muscle and alter the feedback from the muscle-spindle organ to the alpha motor neurons.

SPINAL REFLEXES: SILENT SLAVES

We are not aware of sensory input from our muscles. This may seem surprising at first, but it is true; it relieves us from an enormous amount of decision making. The spinal reflexes we have discussed constitute an extremely efficient and automatic set of *servomechanisms*. The prefix "servo" (from the Latin word *servus* for "slave") indicates that these reflexes follow commands. The general commands are issued from the brain, but the spinal servomechanisms carry out these commands without intruding on our awareness. For example, if there is a general "standing order" to maintain a certain degree of contraction in the muscles of the legs so we do not fall down, a sudden unexpected weight on our backs does not (usually) cause us to fall down, although there must be a rapid change in the degree of muscle contraction to adjust to the new load. P. A. Merton (1972) cites the example of the movie horse which does not sag at the knees when Douglas Fairbanks jumps on it as another example of the silent efficiency of the servomechanisms operative at the cord level. (In fact, the horse collapsing as the hero leaps on his back is so unexpected an event that the concept is immediately ludicrous.) The input from the muscle spindles thus constitutes silent input to the slave systems which have evolved to take care of much of the basic routines of movement. These servomechanisms need to have input from the brain to operate normally, however, as we shall see in the following sections.

TENSION CONTROL

The description of the spinal cord servomechanisms above deals with the system which controls muscle length and, of course, the position of the bones to which the muscles are attached. A somewhat different system exists to control muscle *tension*. The receptors for the *muscle tension control* system are located in the tendons of each muscle. Tendons are the tough, fibrous material that serves to attach the muscle to its joint. The receptors in the tendon are known as Golgi tendon organs. Golgi organs have specialized nerve endings which spray out into the tendon. Their axons enter the spinal cord through the dorsal root and branch several times before making synaptic contacts with other neurons. The function of Golgi tendon organs can be clearly seen in spastic patients. In an extended spastic limb (rigid because of the overcontraction of muscles, in this example dominated by overcontracted extensors), if the limb is forcibly flexed by someone else, there is at first a resistance to further contraction of the flexors, followed by a sudden relaxation, or "melting," of the intense spastic contraction. This is the *lengthening reaction*, and is due to the overriding of the stretch reflex mechanism by an inhibition exerted on the motor neurons supplying the stretched muscle. The Golgi tendon organs are activated under extreme degrees of muscle stretch. When they are activated, they in turn excite *inhibitory internuncial* neurons in the spinal cord. These inhibitory internuncials produce ipsps on the motor neurons supplying the stretched muscle, decreasing the firing rate of these neurons and thus decreasing the degree of contraction of the stretched muscle. The Golgi tendon organ provides the signals for a reflex input-overload system, which automatically prevents overly intense and potentially damaging degrees of muscle stretch.

OTHER SOURCES OF PERIPHERAL INPUT

Scattered throughout the skin and subcutaneous tissue are sensory receptors of different types. The cell bodies of these receptors are clustered together outside the spinal column in a long chain called the dorsal root ganglia. The axons enter the spinal cord through the dorsal root.

There may be as many as 12,000 sensory axons in a single dorsal root ganglion. Since there are 31 pairs of dorsal roots, the total number of sensory axons in a large mammal such as man is 750,000 to 1,000,000. Stimulation of these receptors is capable of exerting some reflex effects even in the spinal animal. There is a wide variety of these skin reflexes, all of which involve internuncial neurons. The *withdrawal reflex* to painful stimulation is a good example of how the spinal reflexes help to provide immediate responses to potentially harmful stimulation. A withdrawal reflex occurs when one has stepped on a tack or touched a hot object. Such reflexes are subject to modification (both inhibitory and facilitatory) via impulses coming to the motor neurons of the spinal cord from higher levels in the brain. For example, if you were to touch a hot cup of tea on a table, the most likely response would be to withdraw your hand quickly. However, if the same cup (heirloom bone china) were passed to you by your great-aunt Sarah, the chances are very good indeed that you would hang onto the cup long enough to set it down somewhere without breaking it, even if it meant burning your fingers. In such a case, your brain has overridden the withdrawal reflex to the advantage of the cup and your family relations but to the disadvantage of your fingers. In a spinal preparation, reflexes are much less flexible. But as a general rule, in the normal animal, any reflex circuit which contains internuncial neurons (as most do) can be influenced by neuronal impulses descending from neurons located higher up in the brain. Reflexes are not invariant but subject to a great variety of influences, both peripheral and central.

HIGHER MOTOR REGIONS IN THE BRAIN

Although much of the brain is concerned with the regulation of movement, the participation of certain brain regions in movement regulation is somewhat better understood than is that of other regions. There are four such regions which deserve special consideration here: the brainstem motor area, the cerebellum, the basal ganglia, and the sensorimotor areas of the cerebral cortex.

Brainstem motor area

Cutting the spinal cord in mammals causes the immediate loss of all voluntary movement and sensation of the limbs below the cut and a loss of reflex response from the isolated lower portion of the spinal cord for the duration of the spinal shock period. Quite different results are obtained if the brain is transected at a somewhat higher level. If a cut is made such that a part of the brainstem known as the *medulla oblongata* is still attached to the spinal cord, the result is termed a *decere-*

brate preparation. The outstanding characteristic of such a preparation is that in place of the abolition of reflexes as seen in spinal shock, there is an *enhancement* of reflexes involving extensor muscles. The result is that the animal's neck, limbs, and tail are rigidly and tonically extended, and the spine is arched. Flexor reflexes are hard to elicit. This phenomenon, in which the entire system of muscles which normally oppose the force of gravity is thrown into tonic hyperactivity, is called *decerebrate rigidity*. It was described by Sherrington in 1898. This overreactivity of the antigravity extensor reflexes is virtually the mirror image of the collapse of these reflexes in the spinal animal. The most obvious explanation is that some important control element is present in the portion of the medulla oblongata that remains attached to the spinal cord. The concept that it is really some antigravity mechanism in the brainstem which has been allowed to dominate the posture of the decerebrate animal is supported by the fact that the sloth (which normally lives in trees and hangs upside down) develops a marked flexor rigidity when it is decerebrated (Mountcastle, 1968).

In addition to the tonic rigidity, decerebrate preparations also display a more varied repertory of reflexes than do spinal animals. In fact (not surprisingly) the higher up in the brain the transection is made, the more variable and complex the behavioral capability left to the animal. The decerebrate animal is capable of displaying some quite complex reflexes which underlie the act of walking. These reflexes involve the whole body and place the animal into appropriate postures for walking. However, such animals cannot walk spontaneously, nor fully right themselves or sit or stand unaided.

The phenomenon of decerebrate rigidity has posed questions regarding brain control of movement from the time of Sherrington to the present. Decerebrate rigidity is manifested by the exaggerated dominance of stretch reflexes in extensor, antigravity muscles; this reflects an imbalance from the normal reflex situation. It is now clear from a variety of experiments that part of this imbalance is due to a release of a *tonic inhibition* of extensor stretch reflexes which comes from parts of the brain anterior to the medulla oblongata. Some of these inhibitory regions of the forebrain can be tentatively identified as being in the frontal lobe and in a group of forebrain structures known collectively as the basal ganglia. The rest of the imbalance can be attributed to the continuing influence of facilitatory input coming from the portion of the medulla oblongata still attached to the spinal cord. There seem to be two different groups of facilitatory neurons in the brainstem. One group lies along the middle portion for quite a distance. The other set is clustered together in a group known as the *vestibular nuclei*, so named because much of the input into these nuclei comes from the vestibular system. The vestibular nerve is made up of axons from the *labyrinth organ* in the inner ear. The labyrinth contains the receptors which provide the animal with the sensory input critical for balance and equilibrium. As you can imagine, such input is of supreme importance to the production of reflexes involved in maintaining normal posture with respect to gravity. The axons from the vestibular nuclei descend to synapse on neurons in the spinal cord principally by way of two tracts: the vestibulospinal tract and the medial longitudinal fasciculus. Destruction of these vestibular nuclei eliminates decerebrate rigidity by removing most of the facilitation exerted on the extensor stretch reflexes. The brainstem also contains neurons which have an inhibitory effect on spinal extensor stretch reflexes. The existence of neurons exerting both excitatory and inhibitory effects on the neurons involved in reflexes illustrates an important functional principle: normal movement is always the result of the integration of excitatory and inhibitory influences.

The cerebellum

In humans, the cerebellum is tucked up under the posterior end of the cerebral hemispheres and attached to the dorsal part of the brainstem. It is extremely highly organized in its internal structure. The cerebellum has been studied rather extensively, and a substantial catalog of facts exists regarding its neuroanatomy and electrophysiological responses (Eccles, Ito, & Szentagothai, 1967; Llinas, 1970). Also, the various disturbances in postural adjustments and movement caused by damage or disease to the cerebellum have been studied in many species, including man.

The cerebellum receives constant sensory information regarding the state of action of all parts of the body. The information enters the cerebellum from hundreds of thousands of sensory receptors in the skin, joints, tendons, and muscles. It is integrated together with sensory input from the vestibular sense organs and from the eyes and ears. Thus, much like the cerebral cortex, the cerebellum receives a great inflow of sensory information concerning the position of the body as well as environmental events. Yet there is a fundamental difference between the effect of sensory input into the cerebral cortex and that into the cerebellum. Simply, we are never aware of the sensory input into the cerebellum: it does not enter consciousness and does not evoke sensations. The sensory input into the cerebellum is used to constantly regulate posture and movement, but it is used without our awareness. Individuals who have suffered damage to the cerebellum such that they are severely handicapped in producing coordinated movements do not experience any sensory abnormalities. Although they may stumble and stagger, they are not dizzy. Whatever the essential neural requirements for the production of consciousness, the cerebellum apparently does not have them. It is interesting, however, and perhaps relevant to discussions of "computer minds" that the cerebellum is a truly elegant neural machine, constantly supplied with a rich, detailed account of various sensory events, performing its computations and sending out commands, yet it seems totally devoid of mind, that is, of conscious awareness.

Nor is the cerebellum disconnected from the cerebral hemispheres, with which we do associate consciousness. It projects to the cerebral cortex via the thalamus and also receives input from the cortex, particularly the sensorimotor regions. This cortical input, coupled with other input from other higher brain motor regions, may allow the cerebellum not only to gain access to information regarding the *result* of motor commands sent out by higher brain regions (via feedback from receptors in the muscles, tendons, etc.) but also to be informed of the intentions of these commands. Any contribution of the cerebellum to the smoothness and coordination of movement could then operate in part *before* the commands were actually executed. Such a correction system would be much more valuable to skilled movements than a system based strictly on feedback. This would be particularly important in the coordination of extremely rapid movements (writing, bowing a violin, playing fast runs on a piano) where there is simply not enough time to correct errors in movement on a feedback basis alone. It is not yet certain that the cerebellum actually operates on the basis of advanced information about motor commands not yet executed, but such a possibility is presently under serious consideration (Llinas, 1970).

The participation, if any, of the cerebellum in higher brain activities such as learning and perception is obscure. Perhaps because it does not seem to participate in consciousness, it has been largely ignored by experimenters in such considerations. Lashley performed a relevant experiment. Recognizing the importance of the cerebellum in proprioception, Lashley investigated the effects of severe cerebellar damage on the retention of a complex maze. Rats rely rather heavily on proprioceptive cues to navigate such mazes. Lashley's experiment demonstrated that the cerebellum does not contribute to the rat's memory of the maze although it does help coordinate the rat's motor capacities. The following is his report of the results on the rat with the largest cerebellar lesion.

Number 4. Adult Female. The performance in initial learning was: Time, 2,388 seconds; Errors, 33; Trials, 35. Preliminary retention tests gave errors in only first two trials: Time, 229 seconds; Errors, 7; Trials, 12. After operation there was extreme contraction of the left hind leg and extension of the right. In walking there was rotation to the left and frequent backward somersaulting. When picked up the animal clutched wildly at anything within reach and gave indications of vertigo. For the first four days she was force-fed, then began to eat spontaneously but showed little improvement in motor symptoms. Thirty days after operation the motor symptoms were still pronounced. She walked as if drawing a heavy weight, with fore and hind legs extended forward and dragging her along in a series of lunges. At this time she was tested in the maze and made a perfect retention record: Time, 801 seconds; Errors, 0; Trials, 10. (Lashley and McCarthy, 1926.)

Lashley's results do not prove that the cerebellum does not normally participate in the learning of various motor skills, only that rat maze learning can survive massive cerebellar damage. More recently, a theory of cerebellar function in the learning of motor skills has been proposed (Marr, 1969). As yet, however, it awaits experimental proof.

A last point about the cerebellum: it is not necessary for the initiation of movement. No paralysis results from cerebellar damage, although the individual's coordination is invariably disturbed. The cerebellum appears to regulate and coordinate movements. It may also play a role in initiation even though it is not absolutely necessary.

The comet, the globe, and the peachstone

The *basal ganglia* are a group of closely related nuclei in the forebrain of mammals. (See Figure 26, Chapter 3.) They are a part of the *telencephalon*, which is more recently evolved than the hypothalamus and thalamus. Since the basal ganglia probably evolved before cerebral cortex, the basal ganglia are among the oldest of the forebrain structures. The basal ganglia in most mammals include at least three major components: the *caudate* (comet) nucleus, the *globus pallidus* (pale globe), and the *putamen* (peachstone). The globus pallidus appears as if it might serve important neural switching functions in this system, receiving input from the caudate nucleus and putamen, and sending axons to a variety of lower brain regions. In man, there are connections from the sensorimotor regions of the cortex and from the diffuse thalamic reticular formation to the basal ganglia. These anatomical connections almost certainly indicate that the functions of the basal ganglia are bound to those of the thalamocortical systems. The nature of this interaction is not clear.

Numerous experimenters have investigated the effects of electric stimulation and/or ablation of the basal ganglia. The results are quite varied. Electric stimulation of various basal ganglia can both facilitate and inhibit movements. It does not seem to be critical whether the movements themselves are naturally elicited (that is, reflexively) or produced by stimulation of sensorimotor cortex. Although many such stimulation experiments have been performed, it is still not possible to discern any obvious functional principles to account for all the data.

Much the same can be said regarding the effects of ablation of basal ganglia structures. One curious phenomenon, called *obstinate progression,* was discovered over a century ago. As the name indicates, the phenomenon is characterized by walking movements which persist even when the animal's head is in a corner and the movements don't take the animal anywhere. This has been observed by several investigators, particularly in cats with large bilateral lesions of the caudate nucleus (Mettler & Mettler, 1942). Other investigators have observed that lesions in the region of the caudate nucleus decrease the ability of both cats and rats to perform normally in a *passive avoidance* situation. In this task, successful avoidance of an electric shock is dependent upon the animal's inhibiting an approach response to a previously friendly but now treacherous (electrically activated) water spout (Fox, Kimble, & Lickey, 1964; Kirkby & Kimble, 1968).

There are at least two recognized disease states associated with abnormalities of the basal ganglia. Both involve pathologies of movement control, but the two diseases differ in the specific nature of the problem. *Parkinson's disease* is characterized by spasticity involving *both* extensor and flexor muscle groups (unlike the spasticity of the decerebrate animal, which involves only the extensor groups). In Parkinson's disease, there is also a marked tremor or shaking of the limbs when the patient is not attempting some movement. This is called a *resting tremor* and is often less marked or absent during voluntary movement.

A second group of diseases, exemplified by Huntington's chorea, is characterized by the appearance of involuntary movements. These can be either quick, jerky movements such as the sudden flailing of an arm or slow, twisting, wormlike movements. This latter condition is called *athetosis.* In these diseases, there is typically no clouding of the consciousness or any other intellectual impairment. The disturbance seems to be in the motor output. However, any conclusions regarding the functions of the basal ganglia must be very tentative. Moreover, the anatomical connections of the basal ganglia with both the thalamus and cerebral cortex have persuaded some investigators that it may not be correct to view the basal ganglia as a separable functional unit.

Motor functions of the cerebral cortex

The neocortex, along with associated thalamic nuclei, is the most recently evolved brain structure. Perhaps for this reason, it is often assumed to control other lower brain structures. Questions concerning what structure controls what in a complex feedback- and feedforward-rich redundantly organized organ such as the mammalian brain may be the wrong approach. Theoretical accounts of brain function based on the principle of hierarchical command systems may be accurate to a first approximation in some nervous system functions but not necessarily the case in general. At the present, we can do little more than identify the most likely areas of the cerebral cortex which are involved in the production of movement and posture.

In man, the main motor area of the cortex, more precisely called the *sensorimotor* cortex, surrounds the central sulcus of each hemisphere, extending down the lateral surface for a considerable distance but restricted to a narrow strip of tissue on either side of the central sulcus (see Figure 60). Electric stimulation of this region of the cortex reliably causes simple movements. Damage to this region causes disturbances in movements, particularly in the performance of precise movements of the fingers. However, even total ablation of this region does not cause a permanent paralysis.

What starts a movement?

What triggers movements? When a cat grooms its fur, or a bird preens its feathers, is the complex pattern of movements which constitute the act of grooming or preening triggered by some peripheral stimulus from the skin; or do these acts start in the brain without any peripheral

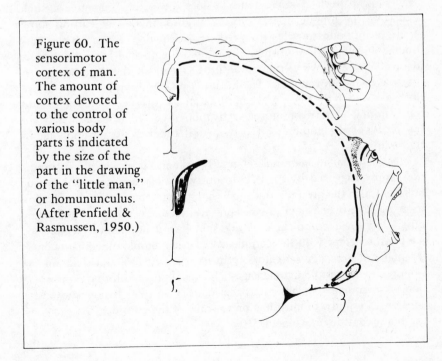

Figure 60. The sensorimotor cortex of man. The amount of cortex devoted to the control of various body parts is indicated by the size of the part in the drawing of the "little man," or homununculus. (After Penfield & Rasmussen, 1950.)

stimulation; or is some combined action of factors responsible? One behavior which has been studied in this regard is birdsong. In some birds, there appears to be a built-in program for song. Both the domestic chicken and the ringdove develop their normal species characteristic clucks and coos (respectively) even if they are deafened immediately after hatching. Thus, even though these birds never hear any birdsong from any species, their central brain program for their species' call develops normally. This is not true for all birds. The white-crowned sparrows, for example, do not develop normal sparrow songs if deafened shortly after birth or raised in isolation so that they hear only their own chirping. This particular species must hear adult sparrow song in order to produce it. Once the bird has developed adult song, deafening is without serious effect on song production (Konishi, 1965). Human beings, of course, are dependent upon hearing both to develop and to maintain normal speech.

There are other behaviors which, although requiring some trigger stimulus, are run off rather automatically once they occur. There are numerous examples of this, such as feeding and escape movements, among invertebrates. Relatively few such automatic, stereotyped behaviors have been carefully studied in mammals. One behavior which has been studied in considerable detail in mammals is swallowing (Doty, 1951; Doty & Bosma, 1956). These workers tried to disrupt the normal swallowing pattern of movements in dogs by various maneuvers, such as placing the tongue in traction or by anesthetizing or cutting some of the twenty-odd muscles involved in swallowing. Although the manipulations must have substantially altered the normal feedback signals involved in swallowing, there was little change in the organization of the swallowing movements. The most reasonable interpretation of these findings is that the temporal coordination of the nerve impulses and the resulting pattern of muscle activation involved in swallowing are the result of the running off of a neural program for swallowing in the brain.

Most behavior in mammals is greatly influenced by peripheral input, not simply triggered by it. We do not walk just because the soles of our feet touch the ground. But the varying input conveyed to our brains from walking over rough gravel is critical to our walking without tripping. The great complexity of the spinal cord and motor regions of the brain together with the complexity of even simple movements have thus far prevented investigators from having a final circuit diagram for even relatively simple manuevers such as walking. Additional information is, of course, available; and the material in this chapter should be considered as only an introduction to some of the considerations of how the brain controls movements.

SUGGESTIONS FOR FURTHER READING

Keele, S. W. *Attention and human performance.* Pacific Palisades, Calif.: Goodyear, 1972.

Merton, P. A. How we control the contraction of our muscles. *Scientific American,* 1972, **226**, 30–37.

Chapter 10

SLEEP, DREAMING, AND ALTERED STATES OF CONSCIOUSNESS

Our normal waking consciousness is but one special type of consciousness, whilst all about it, parted from it by the filmiest of screens, there lie potential forms of consciousness entirely different. No account of the universe in its totality can be final which leaves these other forms of consciousness quite disregarded. They may determine attitudes though they cannot furnish formulas, and open a region though they fail to give a map. (James, 1904.)

So wrote Williams James, the greatest American mind yet to consider psychological phenomena. In this particular case, James was reflecting on altered states of consciousness after having been exposed to nitrous oxide (laughing gas), but his interest in the different states of consciousness was widely based, and included religious ecstasy and hypnosis as well as drug states. Although he wrote in the late nineteenth and early twentieth century, James's views sound very modern. He worked at a time when very little actual experimentation was conducted on these various states of consciousness. James had to base his ideas largely on his own observations and general knowledge, not on laboratory reports.

There is no official catalog of various states of consciousness. There appear to be as many distinctions among functional states of awareness as there are individuals willing to write about them. Ludwig (1966) lists several dozen different altered states of consciousness which can be induced in ways ranging from being caught up in a mob to kayak disease (brought about by long days alone in a kayak). In a similar fashion, the list of chemical substances which can produce altered states of consciousness is virtually endless: anesthetics such as ether, chloroform, nitrous oxide, and halothane; sedatives, hallucinogens (i.e., LSD), and so on through model airplane glue.

Despite the obvious fact that waking is just one of the functional states in which the human brain can exist, until recently American psychologists have largely ignored other states of consciousness. Within the past few years, however, there has been an increase in the interest and investigation of altered states of consciousness.

SLEEP AND DREAMING

The most commonly recognized state of consciousness other than normal waking is, of course, sleeping. We spend much of our life sleeping, as do most mammals. Sleep has been a topic of considerable interest for hundreds of years, and theories and ideas concerning what sleep is, how it is brought about, and what dreams mean have probably always been woven into the fabric of man's musing about himself. But, surprisingly, it is only within the past few years that serious attempts to understand the biological aspects of sleep have been undertaken.

The development of the electroencephalograph (EEG) was critical to the progress of research on sleep and dreaming. Hans Berger (1873–1941), a German psychiatrist, was the first person to record the EEG of man. Berger made his first recordings in 1924 but did not publish his results until 1929. His discoveries opened the way for an immense output of research. Thousands of subsequent research projects have confirmed, amplified, and extended his findings, providing us with a great deal of information about the electrical activity of the human brain.

One of the earliest discoveries made was that the electrical pattern of the brain is different when the individual is asleep from what it is when the individual is awake. Figure 61 shows the characteristic rhythms which would be recorded during waking and sleeping. There is not much difference among most mammalian species in these general characteristics. Two aspects of electrical activity in particular serve to differentiate different brain states: the *frequency* of the brain waves and their *amplitude.* The frequency of brain waves as recorded from the scalp of man varies from less than 1 per second to more than 50 per second. The amplitude of the brain waves is typically about 50 to 100 microvolts, but can sometimes be as large as 200 microvolts. These are still very small potentials, of course, and considerable electronic amplification is necessary to make them readable.

In an awake, alert human, the EEG is characterized by relatively fast (15 to 45 per second) waves of small amplitude (50 to 100 microvolts).

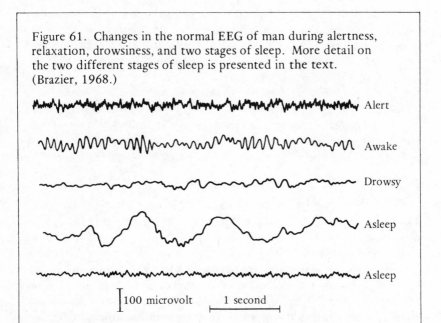

Figure 61. Changes in the normal EEG of man during alertness, relaxation, drowsiness, and two stages of sleep. More detail on the two different stages of sleep is presented in the text. (Brazier, 1968.)

Alert

Awake

Drowsy

Asleep

Asleep

100 microvolt   1 second

The EEG in this state is often described as desynchronized because the record is irregular, arhythmic. In individuals who are awake but not consciously attending to events in the environment around them, there is a characteristic EEG rhythm known as *alpha*. Alpha rhythm is, in man, about 8 to 13 waves per second, and is observed in relaxed but awake brains. It is typically a rather regular synchronized pattern. This synchronized alpha rhythm is desynchronized by attention-getting stimuli or mental activity.

It has been known since Berger's time that the EEG of a sleeping individual is characterized by slower, more highly synchronized brain waves of relatively high amplitude. The species of the sleeper, as long as it is a mammal, doesn't seem to matter very much. The brain-wave record of a sleeping cat and of a sleeping man are very similar. What brain mechanisms account for sleep? The answer is not completely known, but some clues do exist.

Located along the middle of the brainstem is a small cylinder of brain tissue about as big as your little finger. It lies just posterior to the hypothalamus and ends just before the spinal cord begins. It is known as the *brainstem reticular formation* (abbreviated BRF). The BRF receives its input from all of the major sensory systems, either via axon collaterals (audition) or separate neurons (somesthesis). Both single modality and polysensory neurons are present in the BRF. This area of the brain also receives neural input from many other parts of the brain, particularly the hypothalamus, cerebellum, and sensorimotor cortex.

Axons of the BRF project both upstream to the thalamus and other areas, and downstream to the lower brainstem and spinal cord. It is the ascending connections which are of particular importance to the present discussion. Some of these axons apparently go all the way to the cerebral cortex before synapsing. Others project to the nuclei of the generalized thalamocortical system. Still other axons go to the hypothalamus, septal nuclei, and hippocampus. The BRF can be considered as a recipient of sensory input from *all* sensory modalities. It sends axons to widespread areas of the forebrain. The BRF is a complex network, and entire volumes have been devoted to discussing its possible functions (e.g., Jasper et al., 1958). Let us review briefly some experiments which have suggested the importance of the BRF and generalized thalamocortical system for consciousness.

In 1949, Giuseppi Moruzzi and Horace Magoun published a now-famous experiment in a new journal, *Electroencephalography and Clinical Neurophysiology* (mercifully, it is now more typically called simply the EEG journal). It was this experiment which set off a really remarkable surge of interest in the possible brain mechanisms underlying such phenomena as consciousness, sleep, and attention.

When Moruzzi and Magoun performed these experiments, it had been known from Hans Berger's initial discoveries on human brain waves (Berger, 1929) that when a person went from an awake but relaxed, or nonattentive, mental state to an alert, attentive state, the transition in mental attitude could usually be reflected in changes in the electroencephalogram as recorded from the person's scalp. Basically, the 10 to 12 cycles per second frequency, high amplitude, more regular appearing rhythm of the relaxed wakeful state (see Figure 61) called the *alpha rhythm* is abruptly changed to an activated EEG record. This alerted record is characterized by faster frequency (20 to 30 cycles per second), lower amplitude, and less regular, or desynchronized, brain waves. This electrical response of the brain to an alerting signal has been observed in many different mammals, including man. It is generally termed the *alpha block response*. Moruzzi and Magoun's basic discovery was that the alpha block response could be produced by direct electric stimulation of the brainstem reticular formation and portions of the generalized thalamocortical system.

The experiments were performed with cats anesthetized with a nonbarbiturate drug—chloralosane. The type of anesthetic used in experiments of this type is critical. If barbiturates (which are not accurately described as anesthetics but more correctly as general depressants) are used to immobilize the animal, the brainstem reticular formation is itself the main site of action for the barbiturate, and therefore too depressed to allow for its easy electrical activation.

It may not seem overly surprising that one can alert an animal by passing electric current into its brain. But as a matter of fact, stimulation at many points in the brain, with the voltage (1 to 3 volts) and frequencies (50 to 300 pulses per second) used by Moruzzi and Magoun has no effect on the ongoing electrical activity of the cortex. Electric stimulation of the brain is *not* necessarily arousing or painful.

What about electric stimulation of the specific system? Shouldn't this also produce the alerting response? The answer is that it does, but that much higher voltages are necessary to do so than is the case when the stimulating electrode is in the BRF. Moreover, the integrity of the specific sensory tracts is not needed in order to produce the alerting response by BRF stimulation. Such alerting responses can still be produced even when the specific sensory tracts are cut.

The main significance of these discoveries is that the EEG alerting response produced by the BRF stimulation appears to be identical to that seen in the normal, unanesthetized human EEG when an alerting stimulus is presented. The BRF response was not due to inadvertent stimulation of the specific sensory tracts. Moruzzi and Magoun's findings seemed to clear up a related physiological paradox. It had been known for some time that in animals under deep barbiturate depression, it was still quite possible to electrically stimulate the specific sensory tracts in the brain and produce clear and reliable *evoked responses* (complex electrical potentials triggered by the stimulation) in the relevant cortical projection area. In fact, these evoked responses during barbiturate depression were actually much more reliable, consistent, and unvarying from trial to trial than was the case when animals were either unanesthetized or sedated with a nonbarbiturate. The meaning of these open lines to the cortex in a preparation obviously unresponsive to sensory input was now made clear. *It is the activity in the BRF and generalized thalamocortical systems which provides the necessary cortical arousal so that the brain can respond to the information coming to it over the specific thalamocortical system.* Soon after Moruzzi and Magoun's breakthrough, other evidence was accumulated to bolster the concept that there are (at least) two basic components in the mammalian brain related to the processing of environmental input: the specific sensory informational systems (such as the visual system, somesthetic system) and the interlocked but experimentally separable arousal, or alerting, system represented by the BRF and generalized thalamocortical system. The details of the interaction of these systems are not yet completely worked out, but Moruzzi and Magoun's basic observations opened another window on our view of how the brain produces consciousness (Magoun, 1963). In more recent years, it has been suggested that the BRF and generalized thalamocortical systems participate in such different phenomena as sleep, hypnosis, infantile autism, and other states of altered awareness or abnormal responsivity to environmental stimulation.

PARADOXICAL SLEEP AND THE RAPID EYE MOVEMENTS OF DREAMS

More recently, it has been discovered that there are at least three distinct states of consciousness which can be distinguished by their EEG pattern. These three states are wakefulness and two stages of sleep, light sleep and *paradoxical sleep*. Paradoxical sleep, which makes up about 20 percent of the total sleeping time in adult humans, is characterized by a fast, irregular, low-amplitude EEG record, virtually indistinguishable from the pattern seen during normal wakefulness. The animal or person, however, is asleep. Several other indicators serve to distinguish the stage of paradoxical sleep from wakefulness. The muscles of the body become much more relaxed during paradoxical sleep as compared with light sleep. There is a sudden increase in large, rapid eye movements. This aspect of paradoxical sleep is so characteristic and so easily noted that paradoxical sleep is often referred to asrapid eye movement sleep, or simply *REM sleep*. Other indicators, such as the breathing pattern and recordings from depth electrodes in subcortical regions of the brain (in experimental animals), also serve to point up the differences between light sleep and paradoxical, or REM, sleep. Figure 62 illustrates the measurable differences in wakefulness, light sleep, and paradoxical sleep.

What is the significance of paradoxical sleep? One answer is that periods of paradoxical sleep seem to be highly correlated with reports of dreaming episodes by human subjects (Aserinsky & Kleitman, 1953; Dement & Kleitman, 1957). If sleeping human subjects are awakened during periods of light sleep, they report that they had been dreaming. Repeated studies have established the reliability of this relationship between dream reports and paradoxical sleep (Dement, 1965). In animals such as cats and dogs who cannot, of course, give us verbal dream reports, paradoxical sleep periods are also marked by greatly increased frequency of twitching movements of the limbs and whiskers, whines, and fast and irregular breathing. This is probably as far as we can go at present in giving a positive answer to the age-old question, "Do animals dream?"

The discovery that sleep is not a unitary phenomenon has prompted numerous experiments aimed at discovering the brain mechanisms which might underlie the two stages of sleep. One of the leading researchers in this area is Michel Jouvet at the University of Lyons in France (Jouvet,

Figure 62. Some of the characteristic rhythms associated with deep sleep in a cat (group of traces at right) are so much like those of wakefulness (left group) and so different from those of light sleep (middle group) that Jouvet has applied the term paradoxical to deep sleep. Normal cats spend about two-thirds of their time sleeping. They usually begin each sleep period with 25 minutes of light sleep, followed by 6 or 7 minutes of parodoxical sleep. In the latter state they are hard to wake and their muscles are relaxed. (Jouvet, 1967.)

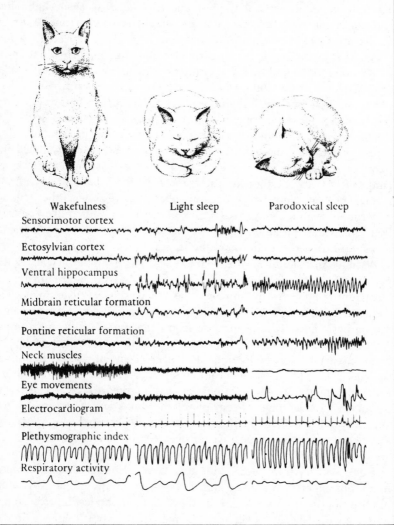

| Wakefulness | Light sleep | Parodoxical sleep |

Sensorimotor cortex

Ectosylvian cortex

Ventral hippocampus

Midbrain reticular formation

Pontine reticular formation

Neck muscles

Eye movements

Electrocardiogram

Plethysmographic index

Respiratory activity

1967). Jouvet has interpreted his own and other's research and concluded that it is possible to identify two systems controlling sleep in the brain of the cat. One of these systems is called the *raphe* (from the Greek word meaning "seam") *system*, a group of brain nuclei located along the midline of the brainstem. The anterior end of this system is just posterior to the hypothalamus and it extends for several millimeters in a caudal direction. The neurons in the raphe system apparently use serotonin as their transmitter substance. On the basis of a variety of physiological experiments, Jouvet has proposed that the state of wakefulness is changed into one of light sleep by the inhibitory action of serotonin on other regions of the brain, particularly the brainstem reticular formation. The activity of the raphe system blocks the fast activity characteristic of the cortex in the waking state, and also blocks most rapid eye movements, presumably by inhibiting the arousal effects mediated by the brainstem reticular formation.

Another system, identified with an area in the pons known as the *locus coeruleus*, appears to be responsible for replacing light sleep with the activated EEG and rapid eye movements of paradoxical sleep. The neurons of the locus coeruleus probably use norepinephrine as their transmitter substance. Paradoxical sleep is, in terms of muscle tone and difficulty of waking, a deeper level of sleep than is light sleep, and it always follows light sleep. Animals do not go from wakefulness directly into paradoxical sleep. The fact that an activated EEG and rapid eye movements characterize this deeper stage of sleep is the reason, of course, that it is termed paradoxical. At present, there is no crucial information about how the raphe system changes wakefulness to sleep, or how the neurons of the locus coeruleus change light sleep into paradoxical sleep. It is quite likely that both systems exert their effects by inhibiting the cortical activation produced by the brainstem reticular formation, but even this point awaits further experimental validation.

Why paradoxical sleep?

Although there are occasional reports of human beings who apparently need very little sleep, most of us sleep roughly one-third of our lives. The biological advantage to sleeping is not entirely obvious, but without sufficient sleep time, health is generally impaired. But why should paradoxical sleep, and the related episodes of dreaming in humans, have evolved? Jouvet (1967) discusses this question and points out that the evidence gathered so far indicates that only mammals spend any appreciable time in paradoxical sleep. In addition, Jouvet found that hunting species, such as man, cats, and dogs, spend more time in paradoxical sleep (about 20 percent) than do the hunted species such as rabbits (5 to 10 percent). The interpretation of this difference is obscure, but one might speculate that the hunting species have been better able to afford the luxury of deep, or paradoxical, sleep. For the hunted species, deep sleep makes them more vulnerable to possible attack. Another rather curious result has been found by depriving both human subjects and cats of paradoxical sleep. William C. Dement (Dement, 1960; Dement & Fisher, 1963) managed to deprive human subjects of paradoxical sleep (but not total sleep time) by waking them whenever they began to show the rapid eye movements and fast brain activity of paradoxical sleep. The subjects were kept awake for a few minutes and then allowed to go back to sleep. This procedure was followed for two to five consecutive nights. As a control procedure, subjects also went through a series of nights in which they were awakened at the same intervals as during paradoxical sleep deprivation but only when they were in light sleep. There were several effects of deprivation of paradoxical sleep, while no significant effects were noted simply as a result of waking the subjects during light sleep. The subjects who were deprived of paradoxical sleep showed progressively more periods of paradoxical sleep on consecutive nights during the experiment. Moreover, on the "recovery" nights immediately following the experimental awakenings, the subjects showed a great increase in such periods, often to more than 50 percent of the pre-experiment baseline. Dement interpreted these results as being due to the interruption of dreaming, which almost invariably accompanies the periods of paradoxical sleep. If this dream deprivation does result in a period of catching up in dream time, then it is possible that dreaming plays some important role for humans. Similar experiments with cats have also shown that paradoxical sleep deprivation leads to a rebound catching-up period in which they too show increased incidence of paradoxical sleep.

BETTER CONSCIOUSNESS THROUGH CHEMISTRY?

Drugs provide an almost endless variety of means to alter our state of consciousness from the ordinary waking state. This change may be relatively mild and short lasting, as with small doses of marihuana, or intense and long lasting, as has been reported for other drugs. The field of psychopharmacology is developing rapidly, and new psychologically active drugs are being produced all the time. As yet, however, very little reliable information is available to indicate how these drugs work on the brain to produce their alterations in consciousness. One generalization is possible, however: It appears that many drugs which alter consciousness interfere with normal synaptic transmission in the brain.

One of the most commonly known and used consciousness-altering drugs is lysergic acid diethylamide (LSD).

In the afternoon of 16 April, 1943, when I was working on this problem, I was seized by a peculiar sensation of vertigo and restlesssness. Objects, as well as the shape of my associates in the laboratory, appeared to undergo optical changes. I was unable to concentrate on my work. In a dream-like state I left for home where an irresistible urge to lie down overcame me. I drew the curtains and immediately fell into a peculiar state similar to a drunkenness, characterized by an exaggerated imagination. With my eyes closed, fantastic pictures of extraordinary plasticity and intensive color seemed to surge towards me. After two hours this state gradually wore off (Hofmann, cited in Goodman and Gilman, 1970).

Thus were the potent effects of LSD discovered. Hofmann, a chemist, had been working with this new compound and had accidentally ingested a minute amount. Suspecting that his bizarre experience had been the result of the accidental taking of the new drug, Hofmann purposefully took a second dose of 0.25 milligram and experienced an even more spectacular trip. We now know that 0.25 milligram is a very large dose of this drug. Descriptions of the psychological effects of LSD are to be found in a variety of sources (see, for example, Ray, 1972).

The exact effect of LSD on the brain has so far eluded investigators. There are some reasons to believe that LSD interferes with the transmission of synapses where *serotonin* is suspected to be the natural transmitter agent. Whether this is true or not remains to be seen. It does seem to be true that drugs which increase serotonin levels in the brain (such as some of the tranquilizers) decrease the psychological effects of LSD. It is also known that LSD interacts with serotonin and related compounds outside the body.

One of the characteristic effects of LSD is its distorting effects on sensory input. Objects appear to change size, their colors are often reported to be more vivid or "emotional," etc. Why should this be true? One possible answer is that LSD seems to lower the threshold for the activation of the brainstem reticular formation by sensory input. How this is accomplished is not known, but it is possible that as the activation of the BRF is abnormally increased, the subjective response to sensory input is also altered. In any event, as we learn more about the normal physiology of synaptic transmission and about the functions of the brainstem reticular formation, we will also gain more insight into how chemicals such as LSD alter normal experience.

Drugs which are known to alter consciousness are also very likely to alter the function of neurons in the brainstem reticular formation. This is not surprising, of course, since we have already discussed the importance of the BRF for the maintenance of a normal level of consciousness. It is very probable that most consciousness-altering substances have other effects in the brain as well, in addition to their alteration of BRF activity. In no case, however, is the complete pharmacological activity of a consciousness-altering drug known. Psychopharmacology is definitely a frontier field.

MEDITATION

There is also a growing awareness and interest by American psychologists in the alteration of consciousness by nondrug means. Specifically, the behavior of Zen meditators and transcendental meditators have attracted considerable attention. A doctoral dissertation by Robert Wallace (1970) proposes that transcendental meditation as practiced by experienced individuals constitutes a fourth major state of consciousness (the other three being waking, light sleep, and paradoxical, or REM, sleep). There is no question that meditation of various sorts produces demonstrable changes in such autonomic nervous system functions as oxygen consumption, heart rate, and blood pressure. Moreover, there is a shift in the EEG record of both Zen masters and experienced transcendental meditators toward an increased amount of time during which alpha is the predominant electrical rhythm. Alpha is closely correlated with states of relaxed wakefulness, and none of these bodily changes are totally unexpected. The overall constellation of autonomic and EEG effects observed during meditation are different from those observed in sleep or normal waking, and thus serve as the basis of Wallace's proposal for meditation as a fourth major state of consciousness. The brain changes which underlie the physiological effects of meditation remain obscure. Wallace offers some speculation that the hypothalamus and brainstem reticular formation are particularly involved in the production of the meditative state, but at the present time we must look to the future for more information on this interesting subject.

SUGGESTIONS FOR FURTHER READING

Jouvet, M. The states of sleep. *Scientific American*, 1967, **216**,62–72.

References

Alpern, M., Lawrence, M., & Wolsk, D. *Sensory processes*. Belmont, Calif: Brooks/Cole, 1967.

Altman, J. Postnatal growth and differentiation of the mammalian brain, with implications for a morphological theory of memory. In G. C. Quarton, T. Melnechuk, & F. O. Schmitt (Eds.) *The neurosciences: a study program.* New York: Rockefeller University Press, 1967. Pp. 723-743.

Anand, B. K., & Brobeck, J. R. Hypothalamic control of food intake in rats and cats. *Yale Journal of Biology and Medicine*, 1951, **24**, 123.

Andersson, B. The effects of injections of hypertonic NaCl-solutions into different parts of the hypothalamus of goats. *Acta Physiologica Scandinavica*, 1953, **28**, 188-201.

Andersson, B., & McCann, S. M. Drinking, antidiuresis and milk ejection from electrical stimulation within the hypothalamus of the goat.. *Acta Physiologica Scandinavica*, 1955, **35**, 191-201.

Aschoff, J. Circadian rhythms in man. *Science*, 1965, **148**, 1427-1432.

Aserinsky, E., & Kleitman, N. Regularly occurring periods of eye motility, and concomitant phenomena during sleep. *Science*, 1953, **118**, 273-274.

Bardwick, J. *The psychology of women.* New York: Harper & Row, 1971.

Barr, M. L. The significance of the sex chromatin. *International Review of Cytology*, 1966, **19**, 35-95.

Beach, G., Emmens, M., Kimble, D. P., & Lickey, M. Autoradiographic demonstration of biochemical changes in the limbic system during avoidance training. *Proceedings of the National Academy of Sciences*, 1969, **62**, 692-696.

Békésy, G. Von. Similarities of inhibition in the different sense organs. *American Psychologist*, 1969, **24**, 707-719.

Bellows, R. T. Time factors in water drinking in dogs. *American Journal of Physiology*, 1939, **125**, 87-97.

Berger, H. Über das elektrenkephalogramm des menschen. *Archiv Psychiatria Nervenkrankheiten*, 1929, **87**, 527-570.

Blackstad, T. W. Cortical grey matter—a correlation of light and electron microscopic data. In H. Hyden (Ed.), *The neuron.* Amsterdam: Elsevier, 1967. Pp. 49-118.

Blass, E. M., & Epstein, A. N. A lateral preoptic osmosensitive zone for thirst in the rat. *Journal of Comparative and Physiological Psychology*, 1971, **76**, 378-394.

Bloom, W., & Fawcett, D. W. *A textbook of histology.* (9th ed.) Philadelphia: Saunders, 1968.

Bonin, G. Von, & Bailey, P. *The neocortex of macaca mulatta.* Urbana: University of Illinois Press, 1947.

Brain, R. *Speech disorders.* London: Butterworth, 1961.

Brazier, M. A. B. The electrical activity of the nervous system. London: Pitman, 1968.

Brobeck, J. R. Food intake as a mechanism of temperature regulation. *Yale Journal of Biology and Medicine*, 1948, **20**, 545-552.

Broderick, C. B., & Bernard, J. (Eds.) *The individual, sex, and society.* Baltimore: Johns Hopkins, 1969.

Brodmann, K. Physiologie des Gehirns. In *Die Allgemeine Chirurgie der Gehirnkrankheiten, Neue Deutsche Chirurgie.* Vol. 11. Stuttgart: Enke, 1914.

Bromiley, R. B. Conditioned response in a dog after removal of neocortex. *Journal of Comparative and Physiological Psychology*, 1948, **41**, 102-110.

Caggiula, A. R., & Hoebel, B. G. "Copulation-reward site" in the posterior hypothalamus. *Science*, 1966, **153**, 1284-1285.

Cannon, W. B. *Bodily changes in pain, hunger, fear and rage: An account of recent researches into the function of emotional excitement.* (2d ed.) New York: Appleton-Century-Crofts, 1929.

Crosby, E. C., Humphrey, T., & Lauer, E. W. *Correlative anatomy of the nervous system.* New York: Macmillan, 1962.

Darley, F. L. (Ed.) *Brain mechanisms underlying speech and language.* New York: Grune & Stratton, 1967.

Delgado, J. M. R. *Physical control of the mind.* New York: Harper & Row, 1969.

Dement, W. C. The effect of dream deprivation. *Science,* 1960, **131,** 1705–1707.

Dement, W. C. An essay on dreams: The role of physiology in understanding their nature. In *New Directions in Psychology II.* New York: Holt, 1965. Pp. 135–257.

Dement, W. C., & Fisher, C. Experimental interference with the sleep cycle. *Canadian Psychiatric Association Journal,* 1963, **8,** 400–405.

Dement, W., & Kleitman, N. Incidence of eye motility during sleep in relation to varying EEG pattern. *Federation Proceedings,* 1955, **14,** 216.

Deutsch, J. A. Appetitive motivation. In J. L. McGaugh (Ed.), *Psychobiology.* New York: Academic, 1971. Pp. 99–128.

De Valois, R. L. Neural processing of visual information. In R. W. Russell (Ed.), *Frontiers in physiological psychology.* New York: Academic, 1966.

Diamond, M. (Ed.) *Perspectives in reproduction and sexual behavior.* Bloomington, Ind.: Indiana University Press, 1968.

DiCara, L. V. Learning in the autonomic nervous system. *Scientific American,* 1970, **222,** 30–39.

DiCara, L. V., & Miller, N. E. Changes in heart rate instrumentally learned by curarized rats as avoidance responses. *Journal of Comparative and Physiological Psychology,* 1968, **65,** 8–12.

Doty, R. W. Influence of stimulus pattern on reflex deglutition. *American Journal of Physiology,* 1951, **166,** 142–158.

Doty, R. W., & Bosma, J. F. An electromyographic analysis of reflex deglutition. *Journal of Neurophysiology,* 1956, **19,** 44–60.

Douglas, R. J. The hippocampus and behavior. *Psychological Bulletin,* 1967, 67, 416–442.

Dowling, J. E., & Boycott, B. B. Organization of the primate retina: Electron microscopy. *Proceedings of the Royal Society, Series B,* 1966, **166,** 80–111.

Eccles, J. C. *The physiology of synapses.* New York: Academic, 1964.

Eccles, J. C., Ito, M., & Szentagothai, J. *The cerebellum as a neuronal machine.* New York: Springer-Verlag, 1967.

Epstein, A. N. The lateral hypothalamic syndrome: Its implications for the physiological psychology of hunger and thirst. In E. Stellar & J. M. Sprague (Eds.), *Progress in physiological psychology.* Vol. 4. New York: Academic, 1971. Pp. 263–317.

Finley, C. B. Equivalent losses in accuracy of response after central and after peripheral sense deprivation. *Journal of Comparative Neurology,* 1941, **74,** 203–237.

Fitzsimons, J. T. The physiology of thirst: a review of the extraneural aspects of the mechanisms of drinking. In E. Stellar & J. M. Sprague (Eds.), *Progress in physiological psychology.* Vol. 4. New York: Academic, 1971. Pp. 119–201.

Fitzsimons, J. T., & Simons, B. J. The effect on drinking in the rat of intravenous infusion of angiotensin, given alone or in combination with other stimuli of thirst. *Journal of Physiology (London)*, 1969, **203**, 45–57.

Flock, A. Transduction in single hair cells in the lateral line organ. In L. M. Beidler & W. E. Reichardt (Eds.), Sensory transduction, *Neurosciences Research Program Bulletin*, 1970, **8**, 492–496.

Fox, S. S., Kimble, D. P., & Lickey, M. Comparison of caudate nucleus and septal-area lesions on two types of avoidance behavior. *Journal of Comparative and Physiological Psychology*, 1964, **58**, 380–386.

Gaito, J., & Bonnet, K. Quantitative versus qualitative RNA and protein changes in the brain during behavior. *Psychological Bulletin*, 1971, **75**, 109–127.

Gardner, E. *Fundamentals of neurology*. (5th ed.) Philadelphia: Saunders, 1968.

Gaze, R. M. *The formation of nerve connections*. New York: Academic, 1970.

Gazzaniga, M. S. The split brain in man. *Scientific American*, 1967, **217**, 24–29.

Geschwind, N. The organization of language and the brain. *Science*, 1970, **170**, 940–944.

Geschwind, N., & Levitsky, W. Human brain: Left-right asymmetries in temporal speech region. *Science*, 1968, **161**, 186–187.

Girden, E., Mettler, F. A., Finch, G., & Culler, E. Conditioned responses in a decorticate dog to acoustic, thermal, and tactile stimulation. *Journal of Comparative Psychology*, 1936, **21**, 367–385.

Globus, A., & Scheibel, A. B. The effect of visual deprivation on cortical neurons: A Golgi study. *Experimental Neurology*, 1967, **19**, 331–345.

Goodman, L. S., & Gilman, A. (Eds.) *The pharmacological basis of therapeutics*. (4th ed.) New York: Macmillan, 1970.

Goy, R. W. Experimental control of psychosexuality. *Philosophical Transactions of the Royal Society, London, Series B.*, 1970, **259**, 149–162.

Gregory, R. L. *Eye and brain: The psychology of seeing*. New York: McGraw-Hill, 1966.

Gross, C. G., Rocha-Miranda, C. E., & Bender, D. B. Visual properties of neurons in inferotemporal cortex of the Macaque. *Journal of Neurophysiology*, 1972, **35**, 96–111.

Grossman, S. P. *A textbook of physiological psychology*. New York: Wiley, 1967.

Groves, P. M., & Thompson, R. F. Habituation: A dual-process theory. *Psychological Review*, 1970, **77**, 419–450.

Hampson, J. L. Determinants of psychosexual orientation. In F. A. Beach (Ed.), *Sex and behavior*. New York: Wiley, 1965. Pp. 108–132.

Hanby, J. The sociosexual nature of mounting and related behavior in a confined troop of Japanese Macaques (*Macaca fuscata*). Unpublished doctoral dissertation, University of Oregon, 1972.

Harlow, H. F. *Learning to love*. San Francisco: Albion, 1971.

Harris, G. W. *Neural control of the pituitary gland*. London: E. Arnold, 1955.

Harris, G. W., & Jacobsohn, D. Functional grafts of the anterior pituitary gland. *Proceedings of the Royal Society, London, Series B*, 1952, **139**, 263–276.

Hervey, G. R. The effects of lesions in the hypothalamus in parabiotic rats. *Journal of Physiology*, 1959, **145**, 336–352.

Hetherington, A. W., & Ranson, S. W. The spontaneous activity and food intake of rats with hypothalamic lesions. *American Journal of Physiology*, 1942, **136**, 609–617.

Hirano, A., & Dembitzer, H. M. A structural analysis of the myelin sheath in the central nervous system. *Journal of Cellular Biology*, 1967, **34**, 553–567.

Hodgkin, A. L. *The conduction of the nervous impulse.* Liverpool: Liverpool University Press, 1964.

Hodgkin, A. L., & Huxley, A. F. A quantitative description of membrane current and its application to conduction and excitation in nerve. *Journal of Physiology*, 1952, **117**, 500–544.

Horridge, G. A. Learning of leg position by the ventral nerve cord in headless insects. *Proceedings of the Royal Society, London, Series B*, 1962, **157**, 33–52.

Hubel, D. H. Effects of distortion of sensory input on the visual system of kittens. *The Physiologist*, 1967, **10**, 17–45.

Hubel, D. H., & Wiesel, T. N. Receptive fields and functional architecture in two nonstriate visual areas (18 and 19) of the cat. *Journal of Neurophysiology*, 1965, **28**, 229–289.

Hubel, D. H., & Wiesel, T. N. Receptive fields and functional architecture of monkey striate cortex. *Journal of Physiology*, 1968, **195**, 215–243.

Hydén, H., & Lange, P. W. S100 brain protein: Correlation with behavior. *Proceedings of the National Academy of Sciences*, 1970, **67**, 1959–1966.

Isaacson, R. L., & Kimble, D. P. Lesions of the limbic system: Their effects upon hypotheses and frustration. *Behavioral Biology*, 1972, **7**, 767–793.

Jacobs, M. S., Morgane, P. J., & McFarland, W. L. The anatomy of the brain of the bottlenose dolphin (*Tursiops truncatus*), rhinic lobe (Rhinencephalon) I. The Paleocortex. *Journal of Comparative Neurology, London*, 1971, **141**, 205–272.

Jacobson, M. Development, specification and diversification of neuronal connections. In F. O. Schmitt (Ed.), *The neurosciences: Second study program.* New York: Rockefeller University Press, 1970. Pp. 116–129.

James, W. The varieties of religious experience. London: Longmans, 1904.

Jarrard, L. E., & Lewis, T. C. Effects of hippocampal ablation and intertrial interval on acquisition and extinction in a complex maze. *American Journal of Psychology*, 1967, **80**, 66–72.

Jasper, H. H., Proctor, L. D., Knighton, R. S., Noshay, W. C., & Costello, R. T. (Eds.), *Reticular formation of the brain.* Boston: Little, Brown, 1958.

Jouvet, M. The states of sleep. *Scientific American*, 1967, **216**, 62–72.

Kaada, B. R., Rasmussen, E. W., & Kviem, O. Effects of hippocampal lesions on maze learning and retention in rats. *Experimental Neurology*, 1961, **3**, 333–355.

Katz, B. *Nerve, muscle and synapse.* New York: McGraw-Hill, 1966.

Keele, S. W. *Attention and human performance.* Pacific Palisades, Calif.: Goodyear, 1972.

Kimble, D. P. (Ed.) *The anatomy of memory.* Palo Alto, Calif.: Science and Behavior Books, 1965.

Kimble, D. P. (Ed.) *The organization of recall.* New York: New York Academy of Sciences, 1967.

Kimble, D. P. Hippocampus and internal inhibition. *Psychological Bulletin*, 1968, **70**, 285–295.

Kimura, D. Right temporal-lobe damage. *Archives of Neurology*, 1963, **8**, 264–271.

Kirkby, R. J., & Kimble, D. P. Avoidance and escape behavior following striatal lesions in the rat. *Experimental Neurology*, 1968, **20**, 215–227.

Kistner, R. W. The pill. New York: Dell, 1968.

Kleitman, N. Sleep, wakefulness and consciousness. *Psychological Bulletin*, 1957, **54**, 353–359.

Klüver, H., & Bucy, P. C. "Psychic blindness" and other symptoms following bilateral temporal lobectomy in Rhesus monkeys. *American Journal of Physiology*, 1937, **119**, 352–353.

Klüver, H. and Bucy, P. C. Preliminary analysis of functions of the temporal lobes in monkeys. *Archives of Neurology and Psychiatry*, 1939, **42**, 979–1000.

Konishi, M. The role of auditory feedback in the control of vocalization in the white-crowned sparrow. *Zeitschrift für Tierpsychology*, 1965, **22**, 770–783.

Kuffler, S. W. Discharge patterns and functional organization of mammalian retina. *Journal of Neurophysiology*, 1953, **16**, 37–68.

Lashley, K. S. *Brain mechanisms and intelligence.* Chicago: University of Chicago Press, 1929.

Lashley, K. S. The mechanism of vision. IV. The cerebral areas necessary for pattern vision in the rat. *Journal of Comparative Neurology*, 1931, **53**, 419–478.

Lashley, K. S. Studies of cerebral function in learning. XII. Loss of the maze habit after occipital lesions in blind rats. *Journal of Comparative Neurology*, 1943, **79**, 431–462.

Lashley, K. S. In search of the engram. In *Society of Experimental Biology Symposium No. 4, Mechanisms in Animal Behaviour.* Cambridge, England: Cambridge University Press, 1950. Pp. 454–482.

Lashley, K. S., & McCarthy, D. A. The survival of the maze habit after cerebellar injuries. *Journal of Comparative Psychology*, 1926, **6**, 423–433.

Lisk, R. D. Estrogen-sensitive centers in the hypothalamus of the rat. *Journal of Experimental Zoology*, 1960, **145**, 197–208.

Llinas, R. Neuronal operations in cerebellar transactions. In F. O. Schmitt (Ed.), rats under massed and distributed trials. *Psychonomic Science*, 1965, **3**, 193–194. 1970. Pp. 409–426.

Ludwig, A. M. Altered states of consciousness. *Archives of General Psychiatry*, 1966, 15, 225–234.

Maccoby, E. *The development of sex differences.* Stanford: Stanford University Press, 1966.

Madsen, M. C., & Kimble, D. P. The maze behavior of hippocampectomized rats under massed and distributed trials. *Psychonomic Science*, 1965, **3**, 193–194.

Magoun, H. W. *The waking brain.* (2nd Ed.) Springfield, Ill.: Charles C Thomas, 1963.

Marks, W. B., Dobelle, W. H., & MacNichol, E. F., Jr. Visual pigments of single primate cones. *Science*, 1964, **143**, 1181–1183.

Marr, D. A theory of cerebellar cortex. *Journal of Physiology* (London) 1969, **202**, 437–470.

Mayer, J. Genetic, traumatic and environmental factors in the etiology of obesity. *Physiological Reviews*, 1953, **33**, 472–508.

McGaugh, J. L. Facilitation of memory storage processes. In S. Bogach (Ed.), *The future of the brain sciences,* New York: Plenum, 1969.

Merton, P. A. How we control the contraction of our muscles. *Scientific American*, 1972, **226**, 30–37.

Mettler, F. A. and Mettler, C. The effects of striatal injury. *Brain*, 1942, **65**, 242–255.

Miller, N. E. Certain facts of learning relevant to the search for its physical basis. In G. C. Quarton, T. Melnechuk, & F. O. Schmitt (Eds.), *The neurosciences: A study program.* New York: Rockefeller University Press, 1967. Pp. 643–652.

Miller, N. E. Learning of visceral and glandular responses. *Science,* 1969, **163,** 434–445.

Miller, N. E., Bailey, C. J., & Stevenson, J. A. F. "Decreased hunger" but increased food intake resulting from hypothalamic lesions. *Science,* 1950, **112,** 256–259.

Milner, B. Brain mechanisms suggested by studies of temporal lobes. In F. L. Darley (Ed.), *Brain mechanisms underlying speech and language.* New York: Grune & Stratton, 1967. Pp. 122–145.

Milner, B. Memory and the medial temporal regions of the brain. In K. H. Pribram & D. E. Broadbent (Eds.), *Biology of memory.* New York: Academic, 1970. Pp. 29–50.

Miner, N. Integumental specification of sensory fibers in the development of cutaneous local sign. *Journal of Comparative Neurology,* 1956, **105,** 161–170.

Money, J. Sexual dimorphism and homosexual gender identity. *Psychological Bulletin,* 1970, **74,** 425–440.

Money, J., Ehrhardt, A. A., & Masica, D. N. Fetal feminization induced by androgen insensitivity in the testicular feminizing syndrome: Effect on marriage and maternalism. *The Johns Hopkins Medical Journal.* 1968, **123,** 105–114.

Montgomery, M. F. The role of the salivary glands in the thirst mechanism. *American Journal of Physiology,* 1931, **96,** 221–227.

Moruzzi, G., & Magoun, H. W. Brain stem reticular formation and activation of the EEG. *Electroencephalography and Clinical Neurophysiology,* 1949, **1,** 455–473.

Mountcastle, V. B. (Ed.) *Medical Physiology.* (12th ed.) St. Louis: Mosby, 1968.

Müller, G. E., & Pilzecker, A. Experimentelle beiträge zur lehre vom gedachtniss. *Zeitschrift für Psychologie und Physiologie der Sinnesorgane, Erganzungsband,* 1900, **1,** 1–288.

Netter, F. H. *A compilation of paintings on the normal and pathologic anatomy of the nervous system.* CIBA, 1962.

Neumann, F., & Elger, W. Permanent changes in gonadal function and sexual behavior as a result of early feminization of male rats by treatment with an antiandrogenic steroid. *Endokrinologie,* 1966, **50,** 209–225.

Olds, J. A preliminary mapping of electrical reinforcing effects in the rat brain. *Journal of Comparative and Physiological Psychology,* 1956, **49,** 281–285.

Olds, J., & Milner, P. M. Positive reinforcement produced by electrical stimulation of septal area and other regions of rat brain. *Journal of Comparative and Physiological Psychology,* 1954, **47,** 419–427.

Olds, J., Segal, M., Hirsh, R., Disterhoft, J. F., & Kornblith, C. L. Learning centers of rat brain mapped by measuring latencies of conditioned unit responses. *Journal of Neurophysiology,* 1972, **35,** 202–219.

Pavlov, I. P. *Conditioned reflexes.* (G. V. Anrep, Trans. Ed.) Oxford: Oxford University Press, 1927.

Penfield, W., & Perot, P. The brain's record of auditory and visual experience. *Brain,* 1963, **86,** 595–696.

Penfield, W., & Rasmussen, T. The cerebral cortex of man: A clinical study of localization of function. New York: Macmillan, 1950.

Peters, A., & Kaiserman-Abramof, I. R. The small pyramidal neuron of the rat cerebral cortex: The synapses upon dendritic spines. *Zeitschrift für Zellforschung.*, 1969, **100**, 487–506.

Poltyrew, S. S., & Zeliony, G. P. Grosshirnrinde und assoziations-funktion. *Zeitschrift für Biologie.*, 1930, **90**, 157–160.

Prestige, M. C. Differentiation, degeneration, and the role of the periphery: Quantitative considerations. In F. O. Schmitt (Ed.), *The neurosciences second study program.* New York: Rockefeller University Press, 1970. Pp. 73–82.

Raisman, G. Neuronal plasticity in the septal nuclei of the adult rat. *Brain Research,* 1969, **14**, 25–48.

Ramón y Cajal, S. Histologie du système nerveux de l'homme et des vertébrés. Paris: A. Maloine, 1909.

Ray, O. S. *Drugs, society, and human behavior.* St. Louis: Mosby, 1972.

Rosenblum, L. A. The development of social behavior in the Rhesus monkey. Unpublished doctoral dissertation, University of Wisconsin, 1961.

Ruch, T. C., & Patton, H. D. (Eds.) *Physiology and biophysics* (19th ed.) Philadelphia: Saunders, 1965.

Russell, W. R., & Nathan, P. W. Traumatic amnesia. *Brain,* 1946, **69**, 280–300.

Sawyer, C. H. Effects of brain lesions on estrous behavior and reflexogenous ovulation in the rabbit. *Journal of Experimental Zoology.* 1959, **142**, 227–246.

Schapiro, S., & Vukovich, K. R. Early experience effects upon cortical dendrites: A proposed model for development. *Science,* 1970, **167**, 292–294.

Schachter, S. Some extraordinary facts about obese humans and rats. *American Psychologist,* 1971, **26**, 129–144.

Sem-Jacobsen, C. W. Depth-electrographic stimulation of the human brain and behavior. From *Fourteen years of studies and treatment of Parkinson's disease and mental disorders with implanted electrodes.* Springfield, Ill.: Charles C Thomas, 1968.

Sherrington, C. S. *Integrative action of the nervous system.* New Haven: Yale University Press, 1906.

Sholl, D. A. *The organization of the cerebral cortex.* London: Methuen, 1956.

Sidman, R. L. Cell proliferation, migration, and interaction in the developing mammalian central nervous system. In F. O. Schmitt (Ed.), *The neurosciences second study program.* New York: Rockefeller University Press, 1970. Pp. 100–109.

Skinner, B. F., *Walden Two.* New York: Macmillan, 1948.

Spencer, W. A., Thompson, R. F., & Neilson, D. R. Jr. Response decrement of flexion reflex in acute spinal cat and transient restoration by strong stimuli. *Journal of Neurophysiology,* 1966a, **29**, 221–239.

Spencer, W. A., Thompson, R. F., & Neilson, D. R., Jr. Alterations in responsiveness of ascending and reflex pathways activated by iterated cutaneous afferent volleys. *Journal of Neurophysiology,* 1966b, **29**, 240–252.

Spencer, W. A., Thompson, R. F., & Neilson, D. R., Jr. Decrement of ventral root electrotonus and intracellularly recorded post-synaptic potentials produced by iterated cutaneous afferent volleys. *Journal of Neurophysiology,* 1966c, **29**, 253–274.

Sperry, R. W. Mechanisms of neural maturation. In S. S. Stevens (Ed.), *Handbook of experimental psychology.* New York: Wiley, 1951. Pp. 236–280.

Sperry, R. W. The growth of nerve circuits. *Scientific American,* November, **201,** 1959.

Sperry, R. W. Selective communication in nerve nets: Impulse specificity vs. connection specificity. *Neurosciences Research Program Bulletin,* 1965, **3,** 37–43.

Sperry, R. W. Hemisphere deconnection and unity in conscious awareness. *American Psychologist,* 1968, **23,** 723–733.

Sperry, R. W. Hemispheric specialization of mental faculties in the brain of man. In M. P. Douglass (Ed.), *Claremont Reading Conference,* 1972.

Sperry, R. W., & Gazzaniga, M. S. Language following surgical disconnection of the hemispheres. In F. L. Darley (Ed.), *Brain mechanisms underlying speech and language.* New York: Grune & Stratton, 1967. Pp. 108–121.

Stellar, E., & Sprague, J. M. (Eds.) *Progress in physiological psychology.* Vol. 4. New York: Academic, 1971.

Stevens, C. F. *Neurophysiology: A primer.* New York: Wiley, 1966.

Teitelbaum, P. Random and food-directed activity in hyperphagic and normal rats. *Journal of Comparative and Physiological Psychology,* 1957, **50,** 486–490.

Teitelbaum, P., Cheng, M., & Rozin, P. Development of feeding parallels its recovery after hypothalamic damage. *Journal of Comparative and Physiological Psychology,* 1969, **67,** 430–441.

Teitelbaum, P., & Epstein, A. N. The lateral hypothalamic syndrome: Recovery of feeding and drinking after lateral hypothalamic lesions. *Psychological Review,* 1962, **69,** 74–90.

Teuber, H. L. Lacunae and research approaches to them. In F. L. Darley (Ed.), *Brain mechanisms underlying speech and language.* New York: Grune & Stratton, 1967. Pp. 204–216.

Thomas, G. J. Maze retention by rats with hippocampal lesions and with fornicotomies. *Journal of Comparative and Physiological Psychology,* 1971, **75,** 41–49.

Tsang, Yü-Chuan. The function of the visual areas of the cortex in the learning and retention of the maze. *Comparative Psychology Monographs,* 1934, **10,** 1–56.

Turner, C. D., & Bagnara, J. T. *General endocrinology.* (5th Ed.) Philadelphia: Saunders, 1971.

Vaughan, E., & Fisher, A. E. Male sexual behavior induced by intracranial electrical stimulation. *Science,* 1962, **137,** 758–760.

Verney, E. B. The antidiuretic hormone and the factors which determine its release. *Proceedings of the Royal Society, London, Series B,* 1947, **135,** 25–106.

Vincent, J. D., & Hayward, J. N. Activity of single cells in the osmoreceptor-supraoptic nuclear complex in the hypothalamus of the waking rhesus monkey. *Brain Research,* 1970, **23,** 105–108.

Wada, J., & Rasmussen, T. Intracarotid injection of sodium amytal for the lateralization of cerebral speech dominance: Experimental and clinical observations. *Journal of Neurosurgery,* 1960, **17,** 266–282.

Wald, G., Brown, P. K., & Gibbons, I. R. The problem of visual excitation. *Journal of the Optical Society of America,* 1963, **53,** 20–35.

Wallace, R. K. The physiological effects of transcendental meditation. Unpublished doctoral dissertation, University of California at Los Angeles, 1970.

Watson, J. D. *Molecular biology of the gene.* (2nd ed.) New York: W. A. Benjamin, Inc., 1970.

Wickelgren, B. G. Superior colliculus: Some receptive field properties of bimodally responsive cells. *Science, 1971,* **173,** 69–72.

Wiesel, T. N., & Hubel, D. H. Spatial and chromatic interactions in the lateral geniculate body of the Rhesus monkey. *Journal of Neurophysiology, 1966,* **29,** 1115–1156.

Wurtz, R. H. Visual receptive fields of striate cortex neurones in awake monkeys. *Journal of Neurophysiology, 1969,* **32,** 727–742.

Zeman, W., & Innes, J. R. M. *Cragie's neuroanatomy of the rat.* New York: Academic, 1963.

AUTHOR INDEX

SUBJECT INDEX

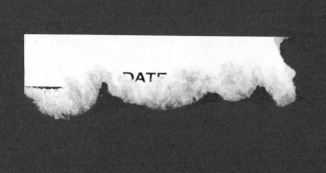

DATE